PERSPECTIVES
ON THE REAGAN YEARS

PERSPECTIVES
ON THE REAGAN YEARS

Edited by John L. Palmer

The Changing Domestic Priorities Series
John L. Palmer and Isabel V. Sawhill, Editors

 THE URBAN INSTITUTE PRESS · WASHINGTON, D.C.

Copyright © 1986
THE URBAN INSTITUTE
2100 M Street N.W.
Washington, D.C. 20037

Library of Congress Cataloging-in-Publication Data

Perspectives on the Reagan years.

  (The Changing domestic priorities series)
  Includes bibliographies.
  1. United States—Politics and government—1981–   .
2. United States—Social policy—1980–   . 3. United
States—Economic policy—1981–   . I. Palmer, John
Logan. II. Series.
JK271.P42 1986   973.927   86-13160
ISBN 0-87766-403-X
ISBN 0-87766-402-1 (pbk.)

Printed in the United States of America

9 8 7 6 5 4 3 2 1

THE URBAN INSTITUTE is a nonprofit policy research and educational organization established in Washington, D.C., in 1968. Its staff investigates the social and economic problems confronting the nation and government policies and programs designed to alleviate such problems. The Institute disseminates significant findings of its research through the publications program of its Press. The Institute has two goals for work in each of its research areas: to help shape thinking about societal problems and efforts to solve them, and to improve government decisions and performance by providing better information and analytic tools.

Through work that ranges from broad conceptual studies to administrative and technical assistance, Institute researchers contribute to the stock of knowledge available to public officials and to private individuals and groups concerned with formulating and implementing more efficient and effective government policy.

Conclusions or opinions expressed in Institute publications are those of the authors and do not necessarily reflect the views of other staff members, officers or trustees of the Institute, advisory groups, or any organizations that provide financial support to the Institute.

THE CHANGING DOMESTIC PRIORITIES SERIES

Listed below are the titles available in the Changing Domestic Priorities Series

AMERICA'S CHILDREN: WHO CARES?
Growing Needs and Declining Assistance in the Reagan Era (1985),
Madeleine H. Kimmich

TESTING THE SOCIAL SAFETY NET
The Impact of Changes in Support Programs during the Reagan Administration
(1985), Martha R. Burt and Karen J. Pittman

REAGAN AND THE CITIES
(1986), edited by George E. Peterson and Carol W. Lewis

PERSPECTIVES ON THE REAGAN YEARS
(1986), edited by John L. Palmer

Conference Volumes

THE SOCIAL CONTRACT REVISITED
Aims and Outcomes of President Reagan's Social Welfare Policy (1984), edited
by D. Lee Bawden

NATURAL RESOURCES AND THE ENVIRONMENT
The Reagan Approach (1984), edited by Paul R. Portney

FEDERAL BUDGET POLICY IN THE 1980s (1984), edited by
Gregory B. Mills and John L. Palmer

THE REAGAN REGULATORY STRATEGY
An Assessment (1984), edited by George C. Eads and Michael Fix

THE LEGACY OF REAGANOMICS
Prospects for Long-term Growth (1984), edited by Charles R. Hulten and Isabel
V. Sawhill

THE REAGAN PRESIDENCY AND THE GOVERNING OF AMERICA
(1984), edited by Lester M. Salamon and Michael S. Lund

CONTENTS

FOREWORD

With the election of Ronald Reagan in 1980, the United States embarked on an experiment with domestic policies that is perhaps as significant as the New Deal. The Reagan administration has raised fundamental questions about the appropriate role of government in national life, and it has been partially successful in implementing a program—one with distinct premises about economic and social behavior—that substantially alters that role. Because this program and the responses to it have had such far-reaching implications for the character of America and its public policies, a rigorous and impartial assessment of the record was clearly needed.

The Urban Institute's Changing Domestic Priorities project (CDP) was begun in early 1982 to help meet this need. The four-year research effort has built on the Institute's long-standing work in assessing the consequences of public actions. Lodged within an established tradition of objective public policy analysis, the effort had drawn on the accumulated expertise of Institute staff, supplemented as needed by that of other researchers. The scope of the project has been broad, relying heavily on collaborative research across disciplines and areas of study in order to capture the interactions among, and public responses to, both the policy changes and their effects.

The CDP project will have produced some two dozen books by the end of 1986. Most of these books center on fairly well-defined policy concerns. Six edited volumes of papers and conference proceedings address budget policy, economic policy, governance, natural resources and the environment, regulatory policy, and social policy; more than a dozen other volumes examine more specifically such topics as state and local impacts, health care financing, housing, and the deficit. Two overview volumes have also been produced under the leadership of project codirectors John L. Palmer and Isabel V. Sawhill, *The Reagan Experiment* (1982) and *The Reagan Record* (1984). These volumes synthesize the project's findings. They document the magnitude and character of the actual shifts of federal domestic policy, as well as some of the policies that the president has proposed but which had not yet been adopted, and they report on the impact of the changes on people, places, and institutions and project probable further impacts.

This third and final CDP overview volume is not an update of the previous two, reporting on the project's ongoing research findings. Rather, it complements the previous documentary and empirical work with interpretive perspectives. The intent of the earlier volumes was to provide fuel for public debate, that is, objective analyses of policy proposals, changes, and impacts that could be used—indeed, were used extensively—by Congress, the press, and the public to assess the undertakings of the Reagan administration. The intent of this volume, in contrast, is to place the policy debates in the larger historical context of America's evolving public purposes and to provide an interpretation of where the nation seems to be going. The concern is less with the Reagan administration per se than with the contribution of the Reagan years to the enduring realities of American public life.

With that concern in mind, contributors to this volume were asked to stand as far back from very recent history as the short passage of time would permit and assess the probable significance of this history for the future. Because this task requires a longer-term perspective than is generally permitted by the Institute's usual work addressing current policies, the volume relies much more heavily on the contributions of academic researchers than did previous volumes. The task is necessarily speculative, and in light of the immediacy of the events being considered, it is also ambitious. But because the political choices being made during the Reagan years may prove profound and far reaching in their impact on the nation's public life, we thought it important to make some effort now at providing a broader interpretive framework for those choices than is possible with policy analysis alone. The resulting volume will at least, I believe, provoke some lively discussion and debate, and that alone will justify its undertaking.

Funding for the volume, as well as for most of the Changing Domestic Priorities project, was provided by The Ford Foundation and the John D. and Catherine T. MacArthur Foundation. Foundations reveal their character in their grants, and in their support of this project these foundations have shown uncommon imagination, willingness to risk, and tenacity. The nation ultimately gains from such models of creative philanthropy.

William Gorham
President
The Urban Institute

INTRODUCTION

John L. Palmer

Since the New Deal, American political thinking has been dominated by a philosophy of federal activism in economic and social affairs, with debate over that philosophy largely confined to academics and political ideologues. During the past decade or so, however, questions about the appropriate role of the federal government have arisen with increasing frequency in popular debate. And with the election of Ronald Reagan, the philosophical issues attained a remarkable purchase on public attention. The Reagan administration has attacked both the general philosophy of federal activism—particularly its generous assumptions about public responsibility for private welfare—and its practical manifestations: rising federal tax burdens, mounting spending for social programs, proliferating federal regulations, the "bloated" federal bureaucracy, and so on. In so doing, the administration has heightened public awareness of a tension among political values that decades of economic prosperity had obscured, namely, the tensions among economic efficiency, social justice, and individual liberty—the reconciliation of which John Maynard Keynes identified as "the political problem of mankind." The Reagan administration has argued that the American version of the "welfare state" has unduly sacrificed both individual liberty and economic efficiency in the pursuit of social justice, and that more diligent concern for the former would inevitably produce the latter. As evidenced by the last two elections, these arguments would appear to have won a lot of converts.

In this volume the other authors and I examine the extent to which the actual experience of the Reagan years illuminates the issues sketched above. To what degree is there in fact a popular conversion in the works, or is it just a historic anomaly? How much have the changes wrought by this ad-

1

ministration addressed real systemic problems in American public life? To what extent are these changes purely ideological in origin and transitory in impact? In what important ways have the economic and social landscape and the domain of federal policy been altered? In short, we are less concerned with what has happened than with what it all means: what can be learned from the Reagan years about the involvement of the federal government in America's economic and social life?

So stated, our interest has been echoed in countless journal and magazine articles and even a few books. What distinguishes our current undertaking, at least somewhat, from these others is that we have consciously tried to push at the boundaries of our own disciplines (political science, sociology, and economics) so as to approximate the perspective a historian might have some years hence. We have wanted to avoid a pure weighting of political "ideas" (as in Richard Reeves' recent book *The Reagan Detour*), the close analysis of particular policy changes (as in previous Urban Institute volumes), or detailed interpretation of political and institutional realignments (as in The Brookings Institution's *The New Direction in American Politics*). We wanted to gain a sense (which ultimately, of course, only time can provide) of what the interactions among these kinds of changes signify for future public life in the United States.

Toward that end, we began with the simplest possible conception of the function of the federal government in economic and social affairs: to provide some framework for the peaceful reconciliation of the competing values of the American people. Hence the chapter by Nathan Glazer on social issues seeks to capture the shifts in value "currents" by examining the course of the New Right's "social agenda." Values (in the larger sense, that is, encompassing economic values) are imbedded in what is often referred to as the "public philosophy." Hugh Heclo defines this term in some detail in his chapter; here I simply characterize it as the prevailing wisdom at any particular time about how values interact in the real world and what approaches the federal government should follow in discharging its reconciliation responsibility.

The public philosophy, in turn, reflects and is reflected in the actual policies the federal government pursues in the social and economic arenas— hence the chapters by Jack A. Meyer and Isabel V. Sawhill. The public philosophy also reflects and is reflected in views of governing institutions: how well adapted are they for doing the reconciliation job? The chapter by Richard Nathan addresses this question. And because our understanding of America's national political experience derives not just from self-observation but also from comparison with other nations, the chapter by Robert Haveman, Barbara Wolfe, and Victor Halberstadt takes a look at the status of the welfare state in Europe. Finally, because we are ultimately concerned with the interaction of all these phenomena, I attempt a synthesis in the concluding chapter.

The resulting volume is thus deliberately speculative. It is not, in general, particularly scholarly—we all paid our scholarship dues before taking on the present task—and it does not aim at detailed forecasts. It is simply our own effort at sorting out the carts from the horses on the current political scene.

THE "SOCIAL AGENDA"

Nathan Glazer

One of the chief ways in which the Reagan administration has tried to make its mark, and ensure that the federal role will be different in the future from what it has been in the past, has been its initiatives in the group of issues referred to as "the social agenda." Abortion, school prayer, and school busing stand at the center of this agenda, but the issues extend beyond these to include school discipline, public pornography, tuition tax credits for and government regulation of private schools, and employment quotas, goals, and timetables.

The position of the Reagan administration with respect to the social agenda marks a considerable break with presidential policy in the past. Indeed, there is no model for it in the past. These issues were considered within the province of states and localities until the Supreme Court decision on school segregation in *Brown* v. *Board of Education* in 1954, on school prayer in 1963, on abortion in 1973. There was no need for a Roosevelt, a Truman, an Eisenhower to involve himself in most of these matters. But by the time of the Carter administration, it was impossible for presidents to avoid "the social issue." Joseph Califano, in his *Governing America*, describes how troublesome the abortion issue and issues affecting the family were for that administration (Califano 1981). With the Reagan administration, for the first time the conservative protesters found allies in the administration to support their stand against liberalizing Supreme Court decisions and against liberal federal regulations interpreting congressional legislation on civil rights and education.

The objective of this chapter is to describe and assess Reagan administration initiatives in these areas and consider whether we may expect the issues of the social agenda to continue to play a significant role in presidential policymaking beyond this administration. Specifically, the chapter compares and contrasts some major issues on the social agenda, looks at the social characteristics of both supporters and opponents of specific issues, describes the position of the Reagan administration, and suggests possible long-range consequences of shifts in opinion for American society and its social problems.

A MIXED BAG OF ISSUES

What are the common elements that bring together the issues of school prayer and abortion, discipline in the schools and pornography, school busing and quotas, as a distinctive domain of policy?

First, they have all become federal issues because of the First and the Fourteenth Amendments. They raise constitutional questions, and thus the federal courts have played a key role in addressing them and setting policy. Legislation on these matters—and there is a great deal of it—generally comes into existence to implement Supreme Court decisions (the Civil Rights Act of 1964) or, more characteristically, to overturn them (the host of legislative proposals and enactments designed to counter school busing, abortion liberalization, school prayer prohibition). Thus the issues all fall into the realm of civil liberties or civil rights. But some key civil liberties have been almost totally absent in the heated disputes around the social agenda—the protection of speech, press, and assembly established in the First Amendment. We have had neither a recurrence of McCarthyism, raising the question of whether unpopular views and organizations would be restricted by federal or state law, nor a resurgence of the social disorder in cities and on campuses of the late 1960s and early 1970s, challenging the limits of freedom to assemble and petition. If the social agenda as I have described it is uncomfortably broad, it at least does not extend to these classic civil liberties issues. For example, we have not seen any effort to ban the teaching of evolution; only efforts to ensure equal treatment for "creationism."[1]

All the issues that make up the social agenda involve what is considered by some to be an unwarranted expansion of judicial power, and by others to be the legitimate protection and extension of civil liberties and rights. Key Supreme Court decisions thus mark the rise and the development of the social agenda—decisions banning school prayer, requiring busing for school desegregation, overruling state laws on abortion, limiting state support to private

---

1. There are exceptions to this generalization—attempts to control the contents of school libraries raise civil liberties questions.

(religious) schools, denying tax benefits to schools that practice discrimination (Bob Jones University), and so on.

A second common feature of the issues on the social agenda is that they primarily concern *values*, though interests are of course involved. Groups with quite different values but with common interests can occasionally be brought together on one or another of these issues. The liberal American Federation of Teachers will argue against quotas as strongly as social conservatives, but it is defending the interests of its members in this case, and values are not at the heart of its involvement. Liberal suburbanites will join with conservative inner-city working-class and lower-middle-class parents if they are brought together in a busing plan. The former are likely defending a better education for their children, rather than the value of the neighborhood school, and neighborhood as such. But at the core of the social agenda are values. The two elements of the social agenda that arouse the greatest controversy and the most intense commitment, abortion and school prayer, are devoid of any interest component. On these issues, social conservatives stand without allies on the basis of some specific interest that is being defended.

A third characteristic of the social agenda is that conflict over its issues generally divides a less privileged conservative element against a more privileged liberal one. The defenders of state limitation on abortion, school prayer, and the neighborhood school are for the most part working-class and lower-middle-class people. These issues have no impact in Ivy League schools, whose faculty, students, and law professors are generally mystified by the uproar. Those of higher education and higher income are generally unaffected personally by the issues; they do not threaten their interests and identity. Admittedly those who oppose the conservatives regarding issues on the social agenda argue that they are defending the rights of the even less privileged and more unfortunate: they argue, for example, for abortions paid by Medicaid to aid the poor, for busing so that black students may obtain a better education, for quotas to provide minorities with access to jobs. Yet to consider the social agenda in classic class terms would be to misunderstand its potency. In part, of course, the agenda does consist of a defense of interests (the quota issue). In even greater part, it consists of the defense of a world, a structure of values, that is perceived by its defenders to be under attack—an attack that comes from the Supreme Court, constitutional scholars and intellectuals, "pointy heads," to use a term that one early explorer in the potency of the social agenda launched. It is true that one or another policy included in the social agenda may harm the poorest and the most unfortunate, but these are seen by the conservatives as in any case deserving their plight, owing to moral inadequacy.

The basic coherence of the social agenda, despite the assortment of specific issues encompassed within it, is given by a rather consistent lineup of social groups on the various issues that form part of the social agenda. On one side are the enlightened and the liberal, those who are better educated, concentrated in the professions, oriented toward career, accepting of modern values or practices (divorce, premarital sex, rights for homosexuals and other sexual deviants), more mobile, less committed to stable family life and neighborhood life and traditional values. On the other side are their opposites. The social agenda is indeed about a social conflict: a conflict over how life should be lived, how it should be controlled, over the relative values of large families versus planned families, of personal fulfillment versus living for family, religion, neighborhood.

Those supporting conservative or traditional (if one will, restrictive) policies find their base in the "Bible Belt" and among the Protestant denominations of lower social status, combined with working and lower-middle-class Catholics. Opponents of restrictiveness—of control or limitation on abortion and contraceptive knowledge, of prayer in school, of aid to private schools, of limited rights of freedom of speech and assembly—and supporters of strong federal action in favor of minorities have generally been found among liberal Protestants and Jews, in the big cities of the East and the West, among occupations based on higher education. Just as there is a class basis to attitude and opinion on economic matters, so there is a class basis to attitude and opinion in these value-laden matters. But here the relation linking income, occupation, and the liberal position is reversed. It is the lower-income and lower-status occupation groups, and the poorer parts of the country, who in general are found as supporters of the conservative position on these issues.

It is this commonality in the social character of support and opposition that links these issues. On a deeper level, it is their connection to an image of the good society—in one case, a society in which community, religion, and family have rights to ensure and preserve common values (a Christian, or conservative, or traditional, or family-based America); in the other case, a society based on individuals, in which freedom from the restraints imposed by family, community, and religion is held to be a key characteristic of the good society.

Choosing the words that appropriately characterize these complexes of values and attitudes is not an easy task. Thus the more "conservative" position is often attacked as not truly "conservative"; for example, it refuses to accept the authority of the Supreme Court. It is attacked as not being interested in the "conservation" of what its opponents consider key elements in the American creed and the Constitution, such as the separation of church and state and freedom of conscience and action flowing from it. The conservatives are indeed often called (and may call themselves) "radical," as in "the radical religious right." The "liberal" position, which opposes government restrictions where individual choice is at stake, is quite willing to support government's strong hand in advancing the interests of minorities (as it conceives them), to the point of busing school children and closely supervising employment and promotion in business and admissions practices of educational institutions.

This lengthy exercise in definition argues for the organic connection among positions on these varied issues. This connection is less to be found in abstract attitudes toward government and its role as such, federalism, or the desirability of maintaining precedent in law. Because such connection cannot be found, it is possible, at a time when being "conservative" is better than being "liberal" or "radical," for the latter to charge the former with the dread accusation of "radical" because they wish to overturn Supreme Court decisions or want government to oversee the treatment by doctors of physically and mentally deformed infants. From the point of view of political logic and consistency, the charge may be correct. From the point of view of the social demographic profile of the lineup on these issues, it is not. It is the social base, and the social vision, rather than an abstract logic that links positions on the social agenda.

Two complications muddy this effort to define the social agenda by the social characteristics of supporters and opponents of the specific issues. The first is that lined up with the social conservatives are constitutional scholars and intellectuals who may share few of the specific values of those they support. The reason for this alliance is that in almost every case the conservatives on the battlefields of the social agenda prefer local to federal control. They favor the state's right to set limits on abortion, the local school district's right to set school prayers or control discipline, the local neighborhood's right to neighborhood schools, individual employers' rights to set terms of employment. In each case, generally at the insistence of the federal courts, the federal government has set a broader, national standard that conflicts with local control. The conservatives on social issues thus often find allies on theoretical constitutional grounds—those who argue that the federal courts have far exceeded their proper powers under the Constitution and that they should be restricted from interfering in the affairs of states, communities, schools, and employers to the degree they have. It is important to clearly separate defenders of strict construction and local control from those who form the heart of the conservative side on social issues. If it should happen that conservatives on social issues gain sufficient power, through judicial appointment or elective strength, that the courts and the Congress set new, but conservative, national standards, the defenders of strict construction—if they are consistent—will move to the other side and defend the liberal inclinations of states, communities, school districts, neighborhoods.

The second, and more serious, complication is that some of these issues (busing, quotas, tuition tax credits for neighborhood schools) either are parts of the classic civil rights agenda or involve a differential racial impact that may affect the interests of the black minority. Busing has become the only means in most cases of advancing the integration of black and white children in the same schools. The opponents of busing say they defend the neighborhood school. It may be their major motivation. As family-oriented people, they may feel threatened by busing their children to racially different neighborhoods. But they also oppose what proponents of busing see as a constitutionally defined right of black children and a policy that is at the heart of black civil-rights litigation.

The conflict with black interests in the case of quotas, goals, and timetables is even sharper. The sharpest conflicts over quotas have arisen over employment and promotion in police and fire forces, favored forms of employment of the conservative social groups I have described. Values are also involved. Expectations—that the hard work in preparing for a test (the typical pattern in big-city police forces, for example) would be rewarded with a job or a promotion, or that seniority would be involved—are all matters of value as well as simple interest. Even the expectation that relatives can and will help one obtain a job (as opposed to the open advertising and recruiting of affirmative action) involves values as well as interests. Thus we deal with a value conflict as well as the old racial struggle between blacks and whites, and the result takes on new forms and new disguises.

A similar running together of the race issue and the value issue is seen in the issues affecting Christian schools. Undoubtedly one motivation for their establishment and growth is the desire to avoid integration and the consequences that integration would have for the social tone of schools—words, actions, and dress allowable in class would have to be broadened, in part because of variant cultures among black and white families, in part because of other constitutional restrictions, quite unrelated to any black-white issues. If one asserted that these schools grow because of racism, it would be hard to deny that is a component. If one argued that they grow because the public schools have changed—religion has been banned from them, dress codes may not be imposed to the same degree, behavior has become freer, discipline has become relaxed—who would deny that too? The interplay between civil rights and the social agenda is close and intimate. It is also ironic because black Americans are the most conservative group in our society when it comes to issues such as school prayer and abortion! The religious heritage that is a major element in the formation of conservatives' beliefs on social issues shapes the views of blacks as well as whites.

The leaders of the conservative or radical religious right try to some extent to reach out to black and Jewish people, groups to which their predecessors and forebears were hostile. Despite this guilt by descent, I would argue that the social agenda is not, or only in small part, a contemporary dress version of the opposition to civil rights for blacks. The basic issues of the social agenda, abortion and school prayer, do not involve the rights of blacks at all. One must expect hostility and suspicion among blacks against a movement whose leaders and adherents so prominently include white southerners of the middle and lower classes, their old oppressors. The balance between racist and other motives among the latter is not easily drawn up to everyone's satisfaction.

THE REAGAN ADMINISTRATION
AND THE SOCIAL AGENDA

From the point of view of the federal government, specifically the Reagan administration since 1981, the complex of elements I have summed up as components of "the social agenda" have certain common features. They do not impinge greatly on the federal budget. They do not involve massive layouts as in the case of defense and public works, or massive transfers as required by the various branches of social policy—Social Security, Medicare and Medicaid, housing subsidies, food stamps, and welfare. The largest budget involved in any social issue is that for the Equal Employment Opportunity Commission and the Office of Federal Contract Compliance Programs. By federal standards they are minuscule (about a fortieth of one percent). For most of the issues I have discussed no governmental mechanism at the federal level is required to oversee regulation. The banning of school prayer does not involve ongoing action by the federal government; nor did the radical recasting by the Supreme Court of state limits on control of abortion. It takes no (or hardly any) federal money to respond to anxiety about school discipline; an occasional study is sufficient. Little money goes to federal aid to private schools. Much more would be involved in the proposed tuition tax credits for private schools that have been steadily supported by the Reagan administration; this support has continued despite massive deficits and major proposals for tax reform that would have (inevitably) complex effects on the significance of tuition tax credits.[2]

---

2. Despite the Reagan tax-reform proposal of 1985, the administration still supports tuition tax credits. Undersecretary of Education designate Gary L. Bauer has asserted: "You could probably name a half-dozen issues that the President is just committed to, and . . . [tuition tax credits] is one of them" (quoted in Hertling 1985, p. 10).

These issues are not tied to the cycle of the budget, as is so much of federal governmental policy. The government can to some extent choose the time to move on these issues, although there is some likelihood that it can be forced to move as private and public litigators demand that it take one or another action, and committed congressmen demand legislative action.

So the administration has been able to exercise a certain amount of discretion regarding how and when to move on these issues. It has been remarkably constant in its *positions* on abortion, school prayer, busing, quotas, tuition tax credits, and indeed on the entire package summed up in the social agenda. But other matters have taken priority in claiming the energy of the president and the executive department—proposing a budget, deciding on the level of military expenditure, on the scale of major spending programs, on how to deal with the deficit, and how all this affects the economy. The administration has been criticized by many of its supporters for moving slowly on the social issues. But when it has moved it has never been in a way to disappoint its supporters. It has also discovered that on some of these issues, particularly those pertaining to civil rights, the liberal opposition has been skillful, effective, committed—and it has lost again and again.

Thus the administration lost in the battle over renewal of the voting rights act, which ended up stronger than it had been before, and much stronger than the administration wanted. It lost in perhaps the best known of its civil rights interventions, the effort to restore tax exemption to Bob Jones University. The case was complicated; in part it bore on the rights of the Internal Revenue Service to make a judgment that Bob Jones University discriminated, and on that basis to challenge its tax exemption. To the social-agenda conservatives, the case was important because during the Carter administration the same Internal Revenue Service had proposed very severe standards for private schools to guarantee nondiscrimination, in which they would have had to pass a statistical test requiring enrollment of a certain number of minority students. The Bob Jones University case was undoubtedly a poor ground on which to take a stand, and the administration lost in the Supreme Court. But it showed its conservative, religious right supporters that it would stand with them.

The administration has opposed, where it could, court-ordered busing, and has proudly presented programs it has hammered out emphasizing magnet schools and other features that depend on choice rather than compulsion. It originally moved cautiously on goals and quotas. Indeed, there it was attacked for the slowness of its moves, and not only by members of the religious political right. Setting goals and quotas was one administrative task in which, in theory, it could perform radical surgery by a "stroke of the pen," to change the regulations defining what is required of government contractors by affirmative action. The administration has not yet changed a jot or a tittle in these regulations (the newspapers report it will change them), though its enforcement of them is less rigorous than was typical under the Carter administration, or indeed under the Nixon and Ford administrations. But after beginning surprisingly slowly, the administration has, following the Supreme Court decision in the Memphis Fire Department case (*Firefighters Local Union No. 1784* v. *Stotts*, decided June 12, 1984), moved against a host of consent decrees—in which it had been a party, in a previous incarnation—that require quotas for minorities. Nevertheless, the administration is not single-minded in its opposition to the entire statistical approach to affirmative action (utilization measures, goals, and timetables).

One may be surprised at either how long the administration took to move against quotas in a major way, or at its foolhardiness in doing so. Quotas, unlike every other item in the social agenda, do involve interests: the interests of employers, public and private, and the interests of employees, majority or minority. As such, the issue of quotas falls into a somewhat different category from abortion or school prayer, or from school busing. It is perhaps not surprising that administrative action in this area has aroused a storm of opposition and denunciation. It is upsetting an apple cart that—whatever the conflicts involved in setting it up—is now accepted by public agencies, private employers, and even (it would appear) by most employees. Quotas have been fought most fiercely primarily in the areas of public employment, and it is there that the administration has tried to make a change. It may have made a serious mistake: whatever its principled arguments, an attack on quotas is too clearly an attack on the interests of members of minority groups, and as such strengthens the case that the administration is indifferent to minority interests if not racist.

On the moral-religious side of the social agenda, less difficult problems have come up. The consistency of the administration has been remarkable, though it has not been terribly effective. There is as yet no amendment allowing school prayer, though the president proposed one as long ago as May 17, 1982, repeatedly called attention to it in his speeches, and called for its passage. The abortion issue has scarcely needed administration support. By 1982 no less than thirty statutes had been passed by Congress, all with the objective of limiting the reach of the Supreme Court decision. In the ninety-sixth Congress (1979–80), seventy-three bills were introduced; in the first six months of the ninety-seventh Congress, fifty-four bills (Davison 1983). But as to the firmness of the president and administration there is no doubt.

A catalog of positions is easy to draw up. An analysis of the effectiveness of administration support of its interests is another matter. In this area, as in others, one suspects that the urgent issues set by international crises and the budget cycle absorb most of the administration's interest and energy. One doubts that the president, having sent down his prayer amendment or proposed tuition tax-credit bill, has spent much time on the telephone "twisting arms," though he has referred to the amendment often in speeches to the nation, remarks at the White House, and speeches to Evangelical and religious audiences.[3]

Action in the courts has been required by many of these issues and has taken place, and it is no surprise that an uproar resulted from the proposed elevation of Bradford Reynolds from Assistant Attorney-General in charge of civil rights to Associate Attorney-General. The greatest steadiness on these issues has been in appointments to positions in the executive branch agencies and in the judiciary branch. Tests to qualify for such positions have often been used—or if not used, have been insisted upon by the defenders of the conservative social agenda. The situation in the executive agencies may change in 1989; the situation in the courts will not. It is there that the most enduring effect of the administration's embrace of the conservative social agenda is likely to be felt.

A large number of judicial appointments have already been made to the district courts and courts of appeals. According to Sheldon Goldman: "With just two terms in office as compared with Roosevelt's three plus, Reagan will accomplish what only Roosevelt and Eisenhower accomplished during the last half century—naming a majority of the lower judiciary in active service." (Note, however, that Carter appointed 40 percent in only one term, Nixon 46 percent in a term and a half.)[4]

Goldman's careful analysis of Reagan's first term appointments reveals some expected and some surprising findings. Ronald Reagan's judges are more affluent than Jimmy Carter's, and include very few blacks. They are as well qualified by A.B.A. ratings, but fewer have been educated in Ivy League law schools (district courts: 8.5 percent versus 17.3 percent for Carter; courts of appeals: 16.1 percent versus 41.1 percent for Carter). Fewer appointees come from public colleges than in the case of Carter's appointments; more come from private colleges. More are Catholic; fewer are Jewish.

All this reflects the double nature of the Reagan administration. As a Republican administration, it draws more heavily than a Democratic administration from businessmen and the wealthy. When compared with previous Republican administrations, however, the Reagan government has a more

3. September 18 and September 25, 1982; January 22, January 31, and March 18, 1983; January 30 and August 23, 1984 (see Office of the Federal Register 1982, 1983, 1984).

4. The quotation and figures are from Goldman (1985).

populist appeal and image; and, as the low proportion of Ivy League appointments suggests, this is not only appeal and image but, in measure, reality.

Has the administration acted as it has because of the personal commitment of the president and his closest advisers or because of political calculation? Do we deal with an accident, whether of personal inclination or the accidental and perhaps temporary political significance of the conservative supporters of the social agenda; or does the remarkable consistency of the Reagan administration on these issues suggest a major change in American opinion and values? Part of the answer depends on just what *is* the state of American public opinion in these matters. There is after all good reason to expect a continuation, after what is perhaps a temporary check, of the long-range shift in public opinion to liberal and secular attitudes that we have seen since World War II. But has something unexpected happened?

THE PULSE OF THE PUBLIC

There is much controversy about just how the public divides on the issues in the social agenda, as well as about the justice or legitimacy of specific policies. The opposition to abortion in Congress and in the Reagan presidency has been contrasted with a majority approval of abortion in public opinion polls. The public support of equal rights for women has been contrasted with the opposition of the Republican party, the failure of the requisite number of states to approve the Equal Rights Amendment (ERA), and the failure of Congress to restart the proposed amendment on its road to ratification after the initial failure. The steady changing of attitudes on civil rights to more liberal ones has been contrasted with the Reagan administration's opposition to busing and quotas and Congress's vigorous attempts, again and again, to ban busing.

In part, this contrasting of public opinion's liberal attitudes to the conservatism of Congress and the Reagan administration is a political ploy: one reads the opinion polls in a way to make one's point. In part, it is a reality. But in each case the Delphic tests set by opinion polls do not plumb the complexity of the issues, as people truly feel about them. Consider, for example, the course of opinion on abortion.

Support for liberalizing conditions for abortion increased from 1965 to 1972. This was a period in which many states were also liberalizing their abortion laws. The Supreme Court's decision in *Roe* v. *Wade* in 1973 outraged conservative constitutional lawyers and opponents of abortion, but one could have expected that a liberalizing trend would continue to be seen in public opinion, that the Court would be, in retrospect, viewed as simply confirming that trend. (This is what happened with attitudes on school segregation after the *Brown* decision.) In some respects, the liberalization of opinion on abortion continued. Thus, "by 1982, an overwhelming 80 percent agreed mildly or strongly that 'the decision to have an abortion should be left to the woman and her physician.' By 1983, 54 percent supported the Court when a Gallup question explained *Roe* v. *Wade* as allowing a woman 'to go to a doctor to end pregnancy at any time during the first three months of pregnancy' " (Sackett 1985, 54). As Victoria Sackett argues, there was a considerable difference of opinion over the legitimacy of abortion for "hard" reasons (because of threat to the woman's health, rape, or a serious defect in the baby) and for "soft" reasons (because of unmarried status, low family income, unwanted children). Opinion also differed greatly over the legitimacy of abortion in the first trimester and in later periods of pregnancy.

Further, as Sackett points out, although Congress agonized over whether to allow federal funding of abortions in extreme cases (such as rape or incest), the majority of abortions are not for such reasons—they fall into just the categories of cases on which the public was uneasy or reluctant to approve abortion. The most recent polls show that majorities support abortion only in the hard cases of rape, incest, or threat to the woman's life. The turnaround is truly striking in more recent years. A sharp trend toward liberalization was checked in 1973, stasis prevailed until the early 1980s, and opinion then began to move against abortion, particularly in the soft cases.[5]

The abortion story has a number of characteristics that hold for other social agenda issues—though for each issue a somewhat different array of participants and factors comes into effect.

A first phase is apparent in the steady liberalization in opinion and law until the early 1970s. This was undoubtedly the case for the ERA and civil rights issues.

A second phase can be seen when some specific implications of a position that had won acceptance by the public in a general way emerge in litigation, Supreme Court decision, or executive or legislative action. Those who write Court decisions or government regulations produce something that many people believe is going too far, and the general and bland acceptance of the course of liberalization collapses on the basis of what one can well call overreaching by liberal advocates. The sharpest example is the 1973 Supreme Court decision on abortion (*Roe* v. *Wade*) and the subsequent chain of decisions on the rights of minors to abortion without parental participation or

---

5. "Opinion Roundup" (1985). Sharp class differences add to the problem of deciding where "public opinion" stands on abortion. A 1974 Gallup poll showed that 70 percent of college-educated respondents supported abortion through the first trimester; 70 percent of the respondents with only grade-school education opposed it. See Skerry (1978, 75).

notification. Such an expansion of the right to abortion breaks what might be considered a previous consensus, as expressed in the passage of liberalized rights to abortion in a number of states (including California, where the then Governor Ronald Reagan signed such a law). But the Supreme Court decisions go further than any state liberalization laws. Similarly with the desegregation issue: until 1971 it was assumed that desegregation meant black children in white neighborhood schools. The busing decisions that have followed require white children in black schools and ignore the claims of neighborhood. In effect, an overreaching has occurred.

When the implications of the liberal position are brought into consciousness by putting a policy into practice, opposition rises. It turns out that the overwhelming majority of abortions are not for rape, incest, the health of the woman, or the prevention of the birth of a baby with serious defects—the kind of cases that have created the initial sympathy for liberalization. In the ERA issue, as Gilbert Steiner demonstrates, there is after all a possibility of serious problems developing that would prevent differential treatment of men and women in their selection for military service and armed combat (Steiner 1985). In civil rights the busing issue is not about accepting blacks into one's children's classrooms—which is what the polls seemed to be asking and what legislation seemed to be requiring—but accepting the busing of one's children to schools in black neighborhoods. The issue in employment moves from acceptance of blacks as equally deserving of jobs and income on the basis of qualifications to a quota requirement. The sequence of stages in the development of public opinion—liberalization, overreaching, the emergence of unexpected implications of liberalized policy, and counterreaction—is common in case after case. One can make the same argument I believe for school prayer, school discipline, rights for (and government aid to) private schools, and other issues on the social agenda.

But there is more to the story of the shifting pattern of public opinion. What we see is a shift not only in relative proportions supporting one or another position, but in the degree to which each position is organized and effective.

Here, too, a common and characteristic story can be told. Initially, whatever the state of public opinion in the large, the liberalizing element is better organized than the conservative one, better entrenched in the elite mass media, and represents the views of respectable opinion, that is, the opinion of the more highly educated, the wealthier, the national offices of the established Protestant churches. What then ensues is not so much a change of opinion—which is why the liberalizers can complain that the new conservative drift does not truly represent opinion change—but improved organization of the conservative forces in reaction to overreaching. Liberalization, proceeding on the basis of well-organized groups, invokes stronger organization in pre-

viously weakly organized or unorganized opposition. The antiabortion movement does not develop into a power of any significance until *after* the Supreme
Court decision of 1973. The antiabortionists were able to muster a paltry four
amicus briefs against the liberalization of abortion law—versus no less than
twenty from the liberalizers—in the legal skirmishing preceding the *Roe* v.
Wade decision. They represented tiny groups and organizations (Luker 1984).
Similarly, when Congress passed the ERA overwhelmingly in 1972 there was
simply no opposition: there was only Phyllis Schlafly. The anti-ERA movement was able to take advantage of the burgeoning antiabortion movement
following the *Roe* v. *Wade* decision (Steiner 1985). The connections between
the two may seem obscure to the rational mind; they were perfectly clear to
the opposition.

Even in the case of civil rights one can argue that, in effect, an overreaching by the better organized created an opposition where one did not exist
before. There was of course overwhelming organized opposition to school
desegregation after the *Brown* decision and to the Civil Rights Act of 1964
in the South, but in the North there was no such organized opposition. Only
after the issues of busing and quotas came up in the early 1970s was opposition
organized in the North, invoked by the unexpected extension of the meaning
of desegregation. Neighborhood movements against busing only organize—
obviously—after busing becomes a threat. They are ad hoc organizations,
with no previous organizational base of any kind. Civil rights activists argued
that this was the same opposition they had met in the South, moving North;
it was of course to their advantage to tar the opposition in the North with the
brush of racism. I would argue it was largely a new opposition. And similarly
with the counterattack on abortion and the ERA: it was an opposition in large
measure created by the offense.

There is thus a dynamics of issue formulation, implementation, and
resistance, and a parallel dynamics of organization, in which better organization seems to create its own opposition. But the underlying social reality
that makes possible these two sequences is the actual condition of opinion.
Here one finds that the liberalizing trends in American society in the 1960s
were deceptive in the sense that they failed to reveal the extent to which a
change in values had taken hold in the American people. First, there was
always firm resistance to these changes among large sections of the population:
the less educated, the less wealthy, the Catholic church, and most significantly, the evangelical and fundamentalist wings of Protestant denominations.
But how did fundamentalism, and the Christian right, revive after its overwhelming defeats over evolution and prohibition in the 1920s and 1930s? In
part because of the dynamics of issue formulation and organization described
above: When liberalization reached into new areas (abortion, school prayer,

school discipline, a higher degree of racial integration) the Christian right turned out not to be simply a decaying force, steadily encroached upon by higher education, East and West Coast cosmopolitanism, and mass media liberalization. It was able to organize and resist.

But second, new and surprising alliances were formed that gave new force to the renascent Christian right. The most important of these was with the Catholic church. Social conservatism was sharply divided in the 1950s and 1960s between urban Catholicism, strong in the Northeast and Midwest, and small-town and rural fundamentalism, strong in the border states, the South, and Southwest. The division of course goes back to the Reformation, but it was strengthened in the United States by nativist resistance to (largely Catholic) immigration in the late nineteenth and early twentieth centuries, a cultural clash over prohibition, and by disagreements over aid to private schools. The racial integration of the schools made the Christian right and fundamentalists as interested in aid to nonpublic schools as were the Catholics; the sharp change in moral climate in the schools and in public life in the late 1960s also drove them together.

This alliance between formerly hostile ethnic and religious elements is the major force that gives such strength to conservatism on social questions today. The issue of prohibition may still divide fundamentalists and Catholics, but on other issues they have joined. The relatively lonely Catholic opposition on abortion, based on clearly formulated church doctrine, now finds support— even more fervent than among its own adherents—from southern conservatives and fundamentalists, whose position is based more on a general social conservatism than on formulated theology. Catholic opposition to school aid now discovers strong support from fundamentalists who are rapidly creating their own schools, whether to escape from integration or from a liberal social environment in the schools in which prayer is banned, and discipline and dress codes are limited by constitutional restraints. Christian conservatives and Catholics are no longer divided by the issue of aid to private schools. I do not suggest an identity of positions: the fundamentalist private schools do not seek financial aid but freedom from government restraints and requirements; the Catholics are less concerned about these constraints, and more concerned about aid. Yet a degree of convergence that would have been unimaginable in the 1950s has occurred.

This convergence is odd in part because Catholics, as they move up socially and educationally, have become more liberal. But on some key issues the Catholic hierarchy, whatever the liberalization of the laity (and the hierarchy's own liberalization, as seen in its statements on nuclear war and the economy), must, by doctrine and interest, retain positions that make it an ally of the fundamentalists. History works in strange ways. Catholics who once created their own schools because they opposed the reading of the Protestant King James Bible are now vigorous supporters of anything that approximates prayer in the schools, even if it is only a moment of silence. Abortion is a key issue, on which a well formulated Catholic theological position joins a fierce resistance, based simply on social and familial conservatism, among fundamentalists.

The alliance has not yet spread to blacks and Hispanics because of the inevitable suspicion that the Christian right has not quite shed its racist attitudes. But if one looks at social attitudes by ethnic group (and by implication, religious group), hints of convergence can be found among the English, Scottish, and Welsh (who are concentrated in the South and the nonestablishment Protestant churches), the Protestant Irish (the Scotch-Irish, also in these areas and denominations), Catholic ethnic groups (Irish, Italian), blacks and Hispanics. So the alliance of fundamentalist churches and the Catholic church hierarchy is somewhat paralleled by attitudes of followers, though in general one will find more liberalism among the Catholic laity ("Opinion Roundup" 1984).

But there is yet a third development in popular attitudes that has added strength to the conservative side on these issues: it is a surprising turn among the young, who are no longer simply the most liberal age category on whatever issue one presents. This has been a pattern of public opinion for such a long time that any change in it is particularly revealing. The commonness of this pattern in the history of public opinion polling has led to much dispute as to whether a long-range secular change is occurring in opinion, with the young representing the most advanced current opinions, opinions they will continue to hold when they grow older, or whether liberalism among the young simply reflects youthful independence and experimentation, and will be replaced by a greater degree of conservatism as age brings family and job responsibilities.

The discussion may now be irrelevant. Aging is no longer invariably accompanied by growing conservatism, and the youngest age groups are no longer the most liberal. On many issues the youngest age group, aged eighteen to twenty-four years, is now more conservative than the group aged twenty-five to thirty-nine years: on abortion, and on a range of civil liberties issues (allowing a person who is against all churches and religion to speak, teach in a college or university, have his book in the library; and the same liberties to a Communist and to a person who believes blacks are genetically inferior).

Youth who attend college show an even sharper turn to conservatism on some issues. Thus, there is a "broad cluster of issues on which the young generally, and the college-trained in particular, now appear more conservative than their counterparts of a decade ago. For example, 68 percent of the college cohort eighteen to twenty-four years of age in the early 1970s described extramarital sex as wrong; 85 percent of the age eighteen to twenty-four college population of the early 1980's say it is wrong. Just 35 percent of the young college-age group of the early 1970's favored the death penalty, 67 percent of the current young college cohort support the death penalty for convicted murderers.'' There still remain issues on which the young are more liberal than the next age-group (ages twenty-five to thirty-nine), in particular the extension of individual rights to blacks and women—which may explain why the college population is more hostile than the group aged twenty-five to thirty-nine to allowing racists to speak, as well as Communists and atheists (Ladd 1985, 21).

Thus the argument that the shift to the right on the social agenda is owing simply to the predilections of the president and his advisers, or to the temporary prominence of the religious right through effectiveness in organization and in publicity, will not, I believe, hold. There is a change. Changes in public opinion can of course be quite evanescent, yet I think these changes will continue. The major reasons are, first, that the conditions of social disorder (crime, teen-age pregnancy, disorder in the schools, the prominence of pornography) continue to lead to some reaction. Second, the liberal response to these conditions of disorder has been discredited. It may well be true that if we do enough to raise the circumstances and prospects of low-income youth there will be less crime, more school accomplishment, less teen-age pregnancy, and so on. But by now there is considerable skepticism on the effectiveness of this course. Maybe not enough was done, maybe we did not stay the course long enough, maybe what we did counteracted what would have been even worse effects. For the most part, however, little support exists for resuscitating or expanding the liberal agenda.

Another agenda is available—and in this remarkably religious country it always has been available. It is the agenda the president has embraced: morality, chastity, religion, prayer in the schools. It is at present limited to exhortation; it may move on to compulsion. The battle is between prayer in the schools and bills of rights in schools, between exhortations to chastity and easier arrangements for contraception and abortion, between setting higher standards in and demanding better discipline in the schools and adapting to the immediate desires and impulses of youth. What has been forgotten during the long upward swing of liberalization is how deeply the first kind of orientation has been felt by the American people. Some of the figures given above (as on attitudes toward premarital sex) will undoubtedly astonish the readers of this chapter. There is a good reason for this: the leadership strata, the better-educated, those who hold higher positions, are much more liberal on these matters than the people in general. A study of American values by the Connecticut Mutual Life Insurance Company a few years ago demonstrated this spread: 65 percent of the public believed abortion to be morally wrong, only 36 percent of the leaders; 71 percent of the public felt homosexuality to be morally wrong, 42 percent of the leaders; 57 percent of the public considered smoking marijuana wrong, 33 percent of the leaders.

A remarkably large base of agreement exists from which leaders—such as the present ones—who agree with the public on these matters can draw.

WITH WHAT CONSEQUENCES?

How do we place these developments in a long-range perspective? We are acquainted with surprising shifts in opinion in this country, accompanied with instant analyses as to their long-range staying power. Who now remembers Charles Reich's *The Greening of America*? What has happened to Daniel Yankelovich's *New Rules*? (In all fairness, some of the public opinion results reported above support some of the "new rules.") Recently these rapid alternations in opinion and their political consequences—Johnson's overwhelming victory in 1964 signalling one kind of country, McGovern's overwhelming defeat eight years later, another—have given rise to interpretations, historical and social-psychological, to explain what seem to be regular alternations in public and private issues (Albert Hirschmann 1981), or regular upsurges of what Samuel Huntington (1981) calls "creedal passion." Depending on one's point of view, there is something satisfying or depressing about any theory that emphasizes the underlying regularity of cycles, dependent on factors that have a longer time-span of effectiveness than the specific passion-arousing issues that initiate and close cycles. Those alarmed by the rise of the right and its increasing self-confidence or arrogance may take comfort in such theories, and wait for the inevitable decline of resurgent traditionalism. That in the long run this must happen no one would dispute. I have suggested above some reasons why we should not expect this decline in the short run. And I am more impressed by the new factors that lie behind the present upsurge than with its similarity with fundamentalism's last big push in American politics in the 1920s.

Certain elements are of course the same. One can locate in the same geographical areas more or less the strength of conservatism in religion and values, and the centers of change. Hollywood and New York were the enemy then, and the enemy is still located on the cosmopolitan coasts. The alarm over changing sexual habits and mores is the same. The resort to an ever-unchanging Bible as the source of truth and values is the same. The fear that the new liberalism will corrupt children and youth in the schools is the same.

But what is different promises to give substantial strength to the movement for conservative practices and values for some time. One reason why things are different is that, as I pointed out above, almost every issue in the social agenda is an issue created by new and path-breaking (and to conservative legal scholars, unfounded) interpretations of the Constitution by the Supreme Court. In the 1920s and 1930s the Constitution and the courts were involved only as defenses against the most egregious attacks on freedom of speech and press. The federal courts played a reactive and defensive role. For a generation since 1954 the courts have played an active role, pushing ahead of public opinion, upsetting practices and expectations long established. If they have checked themselves to some extent in recent years, the battle still goes on, and on any major decision it is touch and go whether a majority of the court can be mustered on one side or another.

The entanglement of the issues of the social agenda with the constitutional structure of the United States is to my mind a new development, one that has made these issues a permanent part of the agenda of Congress and the president, and it is hardly likely they can be so confined that they once again become issues only for state legislatures, city councils, and local school boards.

The issues arise then not only because of a resurgent traditionalism, but because of a long process of judicial (and some legislative) liberalization, which raises serious constitutional issues, and which will not be resolved easily or soon, even if more Reagan appointees begin to change the pattern of judicial decisions in the areas we are considering.

A second reason why things are different: the changes that have taken place in American society in the 1960s and 1970s and that have to my mind been the principal initiating force behind the conservative revival are more extensive and significant than equivalent changes in the 1920s. They include the increase in teen-age pregnancy; the growing number of families with a female head of household; liberalization of law and opinion affecting sexual relations, including homosexual relations; concerns about the effectiveness of the schools, with attention to "discipline" generally first in public opinion polls; widespread use of drugs, spreading to social groups and age groups previously considered immune; questions about the extent to which equal treatment of and equal outcomes for the sexes should be pushed (which come most sharply to the fore in the armed forces); and the scale and openness of pornography.

In the 1920s, one may argue, the changes of the times were as disturbing. And admittedly once one leaves those areas of public policy in which comparative judgments based on economic analyses are possible, no definitive answer can be given as to "more" or "less," "worse" or "better." But there is enough evidence that a large number of Americans feel that the nation is going through a serious moral crisis. The public is sharply divided on these issues. What is to one side healthy liberal change is to the other dangerous decadence. It is hard to see how a strong consensus can be forged that will on the one hand accept these changes as generally for the best, or on the other decide that they are for the worse and drive them underground by official suppression. A permanent combat has been prepared by change: and I do not think those that have, as they see it, been forced into combat will move off the stage, particularly since they already perceive some victories to be within their grasp.

And perhaps a third reason why things are different: the resurgent fundamentalism and traditionalist movement has tried to purge itself of racism, anti-Semitism, and anti-Catholicism. It is now capable of making alliances that help it break out of the confined ground of the Bible Belt. In this increasingly heterogeneous, multiethnic, and multiracial society, this gives the movement the hope of becoming a larger and more permanent part of the American scene than when it was restricted by its racial and religious prejudices.

One can add other differences: I raise these to argue against the tendency to see only recurrence of a cyclical pattern. That is occurring, of course; but the differences in this phase of the cycle may be more important than similarities with previous upsurges.

What are the consequences for American society and its problems?

I consider the effects of the strength of the moral-religious right on, first, the condition of racial minorities, particularly the blacks, who are directly affected by some of the points at issue in the social agenda; and second, on the social problems that have aroused the resurgence and made it so potent.

The black group is the one most closely affected by two of the key points in the social agenda, busing and quotas. On both issues a reversal of position has been initiated by the executive branch, which may have substantial consequences for these policies. No major consequences have yet been experienced, owing to the significant involvement of the federal courts in defining and maintaining these policies and the inability of Congress to make much headway against the courts on these issues.

As a large-scale approach to the problems of education of black children, busing is widely discredited. It continues where it was at some point implemented (an exception being the abandonment of busing in Los Angeles, required under state law, on the basis of change in the state constitution). No major new busing program has been launched for some years. Just how to end existing court-ordered busing is a complicated matter. But a model has recently become available: Norfolk has become the first city in which the court has allowed abandonment of busing where it has been instituted and contested.

But the issue is rapidly losing salience. The aim of busing after all was improvement in the education of black children. Modest improvements have been shown as a result of integration. But the popular resistance to integration by busing is enormous. The extent to which integration will come about through magnet school programs and voluntary decisions, now favored by the administration, is limited. The conclusion must be that the improvement in the education of black children, if it is to come about, will be through other means than public programs aimed at adjusting the proportions of black and white children in the schools. In any case, much informed black opinion has lost enthusiasm for this course (Bell 1980). For this reason, perhaps, the Reagan administration has not suffered serious attacks for its lack of interest in busing. Subsequent administrations will take notice of this.

Forms of race consciousness and race preference in employment and promotion are more extensively established and are institutionalized in major private and in public employment. Support for this is nonexistent in the administration, but the practices are still protected by a large body of administrative requirements and legal decisions, by the political weight of minority groups, and the fact that the programs encompass women as well as minorities. The structure of this system has been considerably weakened under the Reagan administration and will hardly be restored to the vigor with which it was developed, expanded, and implemented in the Nixon, Ford, and Carter years, whatever administration comes to power in 1989.

The effects of the system of affirmative action are much analyzed and somewhat disputed (Leonard 1985 and Welch 1985). Perhaps they have marginally improved the jobs blacks could obtain. Perhaps employer attitudes on what individuals from minority groups they would take a risk on have led to employment losses for others. In any event, the overall economic condition of the black minority gives no cause for satisfaction, owing to high rates of youth unemployment, and higher rates of unemployment generally, which seem hardly affected by affirmative action. Even when affirmative action and major programs of youth employment and training were implemented with the enthusiasm of a Carter administration, it did not seem to have much effect on these serious problems. If they are to be ameliorated, it is likely that it will have to be through other means and mechanisms—those which have been employed by other minorities, in the past, and now. No one can underestimate for blacks and for the society as a whole the gravity and social consequences of the low income and unemployment and consequent family disorder that prevails in poor black communities. That attention must be paid is obvious. It is by no means obvious that the attention that must be paid is in the form of new social programs.

Is the attention defined by the system of exhortation and support for traditional morality and religion now favored by the administration? What about the restoration of school prayer, to the limits that the Supreme Court will allow? And limitations on the right to abortion? Exhortations to chastity and child-bearing as against abortion? Encouragement of adoption? Stronger discipline in the schools, supported perhaps by some limitations in constitutional protection for students' rights? Higher standards in the schools?

It is hard to believe all this will do much to improve the lot of racial minorities, let alone to turn around American society, as is often suggested. However, in substantial pockets of American society in which a somewhat homogeneous moral order prevails, this kind of program may do something to protect it. The passion over the most recent striking down of the moment of silence by the Supreme Court raises the question, what *does* a moment of silence, or of school prayer, or of Bible-reading, do in the schools? I have seen no attempt at a serious analysis of this. Everyone takes it for granted that the issue is purely symbolic. Does the restoration of a symbol change behavior? I am a skeptic because, if the symbol is effective, it is only within a larger order. The school in which prayer was conducted or the Bible was read was one in which the pledge of allegiance was taken by all; teacher and principal authority was respected; dress was in measure prescribed for students and teachers; the curriculum was fixed and unquestioned; and so on. Some parents search for such schools, and one sees considerable response to the establishment of "Christian" fundamentalist schools and considerable enthusiasm, where that option is offered in the public schools, for "traditional" schools. The restoration of the whole package might conceivably have more effects than the minimal moment of silence now so bitterly fought for in some states against the Supreme Court. If the symbol is considered as part of a larger change toward greater authority (which means discipline, homework, and so forth), one can be more optimistic.

I see no reason why the symbol must be given up where it exists and where it is demanded by a community that accepts the values it represents. The argument that the Constitution forbids it is accepted by a scant majority of the Supreme Court, and is hardly compelling. Rather, the Court acts as a participant in a social conflict over the nature of the public schools and the values that may be propagated in them. When Catholics and Jews saw in school prayer the imposition on their children of a dominant and intolerant Protestantism, the Court was acting in the best spirit of its mandate—to protect minorities, define the ground rules for a heterogeneous society. When Catholics and Jews are almost equally disturbed by the conditions in the public schools to which the "moment of silence" responds (if only symbolically), then the Court acts to support a minority position of declining strength and doubtful value in advancing any of the objectives of the public schools.

I would make a similar argument on other elements in the social agenda. The Supreme Court in 1973 in its abortion decision was implementing a majority view defending private choice, and could expect that it would serve, as it has in the past, to mark liberal change in American society, whatever the immediate storm that greeted the decision. This position became harder to maintain as the Court had to rule on the right to abortion for minors without parental involvement or knowledge.

Just as one can ask, will "a moment of silence" do anything to increase discipline in the schools,[6] one can ask, will restrictions on the distribution of contraceptives to minors, exhortations to chastity rather than contraceptive use, the banning of progressive sex education in the schools, measures to increase parental authority over children's behavior do anything to reduce teen-age pregnancy, young families with a female head, or delinquency? It is hardly likely. But where all this is part of an existing conservative order, and in this varied society there are many places in which this is the case, to insist on a national norm based on the Constitution is only to undermine traditional enclaves where these problems may not yet be so severe, or where there is general agreement on how they should be handled. The present social agenda may be seen as one of protection or one of universal conservative change; if the former, the agenda serves a function and defends heterogeneity; if the latter, it threatens a new uniformity and the imposition of a homogeneity that many reject. The first goal is within its powers. The second will meet enormous resistance, and in any case is hardly likely to restore the traditional order.

To restore a traditional order of society seems a hopeless task (although there are historic cases in which that has happened); a program of protection, however, is possible. Protection seems to be the course the Reagan administration has set. The battles over most of the issues in the social agenda concern the protection of traditional norms and practices where they exist, rather than efforts to extend them to the whole society. The administration seems to be engaged in a program of protection of enclaves of traditional values and of political response to the representatives of those enclaves. Its successes in that enterprise (as yet quite minor) may give fundamentalists the hope of taking the offensive and spreading the traditional order to the social groups and parts of the country that now reject it. This is what the liberals

---

6. Discipline in the schools is only one of the objectives of the moment of silence, of course, and as the majority of the Supreme Court argued in the case, the primary objective was to retain a toehold for prayer in the school.

fear—a new Prohibition, and new Eighteenth Amendment initiatives. It may come to that yet. Until now the defensive principle, I believe, has dominated over the aggressive.

What does all this change mean for the political future of the United States? The fundamentalists and traditionalists are only one part of a Republican coalition that (like all governing coalitions in American life) includes many elements who do not support or actively oppose the right wing on the social agenda. The leader of the Republican coalition accepts the social agenda but does not devote his efforts to its advancement; as a result, we find more statements of support than actual change in policies, though these have occurred, and are occurring. But I believe the coalition will hold and the fundamentalist-conservative element will continue to participate actively within it. It brings to the Republican coalition a kind of strength that it has not had for sixty years. Through the social agenda it reaches into low-income and low-status occupation groups, and in particular into the South. Fundamentalists and Evangelicals, as many observers agree, are poorer than other Americans, less educated, less concentrated in professional occupations and high-status occupations, and particularly numerous in the South.[7] In the past, it was argued, Republicans could only gain a presidential majority by appealing to the nationalism of Americans: if they appealed to interests they lost because they were the party of the less numerous, prosperous strata. Under President Reagan, Republicans can now make an appeal to lower-status Evangelicals and Fundamentalists who were once solidly in the Democratic camp. This harbors a major long-range shift in the fortunes of the party of the right, and of liberal social policy.

---

7. For supporting statistics, see Hunter (1983).

REFERENCES

Bell, Derrick. ed., 1980. *Shades of 'Brown'*. New York: Teacher's College Press.

Califano, Joseph A., Jr. 1981. *Governing America: An Insider's Report from the White House and the Cabinet*. New York: Simon & Schuster.

Davison, Roger. 1983. "Procedures and Politics in Congress." In Gilbert Y. Steiner, *The Abortion Dispute and the American System*. Washington, D.C.: Brookings Institution.

Goldman, Sheldon. 1985. "Reaganizing the Judiciary: The First-Term Appointments." *Judicature* (April-May): 314.

Hertling, James. 1985. "Tax Reform Plan Forcing Shift in Tax Credit Rhetoric." *Education Week* May 29: 10.

Hirschmann, Albert O. 1981. *Shifting Involvements: Private Interest and Public Action*. Princeton, New Jersey: Princeton University Press.

Hunter, James Davison. 1983. *American Evangelicalism and the Quandary of Modern Religion*. New Brunswick, New Jersey: Rutgers University Press.

Huntington, Samuel P. 1981. *American Politics: The Promise of Disharmony*. Cambridge, Massachusetts: Harvard University Press.

Ladd, Everett Carl. 1985. "Values: Generations Apart." *Public Opinion* (December-January).

Leonard, Jonathan S. 1985. "What Was Affirmative Action?" In *Selected Affirmative Action Topics in Employment and Business Set-Asides: A Consultation/Hearing of the United States Commission on Civil Rights*. Vol. 1. Washington, D.C.: U.S. Commission on Civil Rights. March 6–7.

Luker, Kristin. 1984. *Abortion and the Politics of Motherhood*. Berkeley: University of California Press.

Office of the Federal Register. 1982, 1983, 1984. "Administration of Ronald Reagan." *Weekly Compilation of Presidential Documents*. Washington, D.C.: National Archives and Records Administration.

"Opinion Roundup." 1984. *Public Opinion* (October-November): 28–29.

"Opinion Roundup." 1985. *Public Opinion* (April-May): 27.

Sackett, Victoria A. 1985. "Between Pro-Life and Pro-Choice." *Public Opinion* (April-May).

Skerry, Peter. 1978. "The Class Conflict over Abortion." *The Public Interest* (Summer).

Steiner, Gilbert Y. 1985. *Constitutional Inequality: The Political Fortunes of the Equal Rights Amendment*. Washington, D.C.: Brookings Institution.

Welch, Finis. 1985. "Affirmative Action in Employment: An Overview and Assessment of Effects." In *Selected Affirmative Action Topics in Employment and Business Set-Asides: A Consultation/Hearing of the United States Commission on Civil Rights*. Vol. 1. Washington, D.C.: U.S. Commission on Civil Rights. March 6–7.

REAGANISM AND THE SEARCH FOR A PUBLIC PHILOSOPHY

Hugh Heclo

By its own account, the Reagan administration has been engaged in a whole-hearted effort to change the prevailing directions of thought about American domestic government. More than any other national leadership group in a number of decades, Ronald Reagan and his active supporters have seen themselves as engaged in a war of ideas. It has been a war on many fronts, ranging from the president's superbly crafted speeches to direct mail campaigns, policy studies by new conservative think tanks, media ventures, and publications funded by probusiness foundations.

Sophisticates have often sneered at the simplifications involved in Reagan claims of "restoring traditional values" or conducting a "second American Revolution." Cynicism, however, is an affliction that has often prevented intellectuals from taking ideas seriously in mass politics. And although the academic community has quibbled about the existence and exact nature of an American public philosophy, the Reagan administration and its advocates harbor no doubt that such a thing exists and is worth fighting for.

This ideological effort, which for shorthand purposes I will call Reaganism, deserves to be taken seriously. Ideas are a source of political power, and for all their avowed pragmatism, Americans are constantly using certain conceptual lenses to understand what is happening around them. In this chapter I try to interpret the larger significance of the Reagan years for America's public philosophy. Assessing contemporary ideological trends is of course a tough assignment, the kind of highly speculative, reputationally risky topic

I am grateful for the advice and comments of Samuel Beer, Henry Brady, Alan Brinkley, Michael Lacy, Aaron Wildavsky, and Melissa Williams.

31

where prudence should overcome any desire to publish. And yet a widespread perception exists that something important is happening over and beyond the particular policy decisions and political maneuverings of the Reagan administration. Ours, like every generation, is engaged in a halting, half-conscious search for the orienting ideas to explain itself to itself. The question is too tempting and too important to be avoided: after all the hoopla and turmoil of everyday politics, what does Reaganism mean for these self-understandings? Is Reaganism more than Reagan?

The first section of the chapter discusses the content and cross-cutting dimensions of an American public philosophy as the Reagan years began. The second section examines the various ways Reaganism has fit into and altered this context of ideas. The chapter concludes with some implications for the future; I take as my premise the notion that Reaganism, like every other mortal effort, can be expected to have unanticipated consequences. No amount of Reagan luck is likely to hold up against that certainty.

VARIATIONS ON A PUBLIC PHILOSOPHY

What is a "public philosophy"? Before going too far, it is important to be as clear as possible about the nature of this slippery concept.

An English writer once said that the most important thing about a person is what he takes for granted. The term public philosophy is a way of trying to capture the outlook on public affairs that seems to be taken for granted in a particular period. It directs attention to ideas in good currency that have a kind of intermediate stability, less fixed than the deeply engrained political traditions of a nation (reverence for the Constitution, individual liberty, and so on) but more rigid than passing public moods (whether or not the country is on the right track, how well the president is doing). A public philosophy is a synthesis of ideas and actions that is persuasive in the particular setting of the times. It is thus a political generation's design for self-understanding, a way of perceiving and responding to events in the political world. A public philosophy invests what would otherwise be disconnected sets of experiences with a particular logic and rationale.

Public philosophies do not come neatly packaged as sudden revelations or sharply defined political creations. A public philosophy is not something "thought up" by anybody. It is an interpretive framework squeezed out as the by-product of real strains in society and the unwinding logic of political ideas.

To say that a certain public philosophy prevails is not to say that everyone agrees—far from it, because the terms of any public philosophy involve essentially contestable concepts such as liberty, justice, and the public interest.

A public philosophy prevails insofar as it provides the dominant framework for defining the field of political argument and interpreting events. Such a phenomenon is "real" even though it may not respond to precise measurement or literal readings. Looking back at the subtexts of the larger American experience, one sees, not just the laws that happened to get passed or a collection of individuals who happened to hold office, but Jacksonian, Gilded Age, Progressive Era, or New Deal approaches to the affairs of state. In short, one sees public philosophies.

There is no point in trying to be dogmatic about such matters. The boundaries separating a political tradition, public philosophy, or public mood are certainly not absolute, and any given intellectual construct may migrate across them. It might be said that a viable public philosophy sinks its roots into the deep soil of a nation's political tradition while also catching the wind of current moods. And this is the interesting feature of Reaganism. After two electoral landslides, there can be no doubt that Ronald Reagan caught the mood of the times. The issue is, were some more fundamental, enduring changes in our ways of thinking about public affairs occurring in the 1980s?

To deal with that thorny question it is useful to have some sense of prevailing intellectual currents before the Reagan years. What one finds is essentially an amalgam with three main perspectives.

Consensus

At the most general level, the American public philosophy has long been characterized by a substantial consensus, roughly encompassed by the term *liberal individualism*.[1] From this perspective a number of historical and intellectual circumstances have combined to create and sustain a distinctively American view of public affairs and the role of government in the nation's social development.[2]

The particular components of this American consensus are familiar. The keystone is the high priority given to the value of personal liberty. Individuals,

1. See Hartz (1957), Hofstadter (1957), and Boorstin (1958, 1965, 1973). More recent statements bearing on this view are in Diggins (1985) and Kramnick (1982).

2. Some have pointed to the nation's Lockean intellectual heritage as a source of pervasive liberal values and institutions. Others have seen the particular sequences of American historical development as being especially important: with mass democracy achieved before bureaucratization of the government or industrialization of the economy, there was less chance of developing a coherent class-based politics or centralized administrative state. Still others emphasize structural determinants. The availability of an unexploited frontier with inexpensive resources and high returns to labor, of a continental mass market, and later of a hegemonic position in the international economy—all these factors have sustained a thoroughgoing public ideology of liberal individualism in an essentially commercial republic. For example, see Katzenstein (1978), Potter (1958), and Rimlinger (1971).

and not some outside authority, are the best judges of their own interests. From this conviction derive some of the most characteristic features of our politics and policies. One strand of thinking argues for limited government, efforts to minimize administrative discretion, a presumption against centralization and for dispersed power. Another strand celebrates private effort, an individually based struggle for self-advancement, a presumption of an economy based on free enterprise and private capital. The social role of government is to keep the rules of the game fair, ensure equality of opportunity, and then stand out of the way.

Without jumping to conclusions, one can find evidence to support the consensus model. The academic community studying public opinion has found enduring structures of ideas that seem little affected by the comings and goings of politicians or policies. Guiding ideas in Americans' approach to public affairs for many years have been belief in the American dream of individual opportunity, support for the free enterprise system, rejection of class-based politics and collectively orchestrated schemes of redistribution, suspicion of government power, and identification of personal freedom with the private sector. These ideas have been found not only in the placid 1950s but also in the so-called turbulent 1960s and 1970s. By the same token, historical studies of the great eras of liberal reform show that New Deal and Great Society policies were characterized by quite familiar appeals and political routines.[3] Initiatives such as the War on Poverty announced in 1964 were framed in terms of advancing individual opportunity. Social Security thrived politically by being sold as a scheme of individual contributions and self-help, not collective redistribution. American politics in the 1970s, as at every other time, was a struggle to occupy the sprawling political center with policies claiming to enhance personal liberty and economic individualism.

Dualistic Conflict

If those who hold the consensus view alert us to elements of stability that are easy to overlook, it is also fair to say that proponents of liberal individualism have never entirely had their own way. Movements in the American public philosophy have occurred through struggles between what are really two great systems of both philosophical thought and historical interpretation. Each offers a distinctive outlook on public affairs and the role of government.

In one corner stands a rights-based individualism founded on the claim that society should be conceived as composed of separate, unique individuals with their own conceptions of what is good. From this follows a refusal to

---

3. For example, see Wood (1972), Derthick (1979), Cates (1983), and Heclo (1985).

affirm any given conception of the good life and moral obligation. Political allegiance is to the framework of basic rights and liberties and not to assorted visions of the ends that people may choose to pursue within that framework. The concept of such rights is ethically prior to any conception of the good. It follows that constitutionalism, the name for such a framework, is fundamentally about limited government, the negative, regularized restraint of power in the collective hands of officialdom.

In the other corner stands a philosophical tradition that denies the idea of separate, freely choosing individuals apart from a social context. Individual rights, like all social meanings, are human constructions derived from the shared conceptions of people in community with each other and not from abstract presumptions about self-contained individuals. This communitarian interpretation calls for fuller recognition of the claims of collective membership in an ongoing social enterprise than any system of rights-based individualism allows. To a self-governing people, constitutionalism is not a negative, self-denying ordinance. Rather it is a positive, empowering device allowing people to take action about their common life together. When periods of upheaval and reform occur, it is not simply because a primordial American instinct has rebelled against public authority; it is because American politics has resolved, in its own messy way (as with the civil rights movement), to keep faith with the idea of America as a socially inclusive rather than exclusive community. Thus American constitutionalism is an affirmation, not a negation of public power. It is a design for people to shape their lives together rather than a nonaggression pact among a random collection of individuals who happen to occupy a geographic space.

The American public philosophy at any period has always been a series of trial balances struck between those two opposing views of individualism and communitarianism.[4] By the end of the 1970s the prevailing amalgam

---

4. The Progressive historians saw a recurring struggle between the forces of privilege and the virtues of the common man. See Hofstadter (1968). More recent radical interpretations suggest an American public agenda dominated by a social and economic establishment that periodically must confront but soon reasserts social control over the grass roots, equalitarian impulses of popular democracy (for example, Piven and Cloward 1979). Of course, it is roughly the same antinomies that have underlaid the Schlesingers's (senior and junior) influential model of alternatives between periods of reformist, liberal energy and periods of stabilizing, conservative reaction. See Schlesinger (1949) and Schlesinger, Jr. (1980). So too another cyclical view presented recently by Samuel Huntington pictures an inherent conflict between the nation's ideals of democratic self-government and the necessity for organized power; this is said to yield a recurring sequence of reforming, moralistic upheaval that subsides into cynicism, complacency and eventual hypocrisy, setting into motion the next reaction of creedal passions (Huntington 1981). A sweeping dualistic interpretation is presented in Kelley (1977). Thoughtful literature reviews are presented in Ross (1979) and Brinkley (1984).

seemed to be essentially one of stalemate and mutual exhaustion between these two world-weary combatants. Everything had become so complex. The channel of individualism branched left and right. On the right was a cost-benefit, economic vision of self-advancement. The individualism of the left spoke for a no less privatized but more antimaterialistic, romantic vision of self-realization. The proliferation of publications in the vein of *Self*, *Lifestyle*, *Money Magazine*, and so on seem to capture the spirit of the times. The strand of communitarianism had also forked left and right, not in any mere theoretical way but in forms embodying real social configurations. Communitarians of the right spoke for exclusive, parochial assemblies of believers while communitarians of the left spoke a language of social inclusiveness and nonjudgmental altruism. Expecting coherent political discourse was like asking the Moral Majority, the Catholic bishops, and gay rights groups to produce a joint communique on human brotherhood.

Disintegration

As the 1970s progressed, what emerged was not so much a structured argument as a babble outside any agreed-upon interpretive framework. At times the confused shouting match seemed to be going on not only between social groups but within each individual. Although consensus and fundamental dualism both had their advocates, the dominating interpretation by 1980 was one of disintegration, a coming apart of what intellectual historians used to call the American mind.

For those living through the times, the 1960s and 1970s seemed a turning point when once-stable public understandings became increasingly incoherent. The exact scope of this disintegration can range quite widely depending on the observers. For some it has been a matter of strategic mistakes made by the generation of American liberals that came after Franklin D. Roosevelt. For example, Samuel Beer has written of the ending of the New Deal public philosophy in the early 1960s and Robert Reich of the liberal abdication.[5] This unravelling of a public philosophy is said to have occurred as the liberalism of the 1960s took on a different and self-destructive quality compared to New Deal liberalism. In Beer's analysis the new liberalism fragmented F.D.R.'s inclusive nationalism into a vast array of groups making claims on government but incapable of constituting a public; instead of the New Deal's meat-and-potatoes focus on personal economic security and countering business power with union power, Great Society liberalism took on technocratic

---

5. See Beer (1978) and Reich (1985). See also White (1982), Matusow (1984), O'Neill (1971), and Schambra (1982).

and romantic qualities that fostered illusions of perfectibility in society and public policy. Reich emphasizes the tendency in the 1960s to base policy on notions of altruism and directionless conciliation, rather than on the sense of social solidarity, mutual dependence, and principled acceptance of hard choices that characterized the older liberalism. The result was a kind of permissiveness that most Americans ultimately found naive and unacceptable.

Other critics consider the disintegration of the public philosophy as the reflection of a deeper moral degeneration. From a more or less leftist political perspective, what is at work is the tendency for welfare capitalism to corrode the social ethic and moral foundations on which its own existence depends. Society loses its ethical bearings as people acquire a shriveled, confused view of themselves as moral agents. Politics loses its normative meaning even as the yearning for valuations beyond the materialistic norms of the marketplace grows apace. Viewed from the political right, it is clear that America's public philosophy has disintegrated because of the moral emptiness that lies at the heart of secular individualism. Contemporary liberal thought is said to have beguiled Americans into mistaking the absence of an ethical order for social tolerance, disunity for diversity, self-indulgence for self-realization, inoffensiveness for civility. These critics point to the futility of any search for a public philosophy that is not grounded in a vision of transcendent moral purpose, whether these be religious values or some refurbished form of civic republicanism.

America before Reaganism

What then was the pre-Reagan state of the American public philosophy—consensus, conflict, or degeneration? Making any simple choice among the three perspectives can easily become a way of prejudging the meaning of Reaganism, a kind of Rorschach test for projecting each observer's hopes, fears, and personal preferences.

From the consensus view the Reagan years can readily be made to fall into place with the long tradition of liberal individualism. The vision of dualistic conflict can also project a plausible story. If one adopts the first perspective of consensus and likes what has been going on in Washington over the past fifty years, then one is likely to talk about a continuing agenda of nation-building: American politics has been at work extending the meaning of citizenship beyond political rights to economic and social rights and in opposition to economic privilege. Reaganism is then set up to take the fall for reneging on this project.

If one does not like what was happening before the 1980s a different kind of argument can be made. The rot sets in, so to speak, with New Deal liberalism. It is then that policymakers in Washington begin their attempt to obliterate the essential condominium of individualistic and communitarian perspectives. Instead of treating the communitarian vision as appropriate for local government levels and private associations and the individual, rights-based vision as appropriate for a national government concerned with personal liberty and economic progress—instead of this traditional pattern, New Deal liberalism sets down the path of using the central government to create one great social community. This perverse project culminates in the 1960s with the liberals' Great Society agenda. The results of attempting to remake society from Washington is government-imposed uniformity, heightened group antagonism, and an undermining of traditional institutions. Following this line of thought, one is then prepared to present Reaganism as restoring America to its true self.

If one simply adopts the third perspective and sees a prevailing disintegration, the Reagan years are likely to take on a significance either as the last gasp of a bankrupt system of welfare capitalism or as the first step in a moral crusade for putting the American public philosophy back together.

The most reasonable position is to recognize that the public philosophy is, and always has been an amalgam. Its three crosscurrents are more or less constant and what changes is the shape of their relationship.

The particular shape that this mixture had assumed by 1980 was, however, clearly troubling to many people. It has become fashionable to dismiss the Carter presidency as a meaningless interlude (with Jimmy Carter playing, as conservatives would like to have it, Buchanan to Reagan's Lincoln). In fact the Carter presidency was significant in giving concrete expression to the troubled state of affairs. The classic consensus impulse was present—a government as good as the people, nothing wrong with us, only "them" in Washington getting in the way of we the people. The appeal to dualistic conflict was also evident, as Carter echoed the old populist and progressive confrontations with special interests and vested privilege. And, a modernized version existed of the old jeremiad call for a people that was falling apart as a people—the malaise problem—to restore their civic souls.

The Carter White House worked hard at symbolic leadership. The three ingredients were there but the amalgam never came together because no real social configurations existed "out there" to underscore what the Democratic Jimmy Carter sought to symbolize. If it was no longer a government of the people, good as they were, it could be readily characterized as a government of the Democrats, dominant as they were for the past two generations. Likewise, special interests and vested privilege seemed more identified with modern Democrats' Washington cornucopia than with progressives' and populists' old enemy, the captains of industry and commerce. Malaise seemed at best a codeword for presidential failure and at worst an attack on the underlying strength of the American spirit.

It was in this context that America entered the 1980s and the Reagan years. Consensus applied with regard to the long American political tradition. Disintegration caught the mood of the moment. But in between there was no focused argument organizing the essential conflict about the meaning of American public affairs. The articulate portions of the Democratic party seemed dumbstruck in the face of events, unwilling to retreat on the New Deal-Fair Deal-Great Society commitments or to go forward toward some more social democratic vision of an egalitarian, solidaristic order. In these ideological terms the economic downturn of 1979 and the subsequent defeat of Jimmy Carter was really beside the point. The 1980 election results merely ended the Democratic agony.

WHERE REAGANISM FITS

At one level the meaning of the Reagan years is quite straightforward. Some time in the 1970s a political reaction against big-government liberalism gathered momentum. The alarm bells could be heard on many sides: tax revolts at the state and local government levels, Washington's cool response to the New York City financial crisis in 1975, the unexpected stampede in Congress to cut capital gains taxes in 1978, the easy defeat of traditional reforms on the Democratic agenda (national health insurance, welfare reform, the Humphrey-Hawkins full employment plan, and so on), the beginning of cutbacks in federal spending for state and local government and for some social programs. Ideas were on the move well before Ronald Reagan arrived in Washington. Reaganism caught this mood and in doing so tapped the enduring verities of the American consensus—individual freedom is the touchstone of good government; government power, especially when it is centralized in Washington, is to be distrusted; free enterprise is the key to economic progress and personal liberty; the role of government is to assure equal opportunity, not to mandate particular results.

In effect, this straightforward interpretation does not take Reaganism seriously as an ideological force in the last quarter of the twentieth century. There can be no impact on the public philosophy because the Reagan administration is already in full accord with it. The problem with this interpretation is that it views the public philosophy as a set of verities rather than tensions. It fails to realize that rearranging and applying old ideas to current circumstances can itself produce a new ideological construct. My view is that Reaganism has been fitting the familiar pieces together in a novel way that deserves to be taken seriously.

It is important not to cast the issue simply in terms of how Ronald Reagan thinks, a sure way of sinking into an intellectual swamp. I say this without prejudice because no successful politician should be expected to think like a social philosopher. (In fact, doing so is probably a good way to become an unsuccessful politician.) Distinctive public philosophies emerge, not from some politician's thinking but from the interactions among political leaders and the movements those leaders symbolize and try to hold together. Reagan is the first president in many years to have come to office heading what might loosely be called a political movement. Putting together this coalition has had the effect of putting together a distinctive collection of ideas capable of making a strong claim on American public thought.

Reaganism grows from a bond forged between groups that previously had little to do with one another. Most visible among these groups is the southern and Sun Belt new right and its Moral Majority, which began to gain force as a self-conscious political movement in the mid-1960s. For this group, Reaganism speaks for school prayer and against abortion, against the corrupt ways of Washington and the redistributive schemes of the liberal "establishment." It speaks for the virtues of traditional America. Ronald Reagan's coalition also makes alliance with the neoconservatives, those disgruntled New Deal Democrats whose intellects crowd the pages of journals such as *The Public Interest* and *Commentary*. For the neoconservatives, Reaganism corrects the liberal permissiveness of the 1960s and 1970s, reintroduces the republican virtues of decentralization, and stands tough-minded on law, order, and national security. At the same time the coalition embraces business, large and small, by promising to reduce government intervention that results in overregulation and high taxes.

In return, each group in the coalition provides valuable political resources for the office-holding representatives of Reaganism. Leaders of the new right provide personnel to man the new government as well as a mass audience accessible through the right's own print, television, and radio networks, voter registration drives, and direct mail fund-raising; neoconservatives offer intellectual leadership in translating middle-class populism into defensible doctrines and policies; business contributes funds.

If Reaganism is to be a genuine amalgam of ideas rather than simply a collective noun for the slogans of a diverse coalition, it must encompass a vast array of tensions among differing interests and outlooks. Tension exists between the young, college-educated professionals—the "yuppies"—supporting individual choice when it comes to economic interests or free-market ideology and the opponents of individual choice when it comes to the social issues of the religious right. A cultural and economic tension separates the Sun Belt country club set, the small-town following of religious radio stations, and the cosmopolitan readership of *Commentary*. Spokesmen for the coalition harbor few doubts about its coherence: "Americans have been mobilizing— some for more than a decade, others for just a few years—against liberalism and in support of traditional values. . . .

Resurgent traditionalism is most dynamic at the grass roots, in life's very private, yet most critical sectors. There, legions of Americans are going back to basics in education, back to Scripture and spirituality in religion, back to trusting the free enterprise system, back to appreciating the nuclear family" (Pines 1982, 15–16).

However, the testimony of enthusiasts can scarcely be the whole story. The ideological impact of Reaganism, whatever it is, will come not from Ronald Reagan's theories or from neoconservative tracts. Any impact will come from the way that a political movement, in its struggle for power and cohesion, intentionally and unintentionally affects Americans' thinking about public affairs. Such a political formula should not be expected to be a consistent set of logically related propositions.

As a contribution to the public philosophy, Reaganism cuts across the grain of conventional categories. It is antigovernment nationalism. It is communitarian individualism. It is free-market radicalism. It is a nostalgic reassertion of futuristic dreams. Reaganism achieves political coherence precisely because it shuns abstract consistency.

Antigovernment Nationalism

Consider first the posture of antigovernment nationalism (and if I make frequent use of President Reagan's words it is only because they are the most publicly available symbols of the movement). Rarely before in peacetime has such a continual effort been made to celebrate the national spirit. As President Reagan stated in his state of the Union address before Congress on January 25, 1984, America is still "number one" and nothing is impossible: "How can we not believe in the greatness of America? How can we not do what is right and needed to preserve this last best hope of man on Earth? After all our struggles to restore America, to revive confidence in our country, hope for our future, after all our hard-won victories earned through the patience and courage of every citizen, we cannot, must not, and will not turn back. We will finish our job. How could we do less? We're Americans." What is at work is more than the high-gloss advertising of Reagan election campaigns designed to make people happy and proud (though there is certainly that). Reaganism aspires to become the carrier of the idea of the nation.

In this conception the nation is portrayed as a collective force, one indivisible mass, composed of millions of individual American dreams. I am not sure when "America" began to be used as a form of personal address in the mass media ("America, we've got your car"), but it fits well the romantic spirit of Reagan nationalism (Tax reform—"Go for it, America"). America is a nation in which people set aside group interests as claimants on government and see the common interest. This challenge in turn goes down easily because contributing to the common interest and general welfare consists of pursuing the American dream to get ahead and advance oneself. Abroad Reaganism advances the idea of a nation that plays the leading role, stands tall, and sees through the communist challenge. Foreign policy experts might wonder what all this means and write about global interdependence and the decline of American hegemony, but Reaganism speaks to the understandings of ordinary people, not experts.

The appeal of this nationalism is not difficult to appreciate. On the one hand, Vietnam broke the twentieth century pattern in which Americans were supposed to win wars and then settle into a postwar era of self-congratulation and bourgeois high living. (Under Eisenhower's amiable management even the standoff in Korea seemed acceptable.) The 1970s, however, were different; the decade brought no victory. The postwar period brought simply more bad news rather than the equivalent of a Roaring Twenties, Swinging Forties, or Affluent Fifties. As if sensing the need to restore the pattern of achievement, Reaganism in effect declared a kind of victory in Vietnam and—through supply-side expectations—anticipatory prosperity. On the other hand, domestic affairs before the 1980s placed an emphasis on particularistic groups as the proper objects of public policy. The black population was the most prominent of those groups but consumer, environmental, and ethnic, gender, and other group advocates soon entered the scene demanding public attention and government response. It was in the context of reacting to the demand for group, rather than individual, rights that Reaganism called out to its "America," collapsing the singular and plural into a homogeneous public in which every American is "the only special interest that counts."[6]

Reaganism argues that government has gotten in the way of the nation. Espousing the Union (as it was called in an earlier century) goes hand in hand with denigrating the central government. This is possible because the inclusiveness of Reagan's nationalism has little to do with the role of the national government. Liberal leaders of an earlier time took pains to make this connection between nationalism and the role of government, as when F.D.R. in his 1937 inaugural address referred to the poorest third of the nation and said

---

6. Presidential television address to the nation on tax reform, May 28, 1985. This reference to the American people as the important "special interest group" repeats the phrases used in Reagan's 1980 acceptance speech for the Republican nomination.

"we are determined to make every American citizen the subject of his country's interest and concern," or Lyndon Johnson in a June 4, 1965, commencement address at Howard University said of the black community, "their cause is our cause." Nation-building, the striving for a fuller inclusiveness, was immanent in the social role of government.

For Reaganism, the nation has been built. Washington is not simply a bungling but an alien force that tries to impose its design on the life of the nation. The nation is full and complete independent of the work of government. As Ronald Reagan put it in his remarks at the March 14, 1982 meeting of the chief executive officers of national organizations: "Did we forget that government is the people's business, and every man, woman, and child becomes a shareholder with the first penny of tax paid? . . . Did we forget that the function of government is not to confer happiness on us, but just to get out of the way and give us the opportunity to work out happiness for ourselves?" In staking out this position, Reaganism revives a rhetoric older than the Constitution itself—the country versus the court—the real nation perceived as morally superior to a corrupt government. Washington is seen to represent corruption in the classic eighteenth-century sense of civic republicanism, namely, idleness and unproductiveness.

The misdeeds in Washington are one obvious link between Reagan nationalism and the historical experience of the 1960s and 1970s. Another common factor is the accumulated resentment against overpromising and underperforming in various Great Society programs. Less obvious is the tie between Reaganism and a younger generation that in the 1960s loudly protested against bureaucratic regimentation and externally imposed restrictions on self-development. Today a number of former campus radicals can be found actively involved in politics carrying forward the Reagan revolution. The Reagan vision of a nation of like-minded individuals, each doing their own thing unfettered by bureaucratic hierarchies, is not too distant from the hopes of campus youths in the 1960s.[7]

The effect of Reaganism is to reinforce and sharpen an already prevailing skepticism about the ability or desirability of the federal government to act on the interests of society through schemes of social engineering. Faced with any internal problem, the preferred course of action is inaction, a reversal of

---

7. Radicals in the 1960s were accustomed to glorifying the people and blaming the system (racism, the capitalist order, and so on). Reaganism embraces system-blame but stands the doctrine on its head. The offending system in this case becomes the anticapitalist order of bureaucrats, "soft-headed" liberals, academics who lean to the left, advocacy groups, and other secular egalitarians. It is the progovernment establishment that is suppressing the people and draining their creative power.

the old adage directed now at government, "don't just do something, stand there." It is the perverse habit of liberals to look for what is wrong within the country when in fact the real threat lies abroad. There is nothing wrong within America that a good dose of antiliberalism will not cure. By contrast, the foreign threat of communism requires immense and continuous exertions—hence the priority that must always be given to defense and national security matters over domestic spending. Reaganism argues that defense commitments advance, not big government, but American nationhood in a threatening world.

Communitarian Individualism

If the nation is fully formed independent of the role of government and the central government best conceived as an onlooker to the social life of that nation, what in the public philosophy of Reaganism allows Reagan officials to use the central apparatus of government to continually harp on certain social values? This brings the discussion to the theme of communitarian individualism. Reagan asserts, it might be said, a politics of the good, not of rights. Public policy is appropriately conceived as the complement to an underlying ethical order and not a neutral realm of moral contingency. As the president remarked at the Convention of National Religious Leaders on February 9, 1982, "Where did we begin to lose sight of that noble beginning, of our conviction that standards of right and wrong do exist and must be lived up to?" Big government in Washington is an alien force to the national life precisely because it seeks to impose a moral relativism that is at odds with traditional American values of the family, community solidarity, law and order, self-help, and free enterprise. Thus, Reaganism perceives itself as standing in direct opposition to the centralized permissiveness of modern liberals.

The parallel is exact. Just as so-called moral education in the schools is empty of substantive morality, so the liberal establishment, fearing the charge of imposing values on others, has sought to indoctrinate political society with the sinister norm of valuelessness. As a special assistant to the U.S. attorney general Edwin Meese put it, "In the values approach, no one need fear a teacher's judgment if his values are wrong, because there are no wrong values (other than, of course, the value of opposing 'values' education). Upon learning that all choices are equally valid, a student will be educated into skepticism about morality, fertile soil for wrong action. . . . Today's 'moral education' fails in the most critical way because it addresses the intellect but not the emotions. No one is taught to dislike and certainly not to hate anything. If young Americans are shaped, they are unfortunately shaped to be moral neuters'' (Eastland 1982). Reaganism as an ideology knows how to hate and what it hates is moral relativism in the public philosophy.

The substance of shared values—the communitarian purpose, so to speak— is ''individualism rightly understood.'' Such individualism is a function of a sharp distinction between the spheres of social issues on the one hand and economic relations on the other. The social agenda of the so-called New Right can be easily accommodated because such questions as abortion and school prayer are social issues of right and wrong, not issues of government power. Welfare reform is another case in point. Previous liberal efforts had proceeded on the morally permissive idea of individual economic ''incentives'' to ''encourage'' work effort, family stability, and other socially approved behavior. Reaganism and the administration's welfare reform initiatives simply presume these traditional norms and unhesitatingly seek to enforce them. This means that any able-bodied person claiming public income support should be required to work and that parental responsibilities for child support should be vigorously enforced. It means that the poor's share of resources should be directed to those who cannot care for themselves rather than to people who are working or capable of working but who happen to have low incomes. As enacted by Congress and implemented by the states, welfare reform and restrictions on income transfers to the working poor were not everything that proponents of Reaganism might have desired. But compared to a previous generation of futile efforts at welfare reform of the permissive, guaranteed-income type sought by liberals, the Reagan administration's success was impressive.

The communitarian ethic argues that people are supposed to look after each other. The attempted mechanization of civic virtue through big government programs suffocates this impulse while promoting dependency among those who are helped. Those who could be good samaritans are relieved of their responsibility to give something back to the country, and those who are on the receiving end of Washington's largesse begin to believe that they have a right to support but no obligation to help themselves. Individualism rightly understood is the individualism of volunteer activity, private sector initiatives, and community-based efforts to meet social needs. Such individualism is therefore an expression rather than a denial of shared values.

The presumption of community-based goodwill makes it possible to believe that being negative toward social spending by big government in Washington is not the same thing as abandoning helpless people to their fate. The American spirit of neighborhood is like, as President Reagan said in his remarks to the New York Partnership on January 14, 1982, ''a communion of hearts that rings the country.'' And so again, one is led back to the idea of the nation complete.

Reaganism portrays a social realm of individuals in caring association and an economic realm of individuals following their own separate dreams for self-advancement. Taken together these conceptions constitute individualism rightly understood: a nation of neighbors and an economy of rugged individualists. Thus given its capacity for nurturing individual autonomy— the source of both community engagement and economic progress—the free market is not just a technically efficient device but also the embodiment of an ethically superior order.

Free Market Radicalism

Because the communitarian impulse can be counted on, Reaganism is able to embrace free market radicalism with a clear conscience. A more paternal, Tory brand of conservatism has always feared the capacity of markets and technological change to destabilize community relations and distort social institutions. Reaganism, by contrast, celebrates the American faith in an unimpeded future of economic and technological progress. The only remnant of a Tory sense of tragedy—the frailty of human ambition and perversity of good intentions—is reserved solely for the public sector, where nothing is said to ever go quite right. For the private sector, Reaganism reasserts a long-standing, somewhat nostalgic American faith in an ever-better tomorrow. Although doubters speak of limitations and trade-offs, the Reagan vision proclaims an era of boundless private market growth with no worrisome, much less tragic, side effects—a kind of space-age, high technology version of Norman Rockwell's America.

Another traditional line of conservative thought, sometimes termed the corporate commonwealth, links seemingly disparate phenomena such as Mark Hanna's National Civic Federation at the beginning of this century and the larger theme of Dwight Eisenhower's political economy; in this vision the acknowledged contradictions of modern capitalism are to be resolved through the nonpartisan negotiations of a corporate society. It is hoped that these central understandings among the major interests will check unbridled acquisitiveness and class conflict (Griffith 1982).

Reaganism goes in a different direction. Just as the 1960s' claim of group rights is rejected, so too corporate conceptions of the economy are passed over in a glorification of individual effort. Just as those who voluntarily help others and give something back to the community are the heroes, so too are those individuals who work at getting ahead. In the final analysis, it is the *producing* members of society who count, and their capacity to produce independently is what most needs protection.

People who fall behind are not necessarily victims thereby entitled to support. The income and property produced by personal effort in the context of a free market is something private that belongs to each productive person and not something lying at the disposal of government or some other distributive power. Teaching people to think of themselves as victims of external circumstances may on the surface appear to be an act of compassion, but in the long run it is an insidious way of destroying personal responsibility. Although some moral claim may well exist at the level of community giving, Reaganism, in its heart, denies that economic losers should have any legally established claim on the body politic. Rights stop at the water's edge of the economy. The president's radio address to the nation on February 23, 1985, carried a message to distressed farmers that was the authentic voice of Reaganism: "Yes, we are sympathetic and we will extend support. But American taxpayers must not be asked to bail out every farmer hopelessly in debt . . . or be asked to bail out the banks who also bet on higher inflation. . . . Over the long haul, there's only one sure solution . . . working our way to a free-market economy. What farmers need and we're determined to provide is less dependence on politicians to supply their incomes and greater independence to supply their own incomes."

Antigovernment nationalism, communitarian individualism, free market radicalism, nostalgic futurism—all are no doubt overly academic terms. They do suggest, nevertheless, how it is possible to reconcile values of country, community, and chasing a buck. Where does Reaganism fit in terms of the American public philosophy? Reaganism fits as an amalgam, taking preexisting ideas and recombining them so as to span the three models of consensus, dualistic conflict, and disintegration. It sounds a tocsin against the incoherence and degeneration that has overtaken American public affairs. To meet this challenge Reaganism paints a picture of polarized conflict between a liberal establishment and popularly based conservative movement, "them" versus "us." Salvation is seen to lie in returning to the bedrock consensus of American politics—the traditional values of family, work, private enterprise, and nation—that have been forgotten. And so the circle is complete. Skeptical academics can easily pick holes in Reaganism as an intellectual doctrine, but that is really beside the point. If Reaganism survives as an important force it will not be because of its theoretical elegance but because of its political persuasiveness, resonating with the hopes and calming the fears of ordinary Americans.

SHADOWS ON THE FUTURE

The danger always exists that in examining the ideas of political partisans, one is engaged in a misguided quest for profundity. Ideas, say some people, are a political convenience used to camouflage interests. Thus some of Reagan's sternest critics on the political left have argued that Reaganism is really a veneer covering a self-seeking alliance of the economically privileged. It allows business to discipline the labor force by forcing the poor and near poor into the work force, depressing wages through higher levels of unemployment and lower social payments, suppressing unions, cutting taxes to starve the public sector, and generally increasing the share of profits relative to labor. Frankly, I have no idea if any of this is true. What I am convinced of is that interests are not self-interpreting. If the mass of Americans is being tricked by such an alliance of the privileged, some fairly potent ideas as well as interests must be at work.

When the 1980s are compared to the 1970s, important differences stand out. Reaganism appears to tap the essential consensus in our long-standing political tradition. It seems to dispel the mood of impending disintegration in the country's political ideas. And in between the tradition and the mood, Reaganism seems to offer a more structured sense of the argument between individualistic and communitarian visions. Indeed, Reaganism combines the ideological components into an amalgam that has tended thus far to squelch any coherent counterargument by the current generation of American liberals. Against the onslaught of Reaganism, a great liberal silence has prevailed as people follow the moral injunction of a commercial republic to enrich themselves. But decadal comparisons are artificial and it is the long-term bends in the public philosophy that are of greatest concern in this chapter. America becalmed is not necessarily America prepared to face the future.

I leave aside the view that certain realities in the world simply preclude a future for Reaganism or, as an author in an earlier Urban Institute volume has put it in a heading of his paper, "Why the Reagan Revolution Will Fail."[8] To my way of thinking we should weigh probabilities, not issue dicta (excluding the dictum just offered). Likewise there is little point in trying to predict unpredictable events. Conservatives are now hostage to economic performance and international developments just as Democrats in command of government once were. The difference is that Reagan's America is more heavily mortgaged at home and abroad than ever before in peacetime. Of course administration supporters claim they have the answers for coping with any resulting problems; but if the world does not cooperate and they do not have the answers, it is not terribly interesting to observe that Reaganism will take it on the chin.

---

8. For examples of this view see Lowi (1985) and Reich (1985).

The task of interpreting the future of Reaganism then becomes one of trying to discern clues about unanticipated consequences that might lie hidden in the present, about strengths and weaknesses in the staying power of Reaganism as a contribution to the public philosophy. My starting assumption is that it is not all one way or the other. Reaganism may have an aleatory contract with the future, but it is also making some of its own luck, good and bad.

The Positives

On the positive side, there is much to cheer Reaganites.

Negative Government Demands Less. Those who promise to solve problems by providing less government can expect to have an easier time dealing with the vicissitudes of public life than those pledged to use government actively for problem solving. Activism requires a constant supply of ideas and interventions, while limiting government requires mainly a consistent willingness to say no. The comparative advantage is symbolized in Ronald Reagan's presidency. Doing less through government is consistent with doing less and knowing less in the White House. As opposed to the hyperactivity of Democratic presidents and the mushrooming expectations placed upon them, President Reagan can work at his dominant priority (limiting domestic government) by not becoming involved, by not thinking up new things to do, by not claiming to solve other people's problems. Blessed is the political movement in which leadership can claim to vary inversely with exertion, where political skill and commitment can be portrayed as the opposite of policy inventiveness. It is the agenda and not just the Reagan persona that has created the so-called Teflon presidency of the past six years.

Negative government demands less not only of presidents but also of Americans in general. The main challenge posed is for average Americans to keep what they have worked for (although this is said to be no small challenge given the redistributive appetite of liberals, big government, and special interest groups). Reaganism seeks to shift the focus of public attention from the relative merits of spending projects to the invariant need for tax restraint. Maintaining past tax cuts and avoiding new revenue measures becomes a new kind of middle-class entitlement that can continually be portrayed as threatened by free-spending opponents. Failure to balance the budget has much the same effect by orienting all major decision making around the problem of deficit reduction. Ronald Reagan may personally object when defense appears on the agenda for cuts, but the basic point remains that Reaganism as an antigovernment orientation is on a favorable playing field when it can argue for spending restraint in the name of economic policy and leave opponents to either condone deficits or argue for higher taxes.

Reaganism, therefore, enjoys an advantage akin to political jujitsu, leveraging the weight of the governmental establishment against itself. The focus on revenue restraint (protection of previous tax cuts, indexation of tax rates) and the enduring deficit problem amount to a kind of institutionalized "no" in the political system. By denying liberals the resources to finance new activities, both tax cut entitlements and deficits create a presumption for negative government, and they do so without the need for constant new exertions from the advocates of Reaganism.

Populism Protects Conservatives. Reaganism contains a populist streak that helps shield it from the conventional attack on conservatives as elitist and isolated from the concerns of ordinary people. It can present itself as conservatism for the little man. Reaganism understands the concerns of people who feel bewildered by the machinations of public bureaucracy and corporate America, who are attached to local concerns and nativistic worries, who distrust the experts and who know a "traditional value" when they see one without the need for philosophical debate. These localist and subcultural attachments—which the intellectual opponents of Reaganism typically dismiss as unmodernized and aberrational—are an enduring part of the American political scene. The available niches of personal autonomy are likely to become more, not less, important to people as modernization proceeds. Just as liberalism made it all right to talk about sex, Reaganism makes it all right to talk about patriotism, parochial allegiances, moral purpose and, yes, imposing middle-class values on others. Reaganism has a future because Americans want to talk about these things in politics.

Assertiveness Helps. Reaganism has an advantage in the future because it is an inherently offensive, not a defensive approach to the political contest. There is a directionality; what Reaganism approves and disapproves is clear. As President Reagan has shown, staking out a purist position (or at least what passes for such in politics) has the effect of not only provoking controversy but also of biasing the inevitable compromises in the preferred direction. Reaganism is pugnacious while decrying adversarialism in American life. Its advocates know what kind of society they want and America needs. By contrast, progressive liberalism is usually defensive and vague with regard to purpose. Rabbit-punched by a Reaganite, contemporary liberals are likely to debate the virtues of tolerance.

Americans Prefer Optimism. Reaganism has an upbeat, positive political message. In this regard there is much in common with the older liberal tradition of the "Happy Warrior," "Happy Days Are Here Again," and "Politics of Joy" (now forgotten as Hubert Humphrey's campaign theme in

1968). It is far more than a similarity of style in the exuberance of F.D.R., Humphrey, and Reagan, although there is plenty of that. Reaganism, like the headiest days of liberalism, offers a vision in which Americans can have it all: world leadership and economic growth without guilt or hard choices. Americans have only to believe in their own dreams. The contrast with both traditional conservatism and post-Humphrey liberalism could not be more striking. Gone are the dour conservative prescriptions of austerity and self-sacrifice and returning to the past. Gone is the Carter era pall of limited resources, complexity, and a world in which "more is not better." Reaganism is kinetic, expansive, and endlessly (critics would say mindlessly) optimistic about the future. In Walter Mondale's 1984 concession speech he identified himself with "the poor, . . . the helpless and the sad."[9] Ronald Reagan's 1985 inaugural address identifies his administration with the nation and the future. It is to capture a spirit and a tradition of political ideas, rather than simply to tweak Democratic noses, that Reagan quotes F.D.R.: "Civilization cannot go back; civilization must not stand still. We have undertaken new methods. It is our task to perfect, to improve, to alter when necessary, but in all cases to go forward."[10]

My conclusion is that Reaganism is likely to have substantial staying power, beyond the political life of Ronald Reagan, as an outlook on public affairs. However, there are also considerable weaknesses that need to be taken into account before any final verdict is reached. It does not require an over-developed sense of irony to see that some of the greatest disappointments in life come about as the result of winning. If Reaganism appears to have been winning in the 1980s, what are the downside clues for its future that lie buried in current events?

The Negatives

The first two potential problems for Reaganism go together. One is the inadvertent but continued nationalization of politics under the Reagan administration; the second is the overt moral emphasis on community and caring. Together these spell trouble for a Reaganite public philosophy in the long run.

---

9. Harvey Mansfield also reminds us that when the Democrats at their convention stopped using their old standard "Happy Days Are Here Again," it was quickly picked up by Republicans in their convention in 1984. See Mansfield (1985, 7).

10. Quoted in the president's state of the Union address before Congress, January 25, 1984. A paraphrased version of this charge to keep moving forward appears in his inaugural address, January 21, 1985.

Nationalization. Reaganism is devoted to reducing the domestic presence of the federal government. The paradox is that Ronald Reagan's genial exertions may have served only to entrench and in some cases expand that presence. The following paragraphs briefly survey some of the more important factors that seem to be at work.

In some respects the performance of Ronald Reagan himself has served as a potent force in further nationalizing American politics. Reagan has done so by capturing media attention, spurring national party offices to organize and counterorganize, restoring vitality and "can-do" presumptions to the presidential office, and putting together national election appeals and victories that cut across regions and groups. The Reagan administration's successes have increased public confidence in government institutions, but the level of distrust regarding private power apparently remains high (Lipset 1985).

Reaganism represents a probing and poking for political soft spots in the larger structure of the American welfare state as it has developed over the decades. Some social functions have been eliminated outright, but it has almost always proven easier to accept the function and cut its customary increment. In effect, the 1980s have witnessed an ongoing national referendum on the social budget that has had the effect of leaving intact—and thereby somewhat legitimating—a scaled-back version of national social commitments.

Reaganism has failed to evolve any principled basis for decentralizing national social programs from Washington. The attempted sorting out of functions under Reagan's New Federalism initiatives in 1981–82 aroused little political interest, and state-rights objections to federal activity are scarcely even a pale imitation of their former selves a generation or two ago. For practical purposes, the real New Federalism of the 1980s has been spelled b-u-d-g-e-t r-e-s-t-r-a-i-n-t, a federal government engulfed in deficits forces the states to pay for whatever domestic policy initiatives people desire. Of course, what fiscal convenience decentralizes it may just as easily recentralize some day, but there is deeper logic unwinding. Washington's more restrained responsibility for education, social welfare, environmental, and economic issues has transferred corresponding pressure to state governors and legislators. Democrats and Republicans have thereby been thrown into a new competition to demonstrate an active concern for the people's problems. Old-fashioned conservatives, with a preference for doing nothing, tend to be driven from the scene by this competition. Whether governed by Republicans or Democrats, more states have undertaken their own initiatives in employment programs, export promotion, educational improvement, and so on. As they do so, greater coordination is likely to be needed to prevent "beggar thy neighbor" cycles from developing in the competition for business, lower tax rates, and skilled labor. Republicans and Democrats will then be engaged in reinventing the federal government and the need for its ordering hand.

Reaganism is prey to the tendency for an antiwelfare state agenda to require more, not less, centralized government. This proves true on any number of fronts. More budget-making authority is required to overcome the power of special pleading. Control over the process of writing government regulations has to be, and has been, enhanced. New ways of centrally rationing or capping the total volume of credit, tax subsidies, or other government beneficences are imposed. Should Reaganites eventually achieve their ultimate objective of amending the Constitution to limit the growth of government (through amendments to require a balanced federal budget limited to a fixed percentage of national income and with a presidential line-item veto) the need for centralized procedures would probably be even greater in order to meet these externally imposed goals.

A generally overlooked fact is that Reaganism's commitment to leaving defense as a favored sector has the effect of increasing, not decreasing, the domestic presence of national government. This occurs directly through the effects of defense spending on patterns of employment, and at community and regional economic development, and indirectly by putting government borrowing requirements at the center of national financial markets.

It certainly has not been Reaganites' intention to leave the kinds of tools outlined in these several paragraphs lying around for others to use, but this has been the result. Some can argue that such tools have a conservative bias, but that is true only if one defines liberalism as an unthinking impulse for big spending. Liberals willing to set priorities can use the same tools for other purposes such as national planning (though none will dare call it that). One might borrow a thought from the 1980 campaign and ask these questions: after an extended spell of Reaganism in Washington, are the basic commitments to major functions of the welfare state more or less firmly entrenched for being tested in the budget battles of the 1980s? Is the tolerance for centralized control in public resource allocations greater or smaller? Is the spirit of reform and presumption of government activism—at the state if not federal level—greater or smaller?

Community and Caring. Reaganism as presented to Americans is not simply a reassertion of nineteenth-century rugged individualism—that is, every man for himself; America is said to be a great national force expressed through a host of small societies (''a communion of hearts that rings the country''). Reaganism speaks the moral language of social obligation. One can give the movement the benefit of the doubt and accept that this is an authentic and not a hypocritical voice. But is it realistic to think that Americans can be taught to think of themselves as caring individuals in association at the level of the family, the local community, in volunteer groups and in business—but not when it comes to the level of national government and policy? Because of its overwhelming appeal to national pride, Reaganism becomes particularly vulnerable to the counterappeal that Americans should not be content to live amid "two nations" of children (25 percent of American children under age six living in poverty), of elderly (economic inequality among the aged being vastly greater than it is among the nonaged) or of its workers (the occupational safety nets in business being strongest for those who already have the most). The call of Reaganism for an "opportunity society" is an open-ended commitment that can leverage huge amounts of national government activity, as it did for the War on Poverty. Reaganism's celebration of a nation of communities has no real answer when such communities reinforce inequality and suppress the individualism of those falling outside the mainstream of particular community leaders' norms. Likewise Reaganism stands mute in the face of the tendency for a kinetic, high-tech society to generate mobilities constantly undercutting community stability. If half of what Reaganism preaches about America's economic and technological future is true, there is likely to be a powerful case for "community action" at the national level in the years ahead. When localism not only brings preferred values to the fore but also serves as a means of validating privilege and social exclusion on the grounds of someone not being "like one of us," when rapid economic and technological change uproots the communities and lives even of people who are working very hard at the American dream— when these things happen, Reaganism has no persuasive answer about what to do next.

"Me First" Politics. To avoid all of this potential trouble, the Reagan public philosophy must have a social vision of very substantial persuasive power and accomplishment. Here a third problem arises because it is not at all clear that what I have called communitarian individualism can produce the promised results. The Reagan administration's private sector initiatives program appears to have operated mainly at the level of symbolic politics. Leaders in the voluntary sector themselves downplay the extent to which they can meet social needs without considerable federal support. The social gospel of Reaganism harkens back to similar ideas in the latter nineteenth century (called variously the new charity, welfare capitalism, social gospel, and so on) without the earlier driving, grassroots religious commitments to produce foot soldiers for the cause. Today's religious activists embraced by Reaganism appear more interested in abortion and school prayer than in home visits to the poor.

Reaganism therefore becomes vulnerable. To do much more in advancing communitarian individualism as a model probably requires a degree of political preaching and exhortation to social duty that is wholly out of keeping with the spirit of the times. It will be much easier for Reaganism to keep preaching the formula but effectively to tune out and disengage from the social issue. But at that point Reaganism risks becoming identified with the much more socially unattractive face of free market radicalism. The economic, as opposed to the social, side of Reagan's individualism can easily be portrayed as playing to the most easily rationalized forms of selfishness—looking out for oneself is the best way of helping the country. There can arise a determined insensitivity that passes for tough-mindedness. The economic losers are not victims, just incompetents. Reaganism then becomes a rationale for the nation to secede from some downcast fraction of its own inhabitants. It would be difficult for political opponents to pin the Scrooge image on Ronald Reagan the man, but his successors in the movement will almost certainly be easier targets.

The Domestic and Foreign Linkage. It is not clear that Reaganism forges an effective relationship between its approach to domestic politics and its vision of America's place in the world. Traditional conservatism has called for a certain quality of self-discipline and a public-regarding quality in domestic affairs to ensure successful leadership abroad. But apart from the vague cajoling of community involvement, Reaganism makes no claims for domestic sacrifice or for collective, public goals. On the contrary, Reaganism brings only the easy message of individual self-advancement with few hard choices. And those choices have been avoided thus far in the Reagan years by borrowing heavily from the future and from abroad to finance current consumption. But if Reaganism does not ask much more of the American people than to enrich themselves and struggle to cut their own taxes, are they really prepared to play the kind of tough-minded, bold role in the world that Reaganism envisaged? If foreign entanglements are Grenada-scale operations, there is no problem; otherwise, the dissonance between privatism at home and nationalistic ambitions abroad casts a noteworthy shadow on the future of Reaganism.

THE PUBLIC NONRESPONSE

Thus far little evidence can be found of any significant turnaround in public attitudes regarding the appropriate domestic functions of government. As noted earlier, confidence in the capacity of government institutions has, if anything, improved since the early 1980s, a change that is apparently more the result of economic cycles than anything else. The real key, however, in any final judgment seems to lie in the answer to this question: what attempted changes in the direction of public affairs—and what ideas represented by those attempts—seem to have resonated and rung true for the American people, and what changes and ideas have not? In the end, a public philosophy has to be material for public digestion, something touching ordinary people and not an abstraction accessible only to professors, columnists, and other pundits. The results of public opinion polls and other passing signs are hardly conclusive, but they offer a few clues. At least there are some trend lines one should reasonably expect to see or not see if Reaganism is having a major impact.

For example, a recent study by the Brookings Institution argues that the terms of public debate have changed decisively in the Reagan years (Ch·;bb and Peterson 1985, 25). From an argument about where to expand public commitments the debate is said to have changed to deciding where to cut federal domestic spending, taxes, and regulation. Have the terms of debate changed for the public? The answer is no, not when you consider how the public responds to questions about spending more or spending less for certain purposes. Certainly the bankrupt state of federal finances has shaped the Washington budget battles and the constraints on new spending without off-setting savings. If, however, a deeper change in public conception has occurred, the trend should be clear. Those in the general public who believe that the issue is still about how much more to expand (that is, those charging that the country is spending too little on social welfare, education, the environment, and so on) should be a shrinking portion of the people polled; those who think the debate is now about the extent of cuts (those asserting that the government is spending, taxing, and wasting too much) should be increasing. In fact the public opinion trends between 1976 and 1985 are roughly the reverse.[11]

By torturing the data long enough, the ideological changes of the Reagan years can be made to look greater or smaller; the revealing point, however, is the amount of effort that must be exerted to find even modest movement in the public's mind toward ideas favored by Reaganism. Most indicators point in a neutral or opposite direction. Thus polls of general policy preferences show pervasive support for the established array of federal social programs—massive support for inclusive programs such as Medicare and Social Security, more tempered support for programs confined to what are perceived as more narrow interest groups. Likewise, exit surveys taken at election polls show that only small proportions of those voting for the Reagan presidency claimed to do so on the basis of the administration's conservative philosophy (5 percent of voters in 1980, 6 percent in 1984). Support for Ronald Reagan

---

11. See Chubb and Peterson (1985, 388). A similar lack of confirming results applies to public attitudes toward government regulation (Shapiro and Gilroy 1984).

did not show any signs of translating into electoral support for other Reaganite candidates for public office. Reagan landslides seem best explained by the particular circumstances of the economy at the time, not by any notions that the American public made conscious ideological choices in 1980 or 1984.[12] Perhaps the one implication relevant to the public philosophy that *can* be teased out of these election results is that (again, paradoxically, against the grain of Reaganism) Americans continue to look to Washington in general and to the presidency in particular for keeping the economy on an even keel. That may mean somewhat less spending and taxing, but the basic New Deal type of proposition remains intact and has been reinforced by the irresistible temptation for Republicans to claim credit for the improved state of the economy in the 1980s. This proposition holds that the health of the American economy is ultimately a public responsibility and the active concern of Washington policymakers rather than an outcome entrusted to any natural order in the private sector.

Another and more indirect way of tracing underlying public views is to look for overall patterns of resistance or acceptance regarding attempts to change domestic government in the 1980s. Where did prevailing assumptions yield to or successfully resist initiatives occurring under the banner of Reaganism? Of course much depended on the particular personalities and circumstances surrounding the events; however, it also seems true that public acceptability, and Washington perceptions thereof, constituted an omnipresent background factor shaping the limits of feasible change. Thus whatever the personal difficulties of a James Watt or Anne Gorsuch, it seems clear that the 1980s will be recorded as a time when the public resisted any major scaling back of federal responsibility for environmental protection and a time when a shift to state-level initiatives for improvement of education, social welfare planning, and industrial policies also was widely accepted. Compared to the heyday of the Great Society, during the 1980s importuning Washington for help went into remission. As noted earlier, this outcome probably had less to do with any new public attachments to the idea of state or local responsibility and more to do with the widespread perception that the federal cupboard was fiscally bare.

If one could tally up all the actions and counteractions of domestic government in the 1980s and the penumbra of public response, the picture would hardly be black or white. However, the overall thrust of the story

---

12. Careful reviews of the 1980 and 1984 election results vis-à-vis the economy, the length of Reagan coattails, and so on are contained in Chubb and Peterson (1985, 69–116). A number of poll results arguing against any major shift in public policy preferences are briefly reviewed in Navarro (1985).

would, it seems, be one of reaffirming the basic structure of federal domestic functions. Efforts to eliminate functions or sharply to reverse the course have aroused little widespread support; efforts to economize, to better target, to abandon the more dotty instances of liberal paternalism and special interest programs have been more widely accepted. These tendencies become clearer the more closely one examines detailed instances of federal policy management in the Reagan era. What follows is a small sampling of changes effected by interest group power, to be sure, but also by the larger contours of public acceptability: at the National Endowment for the Humanities, a scaled-down but more focused federal role in supporting core studies in the humanities and classics; at VISTA and ACTION, a failure to abolish these agencies but a reorientation away from supporting various advocacy groups to continued federal support for more traditional local volunteer programs; at the Federal Trade Commission, a reinforcement of federal rule-making authority based on more thorough economic analysis; at the Labor Department's Employment and Training Administration, stricter standards for contracting to prevent favoritism; at the Bureau of Mine Safety, a deemphasis of pure rule enforcement in favor of more discretion for government inspectors to assure health and safety; at the Highway Traffic Safety Administration, a failed effort to shift from setting stringent vehicle safety standards to greater government emphasis on modifying driver behavior; at the Federal Deposit Insurance Corporation, much more active federal monitoring and enforcement of fiduciary responsibilities in deregulated financial markets.

Such a list can hardly be exhaustive, but it does suggest the kind of developments occurring in Washington with apparent public acquiescence during the 1980s. One could add a general resistance to further major cuts in federal "safety-net" programs, a term scarcely in the public vocabulary before the Reagan administration. Likewise, attempts to put the Reagan stamp on appointments to the federal judiciary may well have a long-term impact on federal policies, but so far at least the general public seems to have broadly endorsed a series of Supreme Court decisions that have turned back efforts by Reagan supporters to lower constitutional barriers between church and state. All in all, Reaganism as doctrine has promised much that could not be sold to the American public by Reaganism as government.

A FINAL VERDICT

The general trend of public opinion and its resonances with events in Washington should be disturbing to true believers in Reaganism for, as noted at the outset of this chapter, theirs is not only a contest for votes but also a battle for the public mind. Reagan officials have in effect tried to have things both ways. On the one hand, they have sought to run "feel good" political campaigns that have avoided troubling discussions of intended budget cuts or their ideology of limited government. On the other hand, Reaganites have claimed a postelection mandate to carry through the major elements of their ideology. The evidence is that any movement in public attitudes and votes has had a great deal to do with economic conditions and President Reagan's personal popularity and very little to do with the ideological messages of Reaganism. Conservative activists will say that this is because the Reagan White House was not pure enough and did not try hard enough to teach their message; liberals will say it is because Reaganism is intellectually vacuous.

Between these two extremes the central tendency seems sufficiently clear. In the 1980s Americans by and large have not come to desire less dependence on Washington, mainly because they want a strong measure of security in their lives—ranging from bank deposits to safety and environmental matters, health care, and retirement income. This underlying desire for security is one of the great frustrations for Reaganism: left free to choose (in Milton Friedman's phrase), people prefer something less risky than free markets and the problematic help of friends, neighbors, and employers.

Any final verdict on Reaganism and the public philosophy will of course be written only some years from now. The struggle of political personalities will affect that legacy to some extent and help to define Reaganism-post-Reagan. In this chapter, I have tried to make the point that the public philosophy and Reaganism are somewhat more complex than conventionally presumed. There are good reasons to be neither dismissive nor overimpressed with regard to the ultimate ideological impact of the Reagan years. Reaganism has tapped major currents in American political tradition, has clearly focused debate with its opponents, and has reassured ordinary people that the country is not coming apart at the seams. In doing so, Reaganism has not so much produced major changes in public thought as it has helped make a changing world seem more bearable to Americans in the 1980s. It has helped many Americans chafe at government as they willingly use it to enhance their security. Amid deep concerns about their weakened bonds of community, Reaganism has reassured Americans that they are not an uncaring people simply because they resist tax increases and big new spending programs. America has been portrayed as number one in the world even while it struggles with the problems of mounting international dependency. Reaganism tells Americans what they have wanted to hear: that the future is as bright as they remember, although the misgivings never quite seem to disappear.

In serving this function of reassurance, Reaganism will eventually prove to have been a consolidating force. Much as F.D.R. and the New Deal had the effect of conserving capitalism, so Reaganism will eventually be seen to have helped conserve a predominately status quo, middle-class welfare state. It will have done so by making the existing system work in a more disciplined, or at least a more broadly acceptable way to the American public. This means a federal government committed to social welfare, environmental protection, economic management, and so on, but not committed in an open-handed way or a manner enshrining advocacy of certain groups' agendas as the standard for good public policy. Whether or not one sees all this as correcting the excesses of the Great Society and its inflated promises of social engineering, the fact is that the base of domestic policy has been more firmly consolidated in what the public can take for granted from a conservative administration.

What has been happening is perhaps best expressed in terms of a before-and-after picture of Reaganism in opposition and after a spell of power. I see a split-screen picture. On half of the screeen is all that in the lexicon of Reaganism was originally thought to be unacceptable. I see the objections to Washington trying to dictate social relations and morality to the states, objections made before and after the civil rights acts of the 1960s were passed. I see objections to the intrusions of big government in the Clean Air Act and to the compulsory welfarism of Social Security, and of federal aid to education, and of consumer protection laws, and all the rest. On the other half of the screen I see all that still remains after eight years of Reaganism in Washington: the civil rights acts, the Clean Air Act, the pledges never to tamper with Social Security benefits—everyone can make up their own list of what has come to be taken for granted.

So there is the final verdict. The 1980s will be seen as a time of consolidation. The ideas embodied in the political movement Reagan symbolized will have helped organize a previous incoherence in our public conversation about the meaning of American national society. But it is an amalgam of ideas rich in implications that will ensure that Reaganism does not have the last word. It is not that Reaganism embraced all the prevailing ideas about the social functions of government, but that by tolerating, marginally adjusting, or simply failing to reverse so many policies and attitudes, the Reagan experience unwittingly served more or less to preserve the base of political argument and domestic policy for future development. And like the other great consolidator of the American welfare state, Dwight Eisenhower, Ronald Reagan and Reaganism will be remembered in large part for things left undone in American society that bedeviled us later. This is another way of mortgaging the future quite apart from the federal deficits, trade imbalances, and foreign borrowing that have characterized the 1980s. Reaganism urges Americans to dream dreams but these are necessarily dreams of private advantage, not public accomplishment. Any ideology of negative government is likely to fall prey in the history books to the collective tasks left undone, and an ideology that simultaneously reasserts public moralism is especially vulnerable to charges of both neglect and hypocrisy. Will President Reagan, whatever might be said about his luck, escape the judgment of having presided over a period when America marked time and stored up problems for the future? One outcome is certain: history will not be much interested in hearing excuses.

REFERENCES

Beer, Samuel. 1978. "In Search of a New Public Philosophy." In Anthony
King, ed., *The New American Political System*. Washington, D.C.: American Enterprise Institute.

Boorstin, Daniel. 1958, 1965, 1973. *The Americans*. 3 vols. New York:
Random House.

Brinkley, Alan. 1984. "Writing the History of Contemporary America."
Daedalus. Summer: 121–41.

Cates, Jerry. 1983. *Insuring Inequality*. Ann Arbor, Michigan: University of
Michigan Press.

Chubb, John E., and Paul E. Peterson. 1985. *New Directions in American
Politics*. Washington, D.C.: Brookings Institution.

Derthick, Martha. 1979. *Policy Making for Social Security*. Washington,
D.C.: Brookings Institution.

Diggins, John P. 1985. *The Lost Soul of American Politics*. New York: Basic
Books.

Eastland, Terry. 1982. "Teaching Morality in the Public School." *Wall Street
Journal*. February 22.

Griffith, Robert. 1982. "Dwight D. Eisenhower and the Corporate Commonwealth." *The American Historical Review* 87(2):87–122.

Hartz, Louis. 1955. *The Liberal Tradition in America*. New York: Harcourt
Brace and World.

Heclo, Hugh. 1985. "The Political Foundations of Antipoverty Policy." In
Sheldon Danziger and Dan Weinberg, eds., *Antipoverty Policy: What Works*?
Cambridge, Massachusetts: Harvard University Press.

Hofstadter, Richard. 1957. *The American Political Tradition and the Men
Who Made It*. New York: Vintage Books.

Huntington, Samuel. 1981. *American Politics: The Promise of Disharmony*.
Cambridge, Massachusetts: Harvard University Press.

Katzenstein, Peter J. 1978. *Between Power and Plenty*. Madison, Wisconsin:
University of Wisconsin Press.

Kelley, Robert. 1977. "Ideology and Political Culture from Jefferson to
Nixon." *American Historical Review* 82(3):531–62.

Kramnick, Isaac. 1982. "Republican Revisionism Revisited." *American Historical Review* 87(3):629–64.

Lipset, Seymour Martin. 1985. "The Confidence Gap: Down but Not Out."
Unpublished document. University of California at Berkeley. April.

Lowi, Theodore J. 1985. "Ronald Reagan—Revolutionary?" In Lester M. Salamon and Michael S. Lund, eds., *The Reagan Presidency and the Governing of America.* Washington, D.C.: Urban Institute Press.

Mansfield, Harvey C., Jr. 1985. "The American Election: Entitlements vs. Opportunity." *Government and Opposition.* (England) 1:3–17.

Matusow, Allen J. 1984. *The Unravelling of America: A History of Liberalism in the 1960s.* New American Nation series. New York: Harper & Row.

Navarro, Vincente. 1985. "The 1984 Election and the New Deal: An Alternative Interpretation." *Social Policy* (Spring): 3–10.

O'Neill, William L. 1971. *Coming Apart: An Informal History of America in the 60s.* New York: Times Books.

Pines, Burton Yale. 1982. *Back to Basics: The Traditionalist Movement That Is Sweeping Grass-Roots America.* New York: William Morrow.

Piven, Frances Fox, and Richard A. Cloward. 1979. *Poor People's Movements.* New York: Vintage Books.

Potter, David M. 1958. *People of Plenty.* Chicago: University of Chicago Press.

Reich, Robert B. 1985. "Toward a New Public Philosophy." *The Atlantic Monthly* May: 68–79.

Rimlinger, Gaston. 1971. *Welfare Policy and Industrialization.* New York: Wiley.

Ross, Dorothy. 1979. "The Liberal Tradition Revisited and the Republican Tradition Addressed." In John Higham and Paul K. Conkin, eds., *New Directions in American Intellectual History.* Baltimore, Maryland: Johns Hopkins University Press.

Schambra, William A. 1982. "The Roots of the American Public Philosophy." *The Public Interest* Spring (67):36–48.

Shapiro, Robert Y., and John M. Gilroy. 1984. "The Polls: Regulation— Parts I and II." *Public Opinion Quarterly.* 48(2–3) Summer: 531–42, 666–77.

White, Theodore H. 1982. *In Search of America.* New York: Harper & Row.

Wood, Robert C. 1972. *The Necessary Majority.* New York. Cambridge University Press.

SOCIAL PROGRAMS AND
SOCIAL POLICY

Jack A. Meyer

My purpose in this chapter is to analyze the changing role of government in the domain of social policy in the 1980s and to assess the likelihood that such changes will endure.[1] To accomplish this, I will examine the extent to which government social programs are being permanently altered in the 1980s and explain the important influence on government social programs of changing attitudes about other national objectives.

The basic issues raised here involve the appropriate role of government in assisting needy citizens in areas ranging from health, nutrition, and housing to education, welfare, and transportation. What groups deserve government aid, and how are competing or conflicting priorities resolved? Is the definition of "need" the same today as a decade ago? If not, which definition is most consistent with American tradition and which one will be likely to endure?

To address such issues and lay the groundwork for analysis, my discussion will establish some basic criteria for ascertaining the proper size, scope, and policy functions of public social programs. Although the chapter is not intended to be a scorecard on the Reagan administration, I will weave an assessment of the objectives, accomplishments, and setbacks of the administration into the fabric of the analysis.

I begin with a brief historical background to place the important changes of this decade in a meaningful context. I then analyze the changing trends in the growth of federal outlays for social programs and explain how other national objectives are driving these changes. This analysis is followed by an

---

1. The term *social policy* has more than one meaning. In this chapter the focus is on the federal government's expenditure programs related to domestic social objectives.

examination of the new approach or social philosophy that characterizes the social segment of federal fiscal policy. The chapter ends with some brief remarks on what I believe will be the enduring features of the Reagan administration's social policy and what remains to be done.

HISTORICAL BACKGROUND

An assessment of the role of government in addressing social problems must begin with an understanding of the broad trends in that role that preceded the 1980s. During the period from the mid-1930s to the early 1960s the key feature of federal social policy was the protection of people at the "back end" of labor force experience—people departing from the work force because of either retirement from work or temporary loss of a job arising from layoff or disability.

The social role of the federal government during that period could be characterized by what Churchill once called "spreading a net over the abyss." The twin pillars supporting this role were the Social Security and unemployment insurance programs providing protection for retirement needs and unemployment, respectively.

In the early to mid-1960s two new federal roles were added to the basic concept of the safety net under what became known as the Great Society. First, the federal government took the lead in encouraging what I call "front end" assistance—efforts to help those who are economically and socially disadvantaged enter the mainstream of economic activity. Both macroeconomic policy and investment in "human capital" were part of this effort. A heightened emphasis on government intervention to assure continuous and strong economic growth was believed to "draw in" the disadvantaged as labor markets tightened. New federal programs for education, training, and job placement were designed to enhance the employability of young and displaced workers. Second, the federal government initiated an effort to rebuild or revitalize certain geographic areas or pockets of deprivation. The notion behind this effort was that disadvantaged inner-city residents could be drawn into the mainstream of economic life by a government-backed campaign to renew the strength of their local economies.

Thus, the one new thrust was federal investment in people; the other, in neighborhoods or areas. Underpinning these policies was the belief that economic growth was vital and necessary to solving social problems, but was not itself sufficient. Pockets of poverty would remain, and some unskilled, low-income people—particularly youth—would be bypassed by buoyant growth even as others were uplifted. In short, a "rising tide" would lift many, but not all boats. The government's job was twofold—to assist as many in economic difficulty as possible and to pull in those who remained adrift.

The key tenets of the human capital side of the Great Society were federally sponsored job training programs, education assistance ranging from preschool years to college, and assured coverage for health care among those outside of the private health insurance market. Also, part of the civil rights movement during this period consisted of an effort to eliminate job discrimination, enabling minority groups to obtain access to the world of work.

Besides the development of these new roles, the more traditional income maintenance role of the federal government was sharply expanded from the mid-1960s to the mid-1970s. Medicare added another dimension to the "back end" safety net while Social Security was enriched through congressional actions in the early 1970s. Unemployment insurance was provided for a more extended period of time. The new funding for these social insurance programs was more responsible for the growth of government spending than was the establishment of the two new roles described above. Finally, the federal cushion was enlarged with the enactment of such programs as food stamps, low-income energy assistance, and a nutrition program for pregnant women, infants, and children (WIC).

President Reagan's policies are marked by a return to the emphasis on economic growth that prevailed in the 1960s. Both a growing economy that could expand the work force and local government and private initiatives were viewed as better suited than national social programs for the supporting role of aiding disadvantaged people. The Reagan administration stressed the continued need for the safety net for the economy's "casualties," but seemed to leave the job of the front-end push to the "invisible hand" of market forces and the private, voluntary helping networks in the local community. In this respect, the Reagan philosophy was not so much a departure into uncharted territory or simply a mean-spirited exercise as a return to the prevailing view of the federal social role during most of the middle third of this century.

The proper role of the federal government, in President Reagan's view, is the provision of basic welfare benefits for those who cannot work, the maintenance of a temporary cushion for those who can work but have lost their jobs, and the provision of basic health and retirement benefits for elderly people. According to this view, many of the "social engineering" functions that characterized the Great Society would be better performed by state or local government or by the private sector.

The scope of government under Reagan's conceptual framework is considerably narrower than under the Great Society. The reduction in the cost of government, however, may not be as large because of the very expensive nature of the commitments made to the elderly and the relatively modest cost of most of the job training, education, and infrastructure programs in the Great Society period.

CHANGING NATIONAL PRIORITIES: IMPACT ON SOCIAL SPENDING

When President Reagan took office, he inherited a situation in which the American people were rebelling against the traditional methods that the government had used for about a decade and a half in its major buildup in federal social spending—reduced outlays for national defense as a share of government, increased taxes, higher inflation, and deficits in the federal budget. Indeed, federal outlays for entitlement programs and other nondefense "mandatory" spending programs rose from 5.6 percent of gross national product in fiscal 1962 to 10.5 percent in fiscal 1980. This growth was facilitated, in part, by the corresponding drop of the budget share attributable to national defense—from 9.4 percent of GNP in fiscal 1962 to 5.0 percent in fiscal 1980 (U.S. Congressional Budget Office 1986).

The accommodation of new government programs and the broadening and enrichment of benefits under existing ones, however, was also facilitated by a small increase in the federal tax burden. Total federal revenues rose from 17.9 percent of GNP in fiscal 1962 to 20.1 percent in fiscal 1981. Moreover, even with a squeeze on defense and somewhat higher taxes, the federal government could not make ends meet, and ran budget deficits in all but one year of this 1960–81 period. Thus the cost of social programs put pressure on other national objectives such as national defense, tax relief, and a balanced budget.

It is important to note that the idea of federal social outlays spiraling out of control is erroneous. This vision of rampant social spending has been seized upon by some observers to justify Draconian policy measures. In reality, social spending in the public sector increased steadily from the mid-1960s through the 1970s (although this spending leveled off as a percentage of GNP in the second half of the 1970s), but at rates that could be explained in part by the gradual implementation of new social programs and in part by decisions made by the Congress to shield beneficiaries under a number of programs from the accelerating pace of inflation. Of course, the real value of benefits per recipient also rose during this period, particularly for elderly participants in the Social Security and Medicare programs. These rising real benefits contributed significantly to a corresponding reduction in elderly poverty.

Thus real Social Security benefits per capita rose by 54 percent between 1970 and 1984 while the corresponding figure for Medicare was 116 percent

(U.S. Congress 1985). The social benefits offsetting such costs are reflected in the halving of the rate of elderly poverty between 1966 and 1984, from 28 percent to less than 13 percent. It is arguable that if increases in Social Security and Medicare benefits had been minimal, other means-tested outlays for public assistance would have been higher.

Indeed, the rising cost of social programs cannot be attributed to a rising bill for welfare, in the conventional sense of the term. Means-tested social programs accounted for only about one out of ten dollars in federal outlays, and in real terms did not increase during the 1970s. In fact, real outlays per capita actually fell significantly under some programs. Between 1970 and 1984 real spending per capita for benefits to recipients of Aid to Families with Dependent Children (AFDC) fell 34 percent (U.S. Congress 1985). The rising cost of food stamps and Medicaid offset this decline and, on balance, low-income beneficiaries received about the same level of benefits in 1980 as they had received a decade earlier.

A dispassionate view of the growth in social spending thus yields the conclusion that program outlays grew substantially as a result of decisions taken by the federal government to raise the purchasing power of senior citizens; to offset declining cash assistance for the nonelderly poor with such benefits paid ''in-kind'' rather than in cash as housing assistance, food stamps and Medicaid; and to experiment with selected new (and for the most part, relatively low-cost) measures such as education and training programs and urban redevelopment designed to reduce poverty among nonelderly, lower-income households.

It is important to observe the contrast between the results of the two clusters of social programs aimed at the elderly and nonelderly, respectively. The former effort reflected the lion's share of the money associated with the Great Society buildup, but seemed largely obscured from public view and debate. Moreover, the enrichment of the elderly's safety net brought clear-cut and favorable results, as noted earlier.

By contrast, many of the programs more typically viewed as Great Society efforts, ranging from Model Cities and Urban Renewal to the Job Corps and Head Start, carried relatively small price tags. As a general rule these programs had a much more mixed record of achievement. Indeed, some of these programs were notoriously wasteful and became symbols of disillusionment with the Great Society.

In one sense, therefore, the Great Society was a quiet, albeit rather expensive success; in another sense, it was a conspicuous ''failure,'' but the cost of the miscarriage of original intentions was not as great as many people believe.

The truth of the matter is that Americans entered the 1980s with a much better idea of how to make inroads against elderly poverty than of how to address the fundamental, growing social problems of the urban ghetto, problems that entangle the nation's disadvantaged youth in a web of crime, poor education, inactivity, and split families. While the barometer of hardship among the elderly steadily fell during the 1960s and 1970s, the mercury rose in the nation's major cities, and the indications of social distress all worsened.

Two difficult challenges thus faced Americans at the beginning of the 1980s. First, could small but important changes be made in the growth path of programs such as Social Security, Medicare, or veteran's assistance that would accommodate and facilitate progress toward competing national objectives? Second, could new ways be devised of addressing the needs of America's "underclass" that avoid the obvious pitfalls of well-intentioned but errant efforts of the 1960s and 1970s?

In my view, what is happening in the 1980s is a fundamental reassessment of the sustainability of continued increases in federal social programs, *given* other national objectives. People do not necessarily believe that the programs all failed or that they were out of control. Rather, there was a growing feeling throughout the 1970s that the price Americans paid for the benefits received was too great—higher taxes, a deteriorating defense posture, and the inflationary effects of stimulative monetary policy. Most people did not want the programs gutted, but rather capped or trimmed to yield a measure of tax relief and to bring the economy under control. Wherever possible, people wanted this reordering of priorities to occur through the elimination of wasteful spending rather than through the slashing of benefits. In short, with the exception of such tarnished efforts as the Comprehensive Employment and Training Act (CETA) or Model Cities programs that became objects of public scorn, most of these programs are popular.

Public opinion polls support this view. The polls also show that people want lower taxes. The challenge is to reconcile these two concurrent streams of thought so that we do not continue to mortgage our future by running massive government deficits.

The Reagan Response: Jolting the System

For years, presidents and congressional leaders in both parties tried in vain to address the growing public sentiment in favor of a reorientation of public priorities. Their policies can generally be described as "rational incrementalism," and with a few exceptions, very little was achieved. The best-laid plans fell victim to the "iron triangle" of vested interests in congressional committees, lobby groups, and federal agencies.

Enter Ronald Reagan. In place of incrementalism, President Reagan tried a more sweeping approach—he jolted the system. Instead of asking for a little bit more here and a little bit less there, Reagan went for broke. In a dramatic and successful campaign in the first half of 1981, Reagan pushed through a new program that, whatever its flaws, captured the public's desire to rearrange federal priorities. Defense outlays were placed on a steep growth path, accelerating the turnaround that had begun in the latter part of the Carter administration. Tax rates were cut across the board by 25 percent, with rates scheduled to be indexed for inflation in early 1985. This spelled the end of the automatic increase in revenue that had always accompanied higher consumer prices.

The new priorities in monetary policy introduced in 1979, with a stronger emphasis on inflation control, were endorsed by the Reagan administration despite some skepticism from ardent supply-siders.

The missing link? A plan to control social spending that would reconcile the president's ambitious defense program with a tax cut that would drain about three-quarters of a trillion dollars from the Treasury during Reagan's first term.

In my view, the lightning rod that transmitted the jolt to government was President Reagan's success in cutting taxes and indexing tax rates to avoid future "bracket creep." With this step, Reagan threw down the gauntlet and put pressure on social spending. From a near-term perspective, the important feature of government social policy in the early 1980s appears to be the failure of the Reagan administration and Congress to devise a coherent plan for cutting entitlement programs that was commensurate with the new tax policies. The result, given the simultaneous buildup in national defense and the 1982 recession, was a whopping deficit.

From a close-up vantage point, a review of the first term of the Reagan presidency would suggest that the president failed to respond to the challenge of bringing overall government spending for social programs under control. At the completion of the first term, the federal government was spending 24 percent of GNP, slightly higher than the 23 percent figure when President Reagan took office.

To be sure, the mix of federal spending had shifted toward a relatively greater emphasis on defense. In fact, federal *domestic* programs will account for an estimated 13.6 percent of GNP in 1986, down 2.1 percentage points from the 1981 figure of 15.7 percent (U.S. Congressional Budget Office 1985). It could still be fairly argued, however, that while the size of social programs had decreased somewhat to accommodate the defense buildup, clearly more could have been done for fiscal soundness. Indeed, the same government that was spending 24 percent of GNP in 1984–85 was taxing its people at 19 percent of GNP, hardly a model of fiscal austerity.

A Long-Term Perspective

A long-term perspective makes the Reagan "game plan" for budget control appear more sensible. This game plan envisions a reduction in the role of government in society not as a simultaneous lowering of taxes and spending, but as a multistage process. The first stage involves the withdrawal of revenue, without commensurate spending control. As this stage proceeds, deficits rise sharply, followed by calls for tax increases, calls that alarm the electorate. Pressure and a consensus build for a more across-the-board program to control expenditures. In subsequent stages, a control program is enacted (in steps, as opposed to all at once), to nail down previous tax cuts and preserve their real value through tax-bracket indexation.

If this game plan is operative, one would expect to observe a *gradual evolution* toward budget cuts that affect middle- and upper-income households and that are targeted to the big-dollar programs. I argue that this is exactly what is happening.

Pulling the Plug

It is in this area that President Reagan's fiscal strategy can be seen as wholly different from those of his predecessors. By leaving the "gravy train" of bracket creep in place and simply chipping away at the edges of entitlement programs (often through cumbersome and feckless controls on social service providers), previous administrations were ratifying the growth of entitlement programs. Quite simply, what Reagan understood was that the only way to stop this seemingly inexorable trend was to pull the revenue plug.

If the scenario I am outlining here actually unfolds (which is by no means a certainty), the Reagan policies will look much more sensible a decade or two from now than they do at the moment. It is hard to tell how good an investment was that you made during the fifth year of a twenty-year loan when the payback seems smaller than the outlay.

The reconciliation of President Reagan's multiple goals of tax relief, defense buildup, and inflation control requires taking on the middle class. Expenditure control means reexamining and changing a system in which some people with little or no financial need are provided with substantial subsidies while others with meager resources receive no government assistance.

Obviously a big gap exists between the initial rhetoric of the Reagan administration and the reality of the federal budget. The rhetoric stressed "the welfare mess," "waste, fraud, and abuse," and the need for improved public management based on sound principles from the private sector. The reality is that relatively low overhead but very costly social insurance programs, national defense expenditures, and interest on the federal debt account for about three-fourths of the federal budget and that outright waste and fraud, while discernible and abhorrent, is a very small contributor to federal expenditures.

Reality also dictates a choice of definitions for the safety net. If it were defined to include and protect the major social insurance programs, primarily benefiting elderly people (rich and poor alike), the short-term political pressure would be minimized, at the cost of any chance of real budget control. If it were defined more narrowly to shield only the "truly needy" in all age brackets, the tax and defense objectives could have been achieved with far less damage to the deficit. Such a policy, however, would require taking on all of the political "untouchables"—Social Security recipients, military retirees, veterans, farmers, and so on. Ironically, although the administration's pronouncements stressed fiscal control and the need to protect only the truly needy, its policy decisions during the first term sacrificed fiscal control to the maintenance of a much broader system of both public expenditures and tax subsidies flowing to all income groups on the basis of categorical status.

The Reagan administration's first term was not an unyielding, unswerving exercise in overpromising what the government could deliver. Instead, in those four years a gradual effort was made to come to terms with the fiscal imperative that the 1981 Reagan policies created for the administration (Meyer 1984). In effect, the administration put itself in a bind by cutting taxes without a serious, broad-based effort to cut spending, and then began, slowly and painfully, to work its way out of this bind.

Evidence on this point can be found in the administration's acquiescence in two tax increases in 1982 and 1984 (while the magnitude of these increases was relatively modest, the administration took considerable criticism from supply-siders for not standing fast and pure). More important, successive administration budgets proposed to Congress during the first term reflected both some easing in cuts geared to the poverty population and some strengthening of proposed cuts in such programs as Social Security, Medicare, and civil service retirement.

Some budget reductions sought by the administration were denied by Congress. For example, in 1981 the administration sought a 25 percentage point reduction in the proportion of full Social Security benefits that an early retiree could receive (a decrease from 80 to 55 percent of full benefits). This proposal, and the larger package of Social Security cuts proposed by the administration at this time, was resoundingly defeated by Congress. The administration's attempts to achieve further cuts in the food stamp program beyond those achieved in 1981 were also rebuffed.

The fiscal 1986 budget proposals of the administration, presented in early 1985, reveal a further understanding of the need to focus on nonwelfare spending.

First, this budget called for some improved targeting of federal benefits in areas never touched before. For example, the health care and housing assistance benefits of veterans would be tightened up in ways that vary the effective subsidy more with actual need. Veterans would have to reach a threshold of out-of-pocket outlays for health care before the federal government stepped in, and health care aid would be tilted toward those with service-connected injuries or ailments.

Second, the Reagan budget proposals would tear into the category of federal spending falling under the title of discretionary outlays. This represents a significant change from the late 1970s and early 1980s when many of these programs were allowed to erode in real terms through nominal spending ceilings, but were rarely slashed or targeted for extinction.

Programs such as general revenue sharing, the Work Incentives Program (WIN), Urban Development Action Grants (UDAG), Job Corps, mass transit, and Amtrak subsidies would have been scrapped under the 1986 Reagan budget agenda. Many of these requests were resubmitted in the administration's fiscal 1987 budget. As of this writing, only general revenue sharing appears headed for total extinction, but the package that emerges from Congress will probably make sharp cuts in most of the other program areas in the discretionary category.

What does all this yield? I suggest that the United States is entering a new phase of expenditure control policy in which it is recognized that the safety net for the poor cannot be cut much further; that the social insurance and retirement functions must at least be on the table for discussion if meaningful fiscal control is to be achieved; and that there will not be too much room in the future for all other federal government social expenditures earlier grouped under such categories as human capital development and infrastructure revitalization. This new phase signals that if taxes remain about where they are now, the federal government will probably be backing out of a number of the new tasks grafted onto its more traditional role during the 1960s and 1970s. This forecast assumes that major changes will not be made in the share of federal expenditures currently accounted for by national defense and Social Security outlays.

Clearly more phases remain before sufficient expenditure control is achieved to reduce federal deficits to safe proportions of U.S. national output. To arrest the continuous rise in the ratio of the national debt to GNP, deficits will have to be lowered from their 1984–85 "take" of 5 percent of GNP to about 2 percent of GNP.

What will the federal government look like a decade or so from now? My conjecture is that it will be much less of a multipurpose, multifaceted operation, and that it will be accounting for between 22 and 25 percent of national output. Its purpose will be largely to take care of our elderly and disabled population and to defend our shores, a vastly more simplified (though by no means easy) charge than the scatter-shot, variegated mandates taken up by the federal government of the 1970s. Functions such as building or maintaining infrastructure or education and training assistance are likely to be carried out by other units of government or by the private sector.

Moreover, I envision a somewhat restricted, or at least limited, role for the government in serving elderly and disabled people. In my view, budget realities, underpinned by taxpayer attitudes, will continue gradually to erode the expanded notion of "entitlement" even in health, retirement, and disability assistance. In a return to the pre-1965 era, the federal role is likely to be characterized by aid that is directed a little more closely to need.

This surely does not presage an end to such programs as Social Security or Medicare. These two programs will—and certainly should—continue to support the elderly and disabled members of society. What it does portend is a movement toward higher contributions to these programs by beneficiaries who can afford it; a redesign of Social Security and other retirement programs to encourage a more active work life for those in their fifties and sixties; a greater emphasis on preventive health care and the delivery of health care in lower-cost settings; and the careful development of criteria for disability programs that stress rehabilitation and the resumption of work activity, where possible, without penalizing those who are unable to return to work.

To complete the unfinished agenda of federal budget control requires, among other things, recognition that the undifferentiated nature of federal benefits to the elderly does not match well with the diversity in their economic circumstances. "The elderly" cannot be treated as a monolithic group. From a variety of perspectives, including income, assets, health status, and age, the elderly population is a very heterogeneous group. With few exceptions, however, public policy affecting elderly people fails to acknowledge this diversity. Flat benefit schedules tend to overcompensate some and undercompensate others relative to their actual needs.

The unfinished agenda may also require devising new ways to reduce poverty among the nonelderly people who comprise about nine-tenths of the poverty population. A measure of income support may be a part of a new strategy. But Americans will also have to address the factors that encourage teenage pregnancies, split families, societal dropouts, and crime if we are to dent this problem.

Finally, if we are going to maintain low tax rates, we may have to apply these rates to more income unless expenditure control fully "earns" us the lower tax rates.

In my view, the 1980s will be viewed as a period in which national priorities are reordered in a significant way through a process of gradual fiscal adjustment to the shock of the 1981 tax changes. This forecast presumes that the elements of the unfinished agenda will be seriously addressed in the near future. A retreat to a doctrinaire supply-side stance, or an unwillingness to take on the more powerful interest groups whose benefits will have to be more properly scaled to actual need, could derail the effort to reorder priorities and leave a legacy of massive debt to the next generation.

THE NEW SOCIAL PHILOSOPHY

Up to this point I have been discussing one major trend in the social role of the federal government—the reordering of priorities within total federal spending, that is, a relatively greater emphasis on national defense and lower taxes and a diminished role for the federal government in the social policy arena. I turn now to an analysis of a second major trend in the federal social role—an altered social philosophy embedded in the nation's federal social expenditure programs.

Of course, the social philosophy underpinning federal programs is not totally unrelated to notions about the desirable size of those programs. For instance, an altered outlook or set of basic values and objectives may yield some new approaches to government programs that will trim federal spending. The important difference is that the change in philosophy reflects more than a desire for lower total outlays. Some policy steps are taken because they are thought to enhance the effectiveness of government programs or render a better value for the money spent. These steps may also be designed to reduce the alleged adverse effects of government programs on the recipients themselves.

Four facets of this new social philosophy are described in this section: (1) a preference for government activities carried out at the state and local, rather than the national level; (2) a heightened emphasis on reducing waste, fraud, and mismanagement in government programs; (3) a greater emphasis on the achievement of successful outcomes in social programs; and (4) a tighter restriction of public assistance to low-income households that excludes the working poor from eligibility for government subsidies.

The philosophical change partly results from a perception that national program structures are unresponsive to variations in local circumstances and regional variations in public preferences. National blueprints, according to this view, are cookie-cutters that stamp out undifferentiated social program models that do not mesh well with indigenous problems. The new philosophy also addresses a belief that government assistance can have a corrosive effect on the human spirit and a deleterious effect on ultimate advancement. According to this conceptual framework, government benefits for working-age, able-bodied people should be quite temporary.

In what follows I present a critical assessment of this new approach to government social policy by grouping the alleged flaws in government social programs into several broad categories and then ascertaining whether or not these flaws are real problems and, if so, how much progress is being achieved to correct them.

Excessive Centralization and Segmentation of Social Programs

The growth in federal spending for social programs was accompanied by the development of a complex, multifaceted system of intergovernmental grants. Federal aid to the states soared from less than $2 billion in the 1940s to well over $50 billion in the late 1970s. These federal grants to states accounted for nearly 40 percent of states' general revenues by 1978, an increase from about 22 percent three decades earlier. Grants from the federal and state governments to local governments rose from $3.5 billion in 1948 to $85.5 billion in 1978 (Barfield 1981).

The size of the intergovernmental revenue flow, however, tells only part of the story. The flow trickled through an elaborate network of roughly 500 categorical grant programs with overlapping, interlocking jursidictions. This network of pipelines was clogged by a complicated set of federal regulations. Although some observers have questioned the need for the federal government to collect and subsequently recycle such vast sums of money, most of the criticism of the system of grants and transfers is directed at the proliferation of categorical programs, with so much decision making and priority-setting centered in Washington, D.C.

To address this situation, President Reagan proposed significant changes designed to make much greater use of block grants. His initial budget proposals envisioned the combination of many relatively small categorical programs into a few larger block grants, with state and local discretion over the apportionment of funds among categories of spending.

For example, the Reagan administration proposed consolidating forty-four elementary and secondary education programs into two packages totalling

$4.4 billion. The Education Consolidation and Improvement Act (ECIA) of 1981 reflected a number of the administration's requests, but did not include the major programs that the administration wanted to consolidate. The Act consolidated twenty-nine categorical grant programs into one simplified program (Doyle and Hartle 1984).

In selected other areas of the budget such as community services and health care, the administration was also successful in obtaining block grants which combined a number of relatively small programs into one grant. Generally speaking, the administration got less than it hoped for from Congress in the area of program consolidation and decentralization, and had to be content with a strategy of level funding in nominal terms from year to year for the programs that it was able to consolidate, gradually eroding their cost in real terms.

The New Federalism Proposal

The President's new federalism initiative, introduced in January 1982, proposed more sweeping changes. Starting in 1984 the federal government would have assumed full responsibility for Medicaid; in return, the states were to take over Food Stamps and AFDC, a "swap" of about $20 billion in program outlays. Also, a new $28 billion trust fund, financed by federal excise taxes and part of the oil windfall profits tax, was to be established for the transfer of other federal programs to the states. The trust fund was intended to cover the areas of education, community development, transportation, and social services (White House 1982).

This plan was billed as "revenue-neutral" for the states, but it contained a ticking time bomb. While the size of the trust fund was to nearly equal the size of the "turn back" programs (about $30 billion in fiscal 1984), after four years the federal revenue base for the turn back of programs would begin to erode, and would disappear completely after 1991. The states would then have to impose their own taxes or shrink the programs. This eight-year time bomb was one that most states wanted to defuse.

After months of negotiations between the White House and groups such as the National Governors Association, the proposal fizzled. It is surprising that, instead of returning to the drawing board to redesign this plan, the administration seemed to drop the idea. Currently there do not seem to be any plans for its revival in the second Reagan term.

The Reagan plan of gradually reducing federal funding after an initial interim funding period ultimately puts pressure on states and localities to raise their own revenues for social services projects deemed worthwhile locally. For projects like downtown redevelopment, sports arenas, and water resource conservation, it may be desirable to encourage regions to become self-supporting. For nutrition, disease control, basic health insurance coverage, or minimal shelter, I am quite uncomfortable with a local option approach. I would not like to see the provision of these needs depend upon where one lives—these are more than amenities.

What is needed is a division of labor among governments in which each level of government "leads from its strength." The federal government has a comparative advantage in carrying out income transfer functions while local governments have a natural edge in delivering services such as education, police and fire protection, and refuse disposal. Moreover, it is difficult to sell such programs as food stamps, Medicaid, or AFDC to local taxpayers who do not benefit directly from such programs in the way that they benefit from bridge and highway construction and repair, downtown redevelopment, or mass transit. Business cannot be drawn into a state with welfare spending.

Although the sweeping proposals that constitute the president's new federalism plan seem moribund, the administration has been active in breathing some life into the "old federalism." In addition to some of the block grants enacted in 1981, as mentioned earlier, the administration has also devolved a considerable amount of responsibility for program administration to the states. The chapter by Richard Nathan in this volume describes a number of the initiatives requiring greater administrative flexibility, decentralization, and innovations at the state level in response to federal cutbacks. In services ranging from job training and education to health and welfare, states have been more active in designing management reforms and in filling in some of the gaps arising from reductions in federal spending.

On balance, the administration's record in decentralizing the authority and responsibility of government is a mixed one. Its formal, comprehensive proposals have flopped, and it seems to have lost the vision of fundamental reform that characterized the beginning of the first term. Yet in some less dramatic and less visible, but still important instances, the administration has made progress toward its goal of returning more funding and authority to local and state governments.

I think it is fair to say that the administration has not yet lived up to the concept of the "Reagan revolution" in decentralization. On a more incremental, evolutionary path, however, some steps have been taken toward local autonomy and away from intrusive decision making by remote regulators.

The Reduction of Waste, Fraud, and Mismanagement

The issue of "waste, fraud, and abuse" in federal social programs generally has been blown out of perspective. The problem is not trivial, and it deserves attention. In my view, however, an objective assessment of the situation that strips away the "welfare queen" imagery and the verbal flourishes reveals a very manageable problem. More important, data presented below suggest that the order of magnitude of the "waste" is not sufficiently large that its reduction could make a substantial difference in the overall budget picture.

Some aspects of wasteful government spending are not addressed here in any detail. For example, the Grace Commission uncovered various methods of government purchasing, money management, or related business practices that were not in accordance with basic, sensible practices of the private sector (President's Private Sector Survey 1984). The recommendations of the commission, where sound, can yield some significant savings, although often a one-time "shake out" is suggested rather than a permanent lowering of the growth path of federal outlays. Other recommendations of the commission indicate policy changes that would achieve savings by reducing federal benefits; this is quite different from "waste and abuse."

I view the challenge to government as one addressing three aspects of government social programs: (1) How large are the payment error rates in safety net programs such as food stamps, AFDC, and Medicaid, and how can they be reduced? (2) How high are administrative costs in operating government social programs, and can they be easily reduced? (3) Are programs poorly managed, and if so, is this a problem of a weak management staff or the wrong management system?

The "waste, fraud, and abuse" campaign has fizzled, in my opinion, because the problem was simply blown out of perspective by the rhetoric. In fact, in 1985 the focus of the waste, fraud, and abuse debate turned from social welfare programs to the Department of Defense. People now seem at least as concerned about what the Armed Services paid for an ashtray or a hammer as they are about welfare fraud.

Program waste and payment errors *do* constitute a problem, and the Reagan administration can be credited with addressing this problem more seriously than its predecessors. However, my assessment is that the administration will probably not be remembered for this accomplishment. Down the road, this issue will fade in importance; as it does, a more fundamental problem will rise to the fore. We will see that government "costs too much" relative to our present willingness to accept higher taxes—not so much because of waste but because the pace of escalation is more rapid in benefits than in taxes. Quite simply, when the veneer of fraud and abuse is stripped away, we will confront the essence of the problem—we have overpromised relative to what we can deliver at these tax rates. Reducing waste can reduce this gap, but it cannot close it.

A few figures help illustrate the dimensions of the problem. Error rates are higher in some programs than others, but do not constitute a runaway problem or a huge drain on federal coffers. The error rate in the food stamp program was particularly high when President Reagan took office (about 10 percent), and has edged down in recent years. Congress enacted the administration's proposal to set targets for states under the food stamp program of 9 percent in 1983, 7 percent in 1984, and 5 percent in 1985 (and thereafter). Federal payments for administrative costs are adjusted upward if these targets are met and downward if they are not. The Medicaid error rate was only half as high as the rate in food stamps in 1980, and it was cut nearly in half in the early 1980s (from 5.2 percent to 2.9 percent).

Taking a weighted average of four such programs—food stamps, Medicaid, AFDC, and Supplemental Security Income (SSI), I calculate a composite 1982 error rate of 5.3 percent. If this composite figure were to hold for the total of all low-income programs, including spending for the relatively small programs such as WIC and low-income energy assistance, program errors in poverty programs would drain an estimated 0.0053 of total federal spending, or about one-half of 1 percent. With the federal budget approaching $1 trillion today, the savings would be about $5 billion, or about 3 percent of the estimated size of the federal deficit! This is the *gross* savings from eliminating errors in welfare programs, which would have to be offset somewhat by the added cost associated with an effort to reduce the error rates.

Of course, payment errors also occur in programs like Social Security and Medicare, not to mention national defense outlays. Reducing these overpayments could add to the potential savings. It is my contention that an error-free government is no more possible than is an error-free private company. One should not expect miracles.

Another myth about federal social programs is that they have bloated administrative costs. Recent figures show that administrative costs under Medicare and Medicaid are 2 percent and 5 percent of total costs, respectively. This is hardly a scandal. Indeed, one could ask how many groups in the private sector could meet these targets? Much of the federal effort in social programs is devoted to mailing out checks to recipients and paying claims (with the latter done through fiscal intermediaries in the private sector). On the whole, it is not a very "top-heavy" system. The important point is that programs that could be viewed as top-heavy, such as Model Cities or CETA, are not typical of federal social programs, and these "bloated" programs have either already been eliminated or are now being scaled down. Such programs are dwarfed by a program like Social Security, which is a relatively low-overhead and efficient program. This is not to say that government has as lean a work force as it could have—but what organization does?

Low Success Rates

Another trend in social programs in the 1980s is a greater emphasis on program success rates as a criterion for continued funding. In previous years the prevailing tendency was to presume that more of the programs were achieving their intended results, or if they were not, that the funding allocated to the effort was probably insufficient. In recent years a bit more attention has been paid to the strategy or basic program approach as a determinant of its probable success, and somewhat less emphasis is placed on the exact amount of funding as the key determinant of outcome.

The current environment demands evidence of successful impact. Particularly for programs outside the basic safety net and social insurance categories, federal social programs are being examined for evidence of success in improving a social problem that would justify the continuation of funding. Earlier this debate might have revolved around a decision about whether to increase funding; today it is more likely to entail a decision about whether to continue the program at all.

It is unfortunate that the tendency exists now to move from unbridled (and perhaps naive) optimism to calloused cynicism. Generalizations from isolated cases are used to discredit programs that actually have a rather mixed record. Generalizations about programs "not working" are very misleading. In attempting to help the disadvantaged in the education system or the labor market, for example, one does not realistically expect that every program enrollee will succeed. Success, in a sense, is relative. Many studies have attempted to track "graduates" of federal social programs against control groups of similarly situated people who did not receive government aid. This helps to answer the question of whether the program participants fared better, as a group, than they would have in the absence of government intervention.

I will offer a few examples of what the scorecard for a social program might look like and address the question of whether the Reagan administration is overhauling programs to improve the chances for success or simply canceling the effort.

In judging the success of social programs, it is useful to return to the objectives I noted at the outset of this chapter. I suggested that the Great Society and its extension through the Nixon period consisted of two separate thrusts: the development of a new public goal of providing a lift at the front end of the labor force to the disadvantaged to help them enter the mainstream of economic life, and an enrichment and broadening of the government's long-standing commitment to protect people at the back end of the labor force who become inactive as a result of retirement, illness, injury, or infirmity.

As noted earlier, most efforts to develop human capital and social infrastructure programs were smaller in scope and produced results that were less clear-cut than the results of social insurance programs. In general most of the former group of programs cannot be said either unequivocally to have "worked" or to have been total failures. More often they help some people and fail to reach others. This makes the total cost of each success seem expensive. Programs such as Head Start, CETA (now the Job Training Partnership Act, JTPA), the Job Corps, Pell grants, and so on have typically been aimed at the hardest people to serve. These programs do not provide direct cash transfers that immediately enhance purchasing power, but rather offer more indirect investments in education, training, or nutrition that are designed to improve well-being and increase future earning power.

A few examples show that these programs yield more ambiguous results than the safety net programs. One study indicates that job training provided in a classroom setting has helped women enrollees in a significant way but has raised the earnings of men only slightly. In the case of women, the favorable effects result largely from more hours worked rather than higher wage rates, a finding that raises questions about how lasting or continuous the progress will be. New entrants (and reentrants) to the labor market have been helped more than those receiving training while on layoff from a job (Burtless 1984).

The Job Corps has been shown by another study to have a favorable "payoff" when all societal benefits are counted (Maller et al. 1982), but critics claim that the favorable results fade quickly if the sizable benefits from crime reduction turn out to have been overestimated.

The Reagan administration's tax cuts, as noted earlier, are forcing painful choices among priorities within the federal budget. This, in itself, is long overdue, although I am concerned about the arbitrary labeling of programs as losers or failures, when the truth is that program results were mixed and resulted from both faulty program designs and the intractable nature of the problems tackled. This labeling creates a convenient but unconvincing cover for a total federal retreat from the "front-end" push for the disadvantaged. Simply dumping the program becomes much easier than redesigning and streamlining to correct past flaws. Operating under this mentality, the federal government would withdraw to a role of helping its citizens only after they are in trouble. It is regrettable that attempts to help people avoid the trouble in the first place have been largely discredited.

Programs like the Job Corps represent a relatively modest federal investment in the nation's most troubled youth. These youths, as potential dropouts, will make more trouble for society in the future unless ways can be found to bring them into the mainstream of economic and social life. Currently about $0.6 billion is allocated toward this effort, less than one-tenth of 1 percent of the federal budget! An objective reading of the evidence is that, although the cost per enrollee is fairly high, a substantial proportion of program participants are being helped, particularly when the concept of a successful outcome is broadened, as it must be, to include not only job placement, but also a return to school or success on the Armed Services entrance examination. To those who contend that the benefit-cost ratio could be higher than it is, I say, "let us find program reforms that achieve this instead of just giving up on these people."

President Reagan's fiscal 1987 budget recommends cutting the Job Corps approximately in half instead of eliminating it, as suggested in 1985. Other programs in the discretionary category, however, are still targeted for elimination as the administration and Congress strive to achieve a substantial reduction in the deficit without touching Social Security and with only minor cuts in Medicare and major retirement programs. National defense seems headed for roughly level funding after a few years of substantial increases in outlays. If the Gramm-Rudman targets for the elimination of the federal deficit over a five-year period are met, these trends in social insurance and defense spending will surely spell the demise of most other programs in the federal budget. Some of these functions that would disappear, such as providing subsidies for urban mass transit or downtown redevelopment, could be better performed by state and local governments. Other functions, such as providing assistance for educating disadvantaged or handicapped youth or cleaning up the environment, would seem more appropriately handled with at least some involvement by the federal government.

Phasing out federal participation in these discretionary programs appears to be inherent in the long-range Reagan game plan. This loss of federal functions might be a little more palatable if a realistic transfer of authority and resources to local governments were envisioned, based on criteria defining the proper roles of each level of government. But, as argued in the previous section, such vision is now quite blurred.

Such action, or lack of it, leads the public to believe government is saying "the safety net works and the rest does not, so let's just provide the safety net." Philosophically this seems to be an odd legacy for an administration that stresses the value of opportunity and self-reliance. Yet, in many ways, this outcome is the inevitable result of conservative cynicism about government, a cynicism that constrains the role of government to the most easily achievable tasks.

Adverse Effect on Work Incentives

The last element in this analysis of the new social philosophy is the development of a new approach to welfare. Because of the tendency for federal benefit levels to compare so favorably with potential earnings for those who can work, but are idle, the concern arises that dependency is more attractive than work. This tendency toward dependency is further strengthened by the rules governing how long benefits may be retained and what types of people are eligible for assistance.

Generally speaking, most observers agree that for a short period benefit levels that permit a decent living standard are desirable, even for people who are able to work. Reasonable people disagree about the earnings replacement rate that should be permitted, even for a short period. It is important to steer a course between benefit levels that are so high that they encourage a worker to give up a job and benefits that are too low to permit a minimally adequate living standard. Observers also disagree on how long earnings replacement should last—four months, six months, a year, and so on.

The real controversy, however, stems from the strategy used to improve adverse work incentives for low-income households that arise from either benefit levels that exceed potential earnings or from an unduly long benefit eligibility period. At the risk of oversimplifying the split between two divergent schools of thought, the essential difference seems to lie in the distinction between two approaches—on the one hand, trying to lure nonworkers into the labor force (or keep low-income workers there) through providing work expense deductions and earnings disregards that allow low-wage workers to retain a small amount of government assistance, and, on the other hand, trying to segment the poverty population in a way that simply denies public assistance to people in certain categories in which self-reliance is deemed feasible. The former approach, which was the prevalent view until the 1980s, favors adjusting the rate at which program benefits are reduced as earnings rise to make work continuously attractive. The latter approach proposes tighter targeting of benefits to nonworking people for whom work is not a realistic alternative (due to disability or child-raising responsibilities) and the establishment of ''workfare'' programs to move low-income people who are not in those needy categories into jobs. The Reagan administration has championed this latter approach, but it also has been tried by a number of state governments. The challenge is to find the strategy that strikes a good balance between fairness to recipients and fairness to the taxpayers supporting them.

In 1981 the Reagan administration sold its own welfare reform position to Congress. The disregard of one-third of earnings for purposes of calculating AFDC benefits was to last for only four months of work, and eligibility requirements and work expense deductions were tightened. More than 400,000 low-income people with jobs lost coverage, and many of these became ineligible for Medicaid.[2]

Although the administration was successful in scuttling the old-style welfare reform plans, it has not been able to fully convince Congress to buy its proposed alternative—mandatory workfare. Congress has been willing to encourage, but not to compel, work requirements.

The Reagan administration's contention that the working poor would generally keep working even without the AFDC-Medicaid package has been largely confirmed by recent studies.[3] The available evidence also clearly shows, however, that these working poor households are significantly worse off than before the changes. President Reagan has won the political battle over welfare, but he cannot claim to have won it without inflicting any casualties.

For example, a mother with three children earning 75 percent of the poverty-line income in 1980 had a total income of $11,150 ($7,958 from earnings). The same woman earning the same amount in 1984 had a total income of only $9,179, a decline of 18 percent. This drop in income, arising from the disappearance of AFDC benefits (offset only to a small extent by food stamps) and higher taxes, moves the family from a position of $539 *above* the poverty line in 1980 to one $1,432 *below* the poverty line in 1984.

Again the issue of balance and fairness arises. Is it fair (even if "it works") to take benefits away from workers at or near the minimum wage while subsidies to higher-paid workers and executives go largely untouched? The Reagan administration has clearly changed the terms of the debate in welfare and dispelled some of the arguments of earlier welfare reformers. But some nagging doubts remain about the basic fairness of a program that penalizes work on a dollar-for-dollar basis for America's lowest-income workers at the same time that the tax penalty is reduced for workers in middle- and upper-income households.

Finally, the segmentation of the poverty population, whatever its short-term fiscal "payoff," does not alter the fact that the poverty rate is higher today than it was at the end of the 1970s. To deny aid to one segment of the

---

2. Some people who lost Medicaid received coverage under certain optional plans such as the federal "Ribicoff children" approach or state plans for the medically needy, but many of the noncategorically eligible poor do not qualify for these programs either.

3. See, for example, U.S. General Accounting Office (1984).

poor and continue aid under a more or less business-as-usual approach to another segment misses an opportunity to refashion and restructure the antipoverty effort in ways aimed at improving outcomes. In fact, a number of features of the welfare system have been characterized as antifamily and antiwork, and little has been done to change these features despite a lot of rhetoric to the contrary. The conversion of welfare payments into temporary wage subsidies or the extension of limited but continuous aid to intact families headed by a working spouse would send a more consistent signal than a paradoxical policy of rewarding work for the nonpoor but rewarding idleness among the poor.

THE LEGACY

In this chapter, I have established several criteria for evaluating a new approach to federal social programs. These criteria are critical to achieving a balance among competing national priorities. By targeting government expenditures more tightly to actual need, sorting out the proper roles of the federal government and state and local governments, improving social program outcomes, reducing waste, and promoting work incentives, this balance among national priorities can likely be achieved.

In my view the 1980s will be remembered more clearly as a period in which these national priorities were altered than as a transition to a fundamentally new social philosophy. The government has brought pressure to bear on total outlays through the unconventional approach of scaling back available revenue. This is a course that I believe will look more prudent years from now than it does in today's climate of huge federal deficits. The system needed a shock, and President Reagan provided it. Whether this process turns out to be successful depends upon whether President Reagan and his successors can continue some recent progress toward tightening assistance to middle- and upper-income beneficiaries of federal social programs. Although President Reagan's strategy of pulling the revenue plug first is risky, it is better than the hopeless program-by-program fights with each constituency group against a backdrop of revenue flows that make government concessions too easy.

Thus the Reagan administration's chief legacy in social policy will be the achievement of greater control over federal outlays for social programs that permits us to give more prominence to other national objectives, such as an improved defense posture and tax relief. This legacy will be unexpectedly large, as the dynamics of deficits and demographics will force future changes in entitlements that were hardly considered at the outset of the Reagan administration.

It is ironic that much of the rhetoric of the times is focused elsewhere—on waste, fraud, and abuse, on decentralization and privatization. The administration seems to highlight its *social philosophy* toward federal programs, an area where most of its accomplishments seem rather marginal. By contrast, it downplays and is defensive about its *fiscal policies* which, while incomplete, herald a major accomplishment for the administration.

I believe that history will record this period as a missed opportunity to restructure the relative roles of federal, state, and local governments in a fundamental way. Early plans appear to have aborted, and bold new thrusts do not appear to be forthcoming.

President Reagan's social policy will be remembered as a turning point in the welfare debate, but only in the sense of successfully scuttling certain approaches to the problem advanced in the previous two decades. The president has a new approach to welfare payments but appears to lack a new approach to the problems of poverty and isolation that continue to plague a significant number of Americans. The simplistic notions of a few popular writers that see "the welfare trap" as the only real cause of poverty may seem attractive in the current political climate. But the problems of family breakup, chronic unemployment, drug abuse, and crime have worsened throughout a period during which the welfare system has essentially remained unchanged. The taxpayers may be saved a few dollars through the new approach of segmenting the poverty population, but these social problems cannot be addressed through welfare rule changes alone.

The 1980s will be remembered as a period during which Americans questioned or even canceled some programs that had grown expensive and produced disappointing results. This is no small accomplishment, considering how much harder it is for government to retreat than to advance, but we are left with the need to develop new approaches to replace those discarded.

In my view the unfinished agenda has two parts. We must remove the contradiction in criticizing "big government" for the poor while condoning and underwriting open-ended government subsidies for middle-income and upper-income households. And we should develop new strategies for all levels of government—and the private sector—in an effort to give the disadvantaged a chance, in the words of Eleanor Roosevelt, to "get into the game."

REFERENCES

Barfield, Claude E. 1980. *Rethinking Federalism: Block Grants and Federal, State, and Local Responsibilities.* Washington, D.C.: American Enterprise Institute.

Burtless, Gary. 1984. "Manpower Policies for the Disadvantaged: What Works?" *The Brookings Review* (Fall): 18–22.

Doyle, Denis P. and Terry W. Hartle. 1984. "Ideology, Politics, and the Education Budget." In John C. Weicher, ed., *Maintaining the Safety Net.* Washington, D.C.: American Enterprise Institute.

Maller, Charles et al. 1982. *Evaluation of the Economic Impact of the Job Corps Program: Third Follow-up Report.* Princeton, New Jersey: Mathematica Policy Research, Inc. September.

Meyer, Jack A. 1984. "Budget Cuts in the Reagan Administration: A Question of Fairness." In D. Lee Bawden, ed., *The Social Contract Revisited.* Washington, D.C.: Urban Institute Press.

President's Private Sector Survey. 1984. *War on Waste: President's Private Sector Survey on Cost Control.* New York: Collier Books-MacMillan.

U.S. Congress. House Committee on Ways and Means. *Background Material and Data on Programs within the Jurisdiction of the Committee on Ways and Means.* Washington, D.C.: U.S. Government Printing Office.

U.S. Congressional Budget Office. 1985. *The Economic and Budget Outlook: An Update.* Washington, D.C.: Congressional Budget Office, August.

U.S. Congressional Budget Office. 1986. *The Economic and Budget Outlook: Fiscal Years 1987–1991.* Washington, D.C.: Congressional Budget Office, February, Table D-6.

U.S. General Accounting Office. 1984. *An Evaluation of the 1981 AFDC Changes: Initial Analyses.* Washington, D.C.: U.S. Government Printing Office, April 2.

White House. 1982. *Fact Sheet: Federalism Initiative.* Washington, D.C.

REAGANOMICS IN RETROSPECT

Isabel V. Sawhill

Capitalism has always had two major flaws according to its critics: a tendency to produce periodic economic crises and a tendency to generate extremes of wealth and poverty. In response to these criticisms, there has evolved over the past fifty years in the United States, as in other industrialized democracies, a role for government in managing the economy and redistributing incomes that has taken the hard edge off laissez-faire capitalism and disarmed its left-wing critics. But by the 1980s such activism had produced a new kind of criticism—a concern that capitalism's edges were becoming overly round. Many now believe that government's commitment to provide full employment and a modicum of economic security has made it more difficult to keep inflation in check and to insure maximum work and thrift among the nation's citizens. In addition, memories of depression and of extreme poverty have faded as an older generation has passed on, and a younger one, born into prosperity, has begun to take its economic security for granted. Finally, the poor performance of the economy in the 1970s left many people dissatisfied. For all these reasons the stage was set in 1980 for the political pendulum, which had been swinging leftward since the 1930s, to swing back again as part of what many would call the Reagan revolution. But to what extent, and in what ways, is it accurate to call it a revolution?

In this chapter, I conclude that the Reagan years are best understood as a philosophical or ideological watershed likely to usher in a somewhat more

I thank George Eads, William Gorham, Robert Haveman, Hugh Heclo, Joseph Minarik, John Palmer, Robert Reischauer, Alice Rivlin, Robert Solow, Charles Stone, and Lawrence Summers for helpful comments on an early draft.

conservative era, including a more conservative set of economic policies. The content of those policies, I argue, remains undefined. The economic policy consensus that had evolved over the postwar period, and that was symbolized by Milton Friedman's statement in 1972 that "we are all Keynesians now," has evaporated.[1] But a new consensus has not yet taken its place. Whatever the virtues of supply-side economics, it has not replaced Keynesian economics as the dominant paradigm. Indeed, I argue that the more extreme version of supply-side theory that was much in evidence during President Reagan's first term has by now been generally discredited as the result of the large deficits it helped to create.

The demise of the earlier postwar Keynesian consensus together with the failure of supply-side economics has left an economic policy vacuum. The truth is that neither liberals nor conservatives have effective solutions to the nation's two most basic economic problems: how to reconcile price stability with full employment and growth, and how to maintain that relative economic position of the United States in the face of increased competition from the rest of the world. These problems would exist with or without current federal budget deficits, and government may or may not be able to solve them. What is new in the 1980s is that, as a result of these deficits, government is not just a potential part of the solution but an increasingly important part of the problem.

POLITICS AND THE ECONOMY

One cannot divorce economics from politics, or vice versa. Politicians are often blamed for economic developments that economists do not know how to control. And economists are often blamed for outcomes that could have been avoided if politicians had listened to economists. An understanding of recent economic history requires an appreciation of these and other interactions. A good starting point for this discussion is what is commonly called the political business cycle.

The Political Business Cycle: An Expanded Definition

As many scholars have observed, presidents regularly ride the tides of the economy into and out of office. Ronald Reagan has been no exception. In 1980 his defeat of Jimmy Carter was in large measure due to the coexistence

---

1. Although this statement is often attributed to President Nixon, according to Herbert Stein (1984, 113), it was made by Milton Friedman. What Nixon said, after announcing an expansionary budget in 1971, was "Now I am a Keynesian" (Stein, 435).

of recession and double-digit inflation in that year. And President Reagan's reelection in 1984 was greatly facilitated by the strong noninflationary recovery then under way.

The proposition that electoral outcomes are sensitive to the economy's performance is confirmed by a number of empirical studies (Kiewiet 1983; Hibbs and Fassbender 1981; Lipset 1984; and Kiewiet and Rivers 1985). The extent to which those in office use this fact to consciously shift policy in ways that maximize their own chances of electoral success is more disputable. However, several analysts claim to have found evidence that unemployment rates fall significantly just before an election, suggesting that incumbents do manipulate the economy for short-term political gain. (See Nordhaus 1975, and Tufte 1978, 21. For a critique, see Barry 1985.) It is this latter, more Machiavellian, proposition that is commonly referred to as the political business cycle.

I use the term in a somewhat expanded and less rigorous sense—expanded because I extend the concept to longer periods of time than an election cycle, and less rigorous because I use it to refer to any interaction between the economy and the political system broadly defined (elections, policies, ideologies). My hypotheses about these interactions are more fully developed in subsequent sections of this chapter. Briefly, defined in this expanded sense political-economic cycles can be thought of as having short-, medium-, and long-term swings. The short-term cycle is dominated by cyclical movements in the economy (recession and recovery) that influence (whether by design or not) how the electorate feels about a particular *candidate* on election day. The medium-term cycle consists of waves of enthusiasm and subsequent disillusionment with particular *policies* once they produce, or are perceived to have produced, negative economic results (depression in the 1930s, inflation in the 1970s, budget and trade deficits in the 1980s). The long-term cycle pertains to shifts in *ideology* that are most likely to occur when there is an accumulation of major grievances about previous policy regimes accompanied by the emergence of a coherent rationale for change.[2]

Using this three-cycle framework, I predict that the outcome of the next election will depend heavily on the state of the economy at the time (the short-term electoral swing); that regardless of who is elected, a reaction will likely occur against the specific supply-side policies of the Reagan administration (the medium-term policy swing); and that regardless of what policies are chosen over the next several decades, they will probably be somewhat

---

2. My thesis about long-term swings is similar to that articulated by Albert O. Hirschman (1982), who argues that there are political cycles of liberalism and conservatism, each in turn creating the seeds of its own destruction.

more conservative than pre-Reagan policies in their goals and assumptions (the long-term ideological swing).

The Cycle in Action: From Keynes to Kemp

The last long-term swing began in 1932. Before that time, periods of boom and bust in industrialized countries had been thought of as temporary and self-correcting. However, the depth and duration of the Great Depression in the 1930s suggested the system was more deeply flawed. Laissez-faire policies were discredited by events and were replaced by a variety of governmental efforts designed to reduce economic and financial instability, relieve suffering, and put people back to work.

These experimental efforts were not all successful. In fact, by 1939 the level of output was no higher than it had been ten years earlier (Stein 1984, 63). This lack of clear success could have led to a rejection of activist measures and a return to laissez-faire if it had not been for two other developments. The first was the emergence of an intellectual rationale for such policies with the publication of John Maynard Keynes' *General Theory of Employment, Interest, and Money* in 1936 and the second was World War II, which proved that big increases in government spending could indeed put an end to high unemployment. These developments ensured that what might have been just another intermediate-term policy swing became a longer-term swing in the public's conception of governmental responsibility for economic welfare.

The commitment to use all of the federal government's powers and resources to prevent another 1930s-style depression was enshrined in the Employment Act of 1946. Initially the commitment did not carry with it a knowledge of what to do. Both Roosevelt's attempts to end the Great Depression and the efforts of the Truman and Eisenhower administrations to continue, in the words of the 1946 act, "to promote maximum employment, production, and purchasing power" had a rhetorical, experimental, and ad hoc flavor that often seems naive by today's standards.[3] But the intellectual rationale for the Keynesian revolution was gestating in the academic community, and by the 1960s a younger generation of economists, thoroughly schooled in Keynesian principles, came to Washington and persuaded President Kennedy to apply these principles in a more systematic fashion. While the Kennedy administration was riding the long-term swing toward greater activism in economic

---

3. The 1954 *Economic Report of the President* is perhaps typical in this regard. It exhorts the private sector to maintain their purchasing power and calls for such ad hoc policies as credit controls, debt management, varying the terms of federally insured mortgages, public works spending, and agricultural price supports to prevent depression or inflation.

and social policy, it also benefited from coming into power after a decade that had produced three recessions and thereby had tarnished Republican economic policies over the shorter run as well.

President Kennedy proposed what would have been unthinkable in a pre–Keynesian era—a cut in taxes in the face of an already substantial deficit in the federal budget.[4] The performance of the economy subsequent to the 1964 tax cut appeared to dispel any lingering doubts about the efficacy of using an activist policy. By 1966, President Johnson was pronouncing that recessions were not inevitable, that fiscal policy could restore high employment, and that expansions need not generate inflation (*Economic Report of the President* 1966, 4).[5] Moreover, the tax revenues produced by a continually growing economy (the so-called fiscal dividend) were to be used to pay for the War on Poverty and other social programs. Optimism was high about government's ability to manage the economy and solve a variety of social problems.

By the late 1960s, however, the long-term cycle had crested. The problem was that expansion, along with the Vietnam War, eventually produced inflation. The Keynesian policies then in favor called for an increase in taxes to prevent inflation, but the short-term political business cycle made this solution impractical. The president and the Congress were unwilling to take the bitter medicine being prescribed by the president's economic advisers because of their concern that it would doom them at the polls. Thus, the 1970s began with inflation out of the box.

Presidents Nixon and Ford might have been expected to reverse policy in an attempt to restore price stability. Republicans have always cared more about inflation and less about unemployment than Democrats, and one would have expected another intermediate-term policy swing as a result. But the willingness of the Republicans to shift gears was tempered by Nixon's conversion to Keynesianism (he, too, was riding the long-term swing); and the success of their policies was limited by a spreading inflationary psychology and an enormous upsurge in agricultural and oil prices in 1973 and 1974. However, it was the short-term political business cycle that again played the major role. Concern over winning the 1972 election led President Nixon to adopt wage and price controls in August 1971, which in turn enabled him to

---

4. This fiscal stimulus was combined with wage-price guideposts to contain inflation and supply-side measures (such as an investment tax credit) to enhance productivity growth.

5. This was not just political overstatement. The text of the report by the Council of Economic Advisors also states "recurrent recession need not be accepted as a necessary fact of economic life (ibid., 182)."

apply excessive stimulus to the economy in 1972–73. This was followed by a period of restraint and a sharp recession in 1974–75 that brought the inflation rate down some but did not put it back in the box.

With the election of President Carter in 1976, a more expansionary policy was once again followed in an attempt to reduce unemployment to about 5 percent. Evidence was accumulating in the academic world that this target might not be consistent with a stable inflation rate, but pressures were being applied in the political world to set the target still lower. In 1978, with strong support from labor and from various liberal constituencies but only lukewarm support from the administration, the Humphrey-Hawkins bill, which called for 4 percent unemployment, was enacted. Its passage was a symbol of the fact that many in Washington had lost touch with growing public concerns about inflation and excessive government intervention.

The Carter administration never succeeded in reducing the unemployment rate to 5 percent, much less to 4 percent. Although it is not clear that its macroeconomic policies were inflationary, its microeconomic policies probably were. These included increasing agricultural price supports, social security taxes, minimum wages, and protectionism (Thurow 1980, 46–47). A second oil-price shock in 1979 ensured that inflation would reach double-digit levels during that year and the next. President Carter decided somewhat belatedly to make fighting inflation a priority, and the tightening of both fiscal and monetary policies put the economy into recession in 1980. Thus, Carter had put the short-term political business cycle into reverse, virtually guaranteeing his own defeat. When candidate Ronald Reagan asked the American voters in the fall of 1980, "Are you better off [now] than you were four years ago?" he knew what their answer would be. And he used this dissatisfaction to instill in their minds a new idea about management of the economy: government needed to do less, not more, to ensure prosperity. It was almost as if the Employment Act of 1946 had been rewritten to state that the federal government should cease and desist from using "all its plans, functions, and resources . . . to promote maximum employment, production, and purchasing power."

Apart from its general emphasis on less government intervention, the Reagan economic program that was put forward in 1981, like the early New Deal experiments, had little intellectual coherence. It was a mixture of traditionally conservative (balance the budget), monetarist (slow, steady growth in the money supply), and supply-side (cut taxes) doctrines.[6] But the centerpiece of the plan was a three-year tax cut, originally advocated by Congress-

---

6. For a more detailed assessment of the Reagan economic program, see Sawhill (1982).

man Jack Kemp. It was based on the supply-side notion that a reduction in tax rates stimulates work, saving, and investment, which in turn increases jobs and productivity, lowers inflation, and leads to a balanced budget. Although the 1981 tax cut was often compared to the 1964 tax cut, their rationales were entirely different: the earlier tax cut was intended to increase spending (demand); the more recent one, to increase production (supply). The long-term cycle from Keynes to Kemp was complete.

THE REAGAN ERA

How should one interpret this shift toward emphasizing government's negative rather than positive contribution together with its corollary, a focus on unleashing supply rather than managing demand? Such a shift would seem to constitute not just the rejection of an unpopular president in 1980 (a turn in the short-term cycle) and a predictable reaction against the inflation associated with previous policies (a turn in the intermediate-term cycle), but a veritable revolution in economic thinking analogous to the Keynesian revolution.

However, it is possible to reject this interpretation on a number of grounds. First, it can be argued that, unlike the Keynesian revolution, this one is based on intellectual quicksand and will have no staying power. Second, a reasonable case can be made that, rhetoric aside, the actual policies pursued under the Reagan administration have been an extension of rather than a sharp departure from earlier policies. Third, as history has shown, successful revolutions require validating events. (The Keynesian revolution was validated by World War II and the success of the 1964 tax cut.) The issue here is *results*. Should they be less than satisfactory they could produce a political backlash, thereby snuffing out the revolution before it has had a chance to imbed itself in the fabric of our history and institutions. I take up each of these issues—the intellectual basis of the revolution, its policy dimensions, and its results—before returning to the larger question of its overall significance.

Ideas and Ideology

Students of economics in the 1950s and 1960s were routinely exposed to what economist Paul Samuelson, in his introductory textbook, called "the neoclassical synthesis"—a kind of marriage between the ideas of Adam Smith and those of John Maynard Keynes. Keynes's contribution was to argue that nothing in a free enterprise system guarantees a level of total spending for the economy as a whole that is both high enough to employ all resources yet not so high as to cause inflation. But once appropriate fiscal and monetary policies have been adopted to ensure full employment of resources without inflation, it is argued, Adam Smith's "invisible hand" (the price system) can once more fulfill its role as an efficient allocator of resources. Thus, the neoclassical synthesis holds that the virtues of a free enterprise system can be preserved by correcting its most serious flaw—a tendency to produce too much instability.

Central to the Keynesian thesis of a macroeconomy that is not self-correcting, and the consequent need for government to manage demand, was the assumption of "sticky"—that is, inflexible—wages and prices.[7] Before Keynes, the classical economists had held that there could never be any lasting excess unemployment because unemployed workers would bid wages down until supply and demand were once again in balance. Keynes observed that such adjustments hardly ever occurred in the real world for a variety of institutional reasons. But his observation was inconsistent with microeconomic theory, according to which markets—including the market for labor—are always assumed to clear, because any excess supply (demand) creates the potential for mutually beneficial transactions between buyers and sellers.

This debate is far from arcane. It is at the core of the controversy within the economics profession today.[8] The modern Keynesian school asserts that wages and prices are not very flexible in the real world for a whole host of reasons. It takes a very long time for markets to clear. Thus, the only way to relieve the human suffering and reduce the economic costs associated with high unemployment is for the government to manage demand. The modern classical school contends that wages and prices are, by and large, flexible. And where they are somewhat inflexible, it is because too many safety nets exist—including a guarantee of perpetual full employment. This guarantee removes the incentive for workers to reduce their wage demands, or businesses their prices, in times of economic slack. If the safety nets can be scaled back and the temptation for government to intervene can be resisted when the economy moves into a recession, any inflexibility will be eliminated and full employment will be restored. Thus, the policy prescriptions flowing from these two different views are diametrically different.

The modern classical school appeals to intuitive beliefs about human behavior in small-scale settings. If a child spends all of his weekly allowance on Monday, he soon learns that this means no movies on Friday. Similarly, removing government's commitment to full employment can change the be-

---

7. It should be noted that there remains some disagreement about the centrality of this assumption to Keynes's thesis in *The General Theory*. See Salant (1985).

8. See, for example, Bator (1982), Bosworth (1984) chapter 1, Nordhaus (1983) and his discussants, Stanley Fischer, Larry A. Sjaastad, and Robert M. Solow.

havior of managers, workers, unions, and other economic actors. In particular, it is argued that constant interventions designed to maintain full employment have produced inflationary behavior. A refusal to intervene would force individuals and firms to pay the price (in higher unemployment or lost markets) of a decision to set wages and prices too high. Faced with such consequences, they would soon learn to behave in less inflationary ways. According to an extreme version of this school of thought, called rational expectations, all that is needed is for the government to announce in a convincing manner that henceforth there will be no bailouts. Less extreme versions of the theory emphasize that the government's noninterventionist stance must be made credible by deeds as well as words.

Modern Keynesians have responded to the modern classical view in part by indicting the harshness of its policy implications. As Arthur Okun put it, should we promote fire prevention by requiring that the fire department refuse to respond to fires (Okun 1981, 358; also cited in Tobin 1983, 298). The Keynesians have also appealed to empirical evidence to demonstrate that the world is replete with institutional rigidities that can only be changed very gradually, if ever; they have rebuilt the microeconomic logic of their own case, stressing that employers may have good reasons for not adjusting wages and prices every time market conditions change.[9] Indeed, such adjustments could lead to inefficiency by, for example, undermining the morale and thus the productivity of workers.

It is unlikely that this debate will be resolved any time soon. Both views have a respectable following within the economics profession. The logic of the new classical view has by and large captured the loyalty of younger members of the profession and is thus likely to become increasingly influential as they move into positions of leadership. The policy implications of this view are profound: there is no role for government in managing the macroeconomy. It is, in effect, a return to the belief prevailing before the New Deal that business cycles are self-correcting—the extreme position being that, without government interference, the corrections will occur quickly and almost painlessly.

The economic program adopted in Reagan's first term was by no means a pure test of these new classical views (no policy ever is). Still, it was a test of sorts. What did the experiment show? Did inflationary expectations and behavior abate once the government moved away from its commitment to preserve full employment?

Inflation dropped from 12 percent in 1980 to about 4 percent in 1984, considerably faster than most people (including those in the administration

---

9. For a review of the literature, see Schultze (1985).

itself) had anticipated. There were wage concessions and a renewed focus on cutting costs and improving productivity in the business sector, but it took a sharp increase in unemployment to accomplish this. Indeed, Keynesian models were capable of fully predicting the decline in inflation (see, for example, Perry 1983). Not only was unemployment very high through this period, but energy, food, and import prices were all moving in the right direction. One would pretty much have to give round one to the Keynesians. Suppose, however, that continuing economic discipline of this sort were to begin to alter our economic institutions in a more flexible direction? How alterable are they in response to a changed policy environment? How long would it take? No one knows. It is quite possible that by the end of round ten, the new classical school would have gained some points.

Whereas the new classical economists emphasize the impact of macro-economic regimes (monetary and fiscal rules) on people's behavior, supply-side economists stress the effects of microeconomic policies (taxes and trans-fers) on their behavior. Although almost all economists subscribe to the notion that incentives matter and that taxes and transfers affect work, saving, and investment, the empirical evidence suggests that any such effects are relatively small, and nothing in the experience of the past few years disproves this thesis (Danziger, Haveman, and Plotnick 1981; Aaron and Pechman 1981; Haveman 1984; Stone and Sawhill 1984; and Bosworth 1984). Yet it is the supply-siders that are largely responsible for the 1981 tax cut, which brought a seemingly unending stream of budget deficits, which in turn helped to produce high interest rates and a high dollar. By extending this thigh-bone-connected-to-the-knee-bone logic, one comes to the conclusion that, contrary to its intentions, supply-side economics is the worst thing that ever happened to the supply-side of the economy—that is, to the nation's ability to compete in world markets and to its prospects for long-term growth.

Why, then, was the supply-side program adopted? The answer seems to be because it was a simple, self-confident, and politically salable approach.

It was simple precisely because it was not burdened by an elaborate theory or the self-doubts of professional economists. Moreover, it stepped into the vacuum left by mainstream controversies and policy failures. During an era in which the reputation of economists was little better than that of alchemists, almost anyone could claim to be an expert, and many did.

Salability was even more important, especially for a party that had been out of power and wanted back in. What could be more salable than a deep cut in taxes and the promise of boundless growth? Indeed, George Bush and Walter Mondale made the same mistake in 1980 and 1984, respectively; they both asked for belt-tightening when Ronald Reagan was preaching the "eco-nomics of joy" (Stein 1984, 232). Moreover, under the cover of an initially rosy supply-side forecast, the Reagan administration (with the critical co-operation of the Federal Reserve) presided over a deep recession and subsequent recovery, the political timing of which could not have been better, ensuring a second Reagan term and a longer period in which to institutionalize the Reagan revolution.

But just what is it, if anything, that has been institutionalized and that is likely to endure? As noted above, the evidence suggests that neither the new classical macroeconomics nor supply-side economics passed muster when put to the empirical test during the first Reagan term. It would be easy to look at their records in practice and to pronounce the intellectual fabric of the Reagan revolution as real as the emperor's new clothes, but I think this would miss their broader significance. Put simply, in large enough doses and over a sufficient time period, common sense tells people that government policies have profound effects on behavior. This is the message, for example, of the Laffer curve showing that at 100 percent tax rates no effort, and thus no revenue, is forthcoming. It is also the message conveyed by such statements as "if you pay people to be poor you will get more poor people." Whatever the empirical evidence may be on these tax and transfer issues, the popular mind tends to dwell on the essential logic of the proposition, unaware or skeptical of countless scholarly papers pointing out that the relevant behavioral responses are small.

Similarly, it seems self-evident that people and institutions would eventually adapt to a firm macroeconomic policy of "doing nothing" in response to high rates of unemployment. It stands to reason that a hungry man will lower the price of his services rather than go without food. Once more the essential logic of the proposition is impeccable and potentially more influential than concerns about how long it would take for such adjustments to occur, how complete they would be in practice, what damage would be done in the interim, and the extent to which a democracy could stay the unpleasant course.

In each of the above cases—whether one is talking about the behavioral effects of macroeconomic policy regimes, of antipoverty policy, or of taxes—the argument is that under an interventionist regime people shift responsibility to the government and do less than they might to cope with their own problems. Thus, government action is self-defeating because it gives rise to countervailing private actions. We cannot improve on the market. Indeed, in the process of trying, it is argued, we may simply make matters worse. Thus, as Ronald Reagan expressed it in his first inaugural address, "government is not the solution to our problem. Government is the problem."

Underlying this general statement is a respectable body of intellectual thought. Human behavior *can* be powerfully influenced by the rules of the game set by government. Although the empirical evidence suggests that any such influence is far smaller than the public has been led to believe, the idea itself, right or wrong, has captured the public's attention and has become the driving force behind the conservative agenda. It is an idea that has become an ideology, but one that conservative intellectuals have made respectable, just as liberal academicians earlier made the New Deal philosophy acceptable.

While I believe that increased intellectual respectability is one reason that conservative ideology has become more influential in recent years, there are undoubtedly other reasons for its popularity, including the success of earlier policies in creating a more middle-class society, a reaction to the excesses of liberalism (especially the perceived failures of liberal economic policy in the 1970s), and the public's desire to reaffirm the traditional values of hard work and family responsibility.

The debate will continue, not just about the reasons for change but also about the extent to which anything fundamental has occurred. Hugh Heclo reviews some of the evidence from public opinion polls elsewhere in this volume and concludes that the electorate has not become more conservative in recent years. He views the Reagan era as a period of consolidation, a time when the public reaffirmed its support for a broad array of governmental responsibilities. Other scholars read the same tea leaves quite differently. John Chubb and Paul Peterson, for example, conclude: "A new direction has already been taken in American government that is comparable in basic respects to realignments of the past. The terms of political debate and the course of public policy have been fundamentally transformed. The forces of institutionalization that had to be overcome in the course of bringing these innovations about not only indicate the political strength underlying them but ensure that they, like the policy transformations of past realignments, will be sustained for a long time to come" (Chubb and Peterson 1985, 30).

My own interpretation is somewhat closer to this latter view. I do not deny the importance of future economic events in determining short-term electoral outcomes. A recession could easily bring the Democrats back in power. Moreover, many of the Reagan administration's specific policies are likely to be rejected in the coming decade. The electorate is not now convinced that these policies are the right ones, and the public's disenchantment will grow should those policies produce unsatisfactory results. However, for all the reasons cited above, the forces that sustained the long swing toward greater governmental activism in economic and social affairs appear to have been dissipated. The public remains quite conservative in its basic values and has become more skeptical about government's ability to solve a variety of economic and social problems.[10]

---

10. Yankelovich et al. argue that values are now more salient than issues in political life. They and others have pointed out that the electorate is more liberal than Ronald Reagan on the issues but that they like the values he articulates.

Policy Evolution or Revolution?

Whatever the outcome of the intellectual and ideological debate, the Reagan administration has been credited with having conducted economic policy differently. In part, this comes from a sense that the policy dials have been reset on fight inflation and encourage long-term growth instead of on reduce unemployment and redistribute income, and in part from a sense that the instruments of policy are different. But just what is new here?

Goals. Few question that the weighting of different policy objectives has shifted. Moreover, the shift was probably sharper than what one would normally experience with a changeover to a Republican administration. But this shift was far greater in the case of social objectives than it was in the case of purely economic objectives such as inflation, unemployment, and growth.

The preeminent goal was to shrink the size of government and curb its tendency to appropriate in taxes income that, according to conservatives, rightfully belongs to individuals.[11] The economic program—including the 1981 tax and budget cuts and the scaling back of social regulations—was in budget director Stockman's words "a Trojan horse" for accomplishing these philosophical objectives (Greider 1981). If actions speak louder than words, the plausibility of this Trojan Horse interpretation increases. Many legitimate functions of government that contribute to better economic performance (for example, spending on education, training, and research) have been curtailed, and the unwillingness to raise taxes in the face of unprecedented peacetime deficits poses an almost certain threat to long-term growth.[12]

By contrast, no revolutionary change took place in macroeconomic objectives. With respect to fighting inflation, some shift had already begun to occur during the Carter administration. By mid-1979, Carter considered inflation the most serious problem facing the nation economically—and himself politically—and was prepared, as a result, to let the unemployment rate rise during the rest of 1979 and 1980 (Silk 1984, 158). The appointment of Paul Volcker to the Federal Reserve in mid-1979 reflected this shift in Carter's priorities. Economic growth was also a concern before 1981. Toward the end of his term, President Carter proposed an expansion of the investment tax credit and more liberal depreciation rules to increase the share of the nation's output devoted to business investment. Overall, however, the Carter program

---

11. Questions of fairness were given little weight. As the 1982 *Economic Report of the President* put it: "Income redistribution is not a compelling justification in the 1980s for federal taxing and spending programs" (*Economic Report of the President* 1982, 92).

12. For evidence on these points see Nichols (1984) and Stone and Sawhill (1984).

sought a balancing of various economic objectives with the result that the sense of strong priorities and an overall strategy for achieving those priorities just was not there.[13]

In sum, the Reagan administration's macroeconomic objectives have not differed sharply from those that had evolved under its predecessors, although under President Reagan some reweighting of these objectives has been accomplished and a clearer sense of priorities developed. Far more significant was the shift in social philosophy and the rationalization of this shift in terms of widely accepted economic goals.

Means. The most notable changes in the means used to achieve these objectives were (1) sole reliance on monetary policy to hold the line against inflation, (2) great faith in fiscal policy (lower taxes) as the way to put the economy on a higher growth path, and (3) a general rejection of other more microeconomic measures such as wage and price controls or industrial policies as possible supplements to macroeconomic policy.

Monetary policy, as previously noted, had already begun to shift toward a more anti-inflationary course in 1979. It remained unusually restrictive until the middle of 1982, at which point the Federal Reserve reversed course in the face of double-digit unemployment, a looming international debt crisis, and a much sharper drop in total spending, and thus a much deeper recession, than anyone had anticipated. Although the administration has certainly had some influence in keeping the Federal Reserve on the anti-inflationary course it began in 1979, nothing in the conduct of recent monetary policy is particularly new or surprising. Paul Volcker is a pragmatist and not a monetarist.

Like monetary policy, the administration's regulatory program was to some extent an extension of what had been begun under the Carter (or Ford) administration, with the important difference that the emphasis was on paring back social regulations affecting health, safety, the environment, and opportunities for the disadvantaged, rather than on eliminating economic regulations governing prices and conditions of entry in such industries as airlines, trucking, railroads, and banking.[14]

Fiscal policy was another matter. Not only were the 1981 tax cut and the deficits that ensued large by historical standards, but the whole operation was justified, as already indicated, on unorthodox supply-side grounds. Quite

---

13. Vacillations were evident in the changing scope of the 1977 stimulus package (a $50 tax rebate was proposed and then dropped), appointments to the Federal Reserve (Miller followed by Volcker), wage-price policies (changing guidelines and uncertain commitment), and the 1980 budget (which had to be submitted twice). For an excellent review of this period, see Silk (1984).

14. For a full discussion of the administration's regulatory program, and particularly its evolutionary character, see Eads and Fix (1984).

apart from the rationale, even the most ardent Keynesian had never suggested that deficits be allowed to grow by this order of magnitude. In sheer size, this shift in policy was unprecedented.

Given its free enterprise orientation, the Reagan administration could have been expected to avoid microeconomic interventions and generally has. However, significant slippage has occurred from time to time in trade policy (for instance, automobiles, steel). The depreciation schedules and other business tax provisions built into the 1981 tax bill constituted an implicit industrial policy that, at this writing, is still being debated in the context of a 1986 tax reform package. Regulatory relief for business could be similarly characterized as a back-door industrial policy.

The net effect of the administration's economic program was that the monetary brakes were on at the same time that the fiscal throttle was wide open. This was just the opposite of what many economists concerned about growth had been advocating. Whatever the theoretical merits or demerits of this particular policy mix, it created an opportunity to observe the actual effects of a novel policy experiment. What did the experiment produce and what lessons have been learned from it?

Results of the Reagan Experiment

With monetary and fiscal policy often pointed in opposite directions after 1979, the first question was, what would the economy do? If monetary restraint prevailed, the economy could be expected to go into a sharp recession. But if the shift in fiscal policy had equally large effects on the level of output, it might not. The experience of the last half decade suggests that monetary policy has powerful effects. The two back-to-back recessions of 1980 and 1981–82 and the subsequent recovery beginning in 1983 are easier to link to shifts in monetary than to shifts in fiscal policy. This does not mean that fiscal policy has no effects—only that its effects may be more on the composition than on the level of spending and output.[15]

The major argument against the Reagan administration's policy mix was its expected negative effects on economic growth. With the government borrowing so much money and absorbing so much of the nation's savings, interest rates were expected to rise, thereby choking off investment and long-term

---

15. Because no satisfactory way has been found to calibrate and compare the amount of monetary or fiscal stimulus being applied and because in some years (for instance, 1981), they were both pointed in the same direction, this observation must remain somewhat impressionistic. I make it as an antidote to what I perceive as a preoccupation with fiscal policy in popular discussions of economic policy. For further discussion, see Stone and Sawhill (1984) and McCallum (1985).

growth. So far, any such impact has been modest. Although inflation-adjusted interest rates remained high during the first half of the decade, investment spending by businesses proceeded at a reasonable pace. One possible reason for investment's strength was the encouragement provided by the business tax incentives introduced in 1981, but probably a more important reason was the surprisingly large inflow of foreign capital without which interest rates would have been far higher.[16] The United States has, in short, borrowed from the rest of the world to maintain domestic investment, and this infusion of funds has thus far protected the U.S. economy from the bleak consequences that might otherwise have occurred.

The inflow of foreign capital has done more than maintain investment; it has meant continuing good news on the inflation front. Foreigners who want to invest in U.S. assets to take advantage of the relatively high interest rates here must first buy dollars, and this demand for dollars strengthens the value of U.S. currency relative to other currencies and cheapens the price of imports to U.S. consumers.

Most economists think it is only a matter of time before the large inflow of foreign capital abates, interest rates rise, and inflation returns. But there is a clear lesson for future administrations. The current monetary-fiscal policy mix is a good way to reduce inflation quickly and to maintain a noninflationary recovery. Whatever its long-run consequences, much of the Reagan administration's short-run success must be attributed to this policy mix. Indeed, it is ironic that an administration that rejected short-run stabilization goals in favor of promoting long-run growth should have succeeded so handsomely in the former at the probable expense of the latter.

Another interesting and ironic facet of this experience is its negative impact on the country's sense of its position vis-à-vis the rest of the world. Most experts agree that the overvalued dollar accounts for most of the deterioration in the U.S. trade balance since 1980 and that the appreciation of the dollar, in turn, is related to U.S. deficits (see Congressional Budget Office February 1985, chap. 3, and August 1985, chap. 1; and Stone and Sawhill 1985). The upshot is that the United States can no longer compete in world markets. So whatever the defense buildup has done to restore America's stature in the world, the nation is not standing tall among its trading partners. The United States may be winning the arms race but losing the economic marathon.

---

16. The evidence on the impact of the business tax incentives is mixed. See Bosworth (1985), Blinder (1984), and Boskin (1985).

In addition to their effects on international competitiveness, the Reagan administration's macroeconomic policies has had one other significant unintended consequence: their influence on the distribution of income. The Reagan administration has argued that the growth of social welfare spending has a negative impact on economic growth. As already noted, at some level of abstraction, this is a correct proposition, although little evidence exists that the disincentives associated with the current level of taxes and transfers in the United States are having substantial economic effects.

Although redistributional policies are not having a major impact on macroeconomic performance, macroeconomic policies are having major consequences for the distribution of income. Of all the variables that have influenced the incidence of poverty and the degree of income inequality among the working-age population, the overall condition of the economy has tended to be the dominant one historically, and analysis of the experience of the early 1980s has confirmed the strength of this relationship (Ellwood and Summers 1986; Blank and Blinder 1986; Moon and Sawhill 1984; Bendick 1982; Gottschalk and Danziger 1984). High unemployment, in short, was a prescription for growing disparities between rich and poor, old and young, white and black. As long as maintaining high unemployment is the principal means of controlling inflation, such disparities are likely to grow.

The Reagan administration's push for more economic growth as the single best solution to the problem of poverty is the right policy;[17] it has simply not produced much economic growth. But this was predictable, given Reagan's commitment (and Carter's before him) to reducing inflation. It was that commitment, even more than the 1981 tax cut or the scaling back of income transfers, that has produced greater inequality since the late 1970s. Thus, the real trade-off is not so much between equity and growth as it is between equity and price stability. The failure to understand this has sometimes left liberals tilting at the wrong windmills. Fairness requires, first and foremost, different macroeconomic policies, not simply more spending on the poor.

Distributional and other unintended consequences aside, has Reaganomics been a success? In particular, are most people better off because of it? This is not the place to attempt a complete evaluation of the results of the Reagan experiment with economic policy, since such an assessment has been the focus of other research.[18] Moreover, the experiment is not over and the results are not all in. Nevertheless, I am willing to speculate that the results

---

17. More precisely, the evidence suggests that it is high employment rather than rapid growth that helps the poor disproportionately.

18. See, for example, Sawhill and Stone (1984); and Moon and Sawhill (1984).

will be disappointing—largely because of the deep recession at the start of
the decade and the effects of the deficits on international competitiveness and
growth toward the end of the decade. Inflation has been tamed, but there is
little reason to believe it has been permanently exorcised. As I have shown
elsewhere, on almost every key indicator—unemployment, economic growth,
and increases in family incomes adjusted for taxes and inflation—the 1980s
are likely to be no better than the 1970s (Sawhill and Stone 1984, 93–94).
If I am correct, and the political business cycle has longer as well as shorter
swings, a negative response to current policies and those who espouse them
can be expected—sooner or later.

THE REAGAN ERA INTERPRETED

Recent economic history is replete with examples in which results have
fallen short of initial promises. The variables that can intervene between what
is promised and what is produced include politics, ideology, and lack of
knowledge, but politics appears to be the primary culprit.

President Reagan did not intend to create a sea of red ink; in fact, he
promised to balance the budget before the end of his first term. But to
accomplish this objective in the face of a deep tax cut and rapid military
buildup, one of two things needed to happen. Either a supply-side miracle
had to occur or nondefense expenditures had to be cut more than in half. The
first was wishful thinking and the second was impossible, given the high
proportion of social welfare expenditures benefiting the middle class.

But this is an old story in the history of economic policymaking. To
gain support, presidents both exaggerate what their policies can actually produce and bow to political pressures in choosing their strategies. Thus, the
first intervening variable between intentions and results is politics.

Lyndon Johnson promised to end poverty and tame the business cycle.
Instead his refusal to raise the taxes needed to pay for both the Vietnam War
and the War on Poverty set off the inflation that plagued the economy for
the next decade, and that, in turn, discredited Keynesian-style liberal economics. Similarly, Ronald Reagan's failure to successfully tackle middle-
class entitlements, including Social Security, contributed in part to deficits
that have already begun to discredit supply-side economics.

Politics is even more evident in the choice of microeconomic policies.
Although conservative administrations often argue in favor of free enterprise,
in practice their tax, trade, and regulatory policies often remain responsive
to the business interests and upper-income groups they represent just as liberal
administrations tend to favor organized labor, farmers, and other (less powerful) constituencies. The conservatives invoke economic efficiency and the

liberals fairness as justification for their actions—even when there is little evidence that such objectives are being well served in practice. For example, almost all economists agree that across-the-board reductions in personal tax rates, individual retirement accounts (IRAs), and vastly different effective tax rates on different types of business income are not the best way to improve economic performance, and that such measures as increasing the minimum wage and extending student financial assistance to middle-class families are not well-designed to achieve "fairness." Yet the former actions were all taken during Reagan's first term and the latter under President Carter. Thus, as Mancur Olson argues, it may be only the form of assistance and the specific beneficiaries that change from one administration to the next. Moreover, economic policy in the service of special interests tends to reduce efficiency and slow economic growth (Olson 1984). It is not the size of government that matters as much as its susceptibility to lobbies attempting to promote their own interests.

If it is special interests that undermine the efficiency of the economy and reduce the general welfare, then one way to improve matters is to keep the policy tool box as lean and simple as possible. In fact, it is fear of their susceptibility to political manipulation that has led many economists to be wary of microeconomic interventions, such as industrial policies, trade policies, incomes policies, and a tax code designed to achieve a variety of social and economic objectives beyond simple revenue-raising.

A second intervening variable that may lead to disappointing results relative to initial promises is ideology. (Although politics and ideology often overlap, the distinction is that politics is what an administration puts off limits because of its perceptions about what the electorate will support, and ideology is what it considers non-negotiable because of its own philosophical predilections.) Most administrations have ideological agendas that contaminate their economic policies. Ideology aside, the economy would have been better off if Johnson had scaled back the Great Society to pay for the Vietnam War and if Reagan had raised taxes to reduce deficits. Moreover, both discovered that the economic consequences flowing from these decisions served ideological purposes. The inflation produced by Johnson's policies created a fiscal dividend that was used to fund an expansion of social programs in the late 1960s. And the Reagan deficits are being used to squeeze down social welfare expenditures in the mid-1980s. Thus, what may appear as "mistakes" in economic policy are sometimes allowed to occur or persist because they further ideological objectives.

The third intervening variable between promises and results is lack of knowledge about how the economy works. But for all the talk about disarray among economists, it may not be their advice that has been wrong as much as it is what politicians have done with it in practice. Most economists have never maintained that policy is the only variable impinging on the economy's performance or that easy remedies exist for inflation or other economic problems. Politicians have either distorted the message received from their economic advisers or chosen to listen only to the minority promising quick and painless results.

In sum, of all the variables that can intervene between what is promised and what is produced, politics is probably the primary culprit. Politics, along with occasional streaks of bad luck, lead to disappointing results, and these results in turn give rise to a new political cycle. At some points in history they can even destroy revolutions and set the stage for counterrevolutions as seems to have happened in the late 1970s.

Put somewhat differently, economics cannot deliver what politics requires. Although, as I argue below, there is a critical need for better economic mousetraps, there is also a need for public understanding of the limits of existing policies. The person in the best position to educate the public is the president of the United States. In this sense, what President Reagan has said—and not said—to the American public about the complexity of the issues and the hard choices that must be made may be as important as the policies he has pursued.

If politics is a critical actor in this story, its supporting characters have been events and ideas. In the category of events, the turning points were the 1930s depression and the 1970s stagflation. These events (the result of both past policy errors and random shocks to the system) gave rise to new ideas and new policies. In the category of ideas, liberal Keynesian thinking replaced an earlier laissez-faire ideology and is now being challenged by more conservative economic doctrines. These new ideas were made possible by historical events, but it is the ideas rather than the events that are likely to sustain what might otherwise be ephemeral redirections of policy.

My view is that the nation is near the peak of a short-term cycle that contributed to Reagan's reelection, is heading into the declining phase of a medium-term cycle that will see the rejection of supply-side economics and the conservatism of the New Right, and is at the beginning of an upswing in a long-term cycle that will tilt elections in favor of Republicans and make any Democratic administration that is elected more conservative in its orientation.

Of course, any number of unforeseen events could alter this scenario. Thus, a much safer prediction is that the political-economic cycle will continue to operate in some form. Short swings will occur because the public has little understanding of the nature of the relation between economic policy and economic conditions and thus tends to give short-term credit or blame where none is due. Intermediate term swings will occur because no set of economic policies has yet been devised that simultaneously guarantees price stability, full employment, and steady growth, a situation that inevitably leads to disappointed public expectations and a search for new solutions. Long swings will occur because any society must continually struggle toward a more mature set of collective judgments about the appropriate balance of personal versus social responsibility for various problems.

BEYOND REAGANOMICS: THE PROBLEMS THAT REMAIN

Anyone reading the daily newspapers circa early 1986 might be left with the following impressions: inflation is well under control; unemployment is a bit high but most of it is structural in nature; productivity growth has revived and the economy is back on a stronger growth path than during the 1970s; deficits are *the* major problem and could produce an economic crisis at any time; but when and if budget deficits, and associated trade deficits, are brought under control, prosperity will be more or less assured.

A more accurate view, in my opinion, might be summarized as follows. Inflation has not been eliminated, only suppressed, and is likely to accelerate again if unemployment should drop substantially and the dollar depreciate.[19] The nation still has some cyclical (not just structural) unemployment and considerable idle plant that is being used to keep inflation under control, and this excess capacity is a major drag on economic growth (Sawhill 1985). The trend rate of productivity growth (adjusted for the effects of the business cycle) is no higher now than it was in the 1970s. If this dismal performance continues, standards of living will creep upward during the next decade at rates well below historical experience and well below those of other countries (Gordon 1984; Clark 1984). Although these problems are exacerbated by the huge accumulation of federal debt and swollen trade deficits in recent years, they will not disappear if the budget and trade deficits are eliminated; they are endemic.

In short, the problems of inflation, unemployment, and a disappointing rate of productivity growth remain. The flirtation with supply-side economics, concern about the resulting deficits, and an unusually fierce ideological debate

---

19. Thurow (1985, 40), for example, estimates that the direct effects on import prices of a 30 percent fall in the value of the dollar (the amount needed to eliminate the trade deficit) would be to increase the inflation rate by 3 or 4 percentage points. Adding in the indirect effects on other domestic prices could mean a return to double-digit inflation. Some of this increase in inflation, however, might be temporary.

have simply diverted people's attention from these more fundamental problems. The nation is no nearer to solutions now than it was before the Reagan administration took office.

Liberals offer a remedy for high unemployment and slow growth (use fiscal and monetary policy to expand the economy) but they do not have a satisfactory way to control inflation. Fine tuning (moving the economy to the inflation trigger point but no further) has been tried and has few remaining defenders. Wage and price controls have also been tried and found wanting (Sawhill 1981). It can be argued that the failures were not inherent in the policies themselves but were related to the way they were applied in practice (politics as the intervening variable again). However, at a minimum, these experiences are likely to discourage new experiments with traditional liberal policies.

Conservatives have a solution to inflation (use fiscal and, especially, monetary policy to maintain sufficient economic slack so that any resurgence of inflation can be prevented), but it is not clear that they know what to do should the resulting rates of unemployment and economic growth be unacceptable. The view that there need be no long-run trade-off between inflation and unemployment has gained respectability in the academic community, permitting conservatives to argue that policymakers can focus solely on containing inflation and can allow the unemployment rate to seek its "natural" level set by various imperfections in the labor market. But if, in a world of market imperfections and price shocks caused by fluctuations in both supplies of basic commodities and the value of the currency, it turns out that preventing inflation requires continuing high unemployment, this is not a very happy prescription. Moreover, if rates of unemployment and capacity utilization affect decisions to work and to make investments in both human and tangible capital and influence the willingness to reallocate resources to more productive uses, it is also a prescription for slow growth. The record of the past few years should make clear that supply-side incentives do not work in a slack economy. Thus, by restraining demand one can end up winning the battle against inflation but losing the far more important war to improve standards of living. What is often called the inflation-unemployment dilemma is also an inflation-growth dilemma.[20]

---

20. According to a review of the available evidence conducted by the U.S. Bureau of Labor Statistics, economic slack was the single most important factor responsible for the slowdown in labor productivity after 1973. Less well-known, but well-documented by Michael Bruno and Jeffrey Sachs, is the pronounced slowdown in productivity growth that occurred during the Great Depression in virtually all industrialized countries. They also argue that the more rapid productivity growth in the middle-income, developing countries relative to the OECD countries after 1973 was due to the more expansionary policies pursued by the former countries (see U.S. Department of Labor 1983, 25–31; and Bruno and Sachs 1985).

The fact is that price stability and full employment cannot be fully reconciled by drawing from our current arsenal of macroeconomic weapons (except perhaps during periods when commodity prices are falling and the dollar is appreciating). Given this dilemma, liberals are forced to practice benign neglect of inflation and conservatives, benign neglect of unemployment. Where one stands in this debate hinges largely on which economic malady is perceived to be the greater evil. Although economists have never been able to establish any strong linkage between the moderate rates of inflation found in industrialized countries and real economic performance (that is, improvements in standards of living), the fact remains that people do not like living with the uncertainty of inflation, and any government that tolerates it will appear to be ineffectual.

With respect to unemployment, conservatives argue that most of it is voluntary. The problem comes in defining the word "voluntary." If by voluntary we mean that people could find work *on some terms* (for instance, work well below their customary wage, in a different location, or in a new line of work), then it is probably true that much unemployment is voluntary. So the debate about the seriousness of unemployment, from a social welfare perspective, revolves around beliefs about what kinds of compromises workers should be expected to make in their search for work. Conservatives argue that workers do not make many compromises because in today's world they have other options (such as unemployment insurance). Liberals contend that the human costs of unemployment have been neglected. What both liberals and conservatives have failed to emphasize is the purely economic costs of unemployment—the loss of output and slower growth associated with unutilized resources.

The dilemma remains: how can the nation eliminate the sheer economic waste of unemployed labor and capital and the drag that they exert on economic growth, while simultaneously keeping the rate of inflation under control? The solution, if there is one, will probably not come soon. The possibilities of improving public understanding of the costs of inflation and unemployment and of making the economy more inflation-resistant exist, but such a goal will not be easy to achieve and will require the kind of national leadership and debate that has been sorely lacking in recent years.

As if the dilemma of inflation versus unemployment and growth were not serious enough, the nation now faces a new threat to its long-run sense of well-being: increased economic competition from other countries that is likely to reduce relative if not absolute standards of living for Americans. It would be a mistake to attribute current trade deficits to this factor alone; they stem primarily from an overvalued dollar, which can be, and is being, corrected. Even after such a correction has taken place, however, the question remains whether the United States can still compete in world markets over the longer run without accepting a decline in relative wage levels and standards of living. Wages in other parts of the world have always been low by American standards, but they were matched historically by equally low productivity. What is new is that many other countries—both developed and developing— now have access to much the same technology and capital as the United States. As a result they have experienced a faster rate of productivity growth than the United States during the past dozen years, enabling them to sell goods that are increasingly cheaper or better than those of the United States. The issue is not whether the U.S. economy is competitive under these circumstances; it will be if relative wages adjust (that is, U.S. wages rise more slowly than wages in other countries) or, as seems more likely, if the value of the dollar gradually declines. But a decline in the value of U.S. currency will mean an increase in what Americans have to pay for imports, along with a decline in what is paid for U.S. exports, and will adversely affect relative standards of living in this country just as much as an adjustment in relative wage levels. Thus, if the United States wants to maintain its relative economic position, it will have to restore the productivity growth rates that were enjoyed during the 1950s and 1960s.

Again, there are no easy answers, no correct or agreed upon policy responses, only a problem crying out for national leadership and debate. Americans could decide that more expansionary macroeconomic policies are an important part of the solution and focus on innovative means of constraining any resulting inflation. They could decide that Reagan-style supply-side measures such as keeping marginal tax rates low are a useful contribution, even though the payoff so far has been small. They could go further and adopt the Democratic version of supply-side economics—some form of an "industrial policy." Or they could decide they no longer want to be "number one" in the world, which would make economic growth of less concern. However, as long as Americans aspire to remain an economic as well as a military power and to face a future that is materially far better than the past, this latter choice is unlikely.

It has become fashionable in these conservative times to preach the virtues of laissez-faire. But there is no such thing as laissez-faire where macroeconomic policy is concerned—for at least two reasons. First, even strict libertarians see some positive role for government—to maintain law and order, define property rights and other rules of the economic game, and provide for the common defense (Friedman 1962). Nevertheless, because some of these activities—defense, in particular—are quite costly, a major industrialized power like the United States is bound to have a sizable public budget and thus a fiscal policy. Second, the Constitution establishes the power of Congress "to coin money" and "regulate the value thereof," and no modern economy could function without some government regulation of the money supply—that is, a monetary policy. Thus, the issue is not whether government will have a role in the macroeconomy but what that role will be. The federal government has, at all times, a fiscal (budget) and monetary policy, if only by default. It can try to consciously manage these instruments in ways that respond to economic circumstances, or it can abdicate such responsibility by adopting rules for balancing the budget or managing the money supply. However, it cannot thereby avoid influencing the economy.

Government may or may not be able to solve the problems of inflation, unemployment, and growth in an increasingly competitive world economy, but one could hope that it would at least not make matters worse in the process of trying to make them better. Yet this is the true legacy of the Reagan years. The United States has experienced periods of economic mismanagement in the past, but few, if any, of these instances can rival the current government's tolerance of budget deficits that virtually guarantee poorer productivity performance in the future and a further erosion of America's relative standard of living. The nation's first priority should be to correct this mistake. Even after this is done, however, the problems that remain must still be addressed with a full understanding that there are no Keynesian or supply-side panaceas.

CONCLUSIONS

Although only history can render a final verdict, it seems likely that the Reagan era will be remembered as a turning point in a long swing from liberal to conservative ideas and policies. It has been a period during which some of the excesses of liberalism have been checked, and during which a useful debate has taken place about how—and especially how much—government policies influence private behavior.

While one should not ignore such influences in setting either macroeconomic or microeconomic policy, New Right conservatives have greatly exaggerated their magnitude. As the nation gains more experience with supply-side policies, the results are likely to prove disappointing, paving the way for the emergence of a new and more moderate consensus.

The next generation of economic policies (ushered in during the medium-term swing) should benefit from the lessons of the Reagan years. As I see it, these lessons are that supply-side economics does not work; there is no painless cure for inflation; monetary policy is a powerful influence on the level of economic activity; deficits are not inconsistent with short-run growth but have devastating effects on America's ability to compete in world markets;

and efforts to achieve and maintain price stability may create, as a byproduct, a more uneven distribution of income.

   As useful as the lessons may be, they will not solve the unemployment-inflation dilemma or guarantee faster economic growth. The nation must either lower its expectations or find new strategies for coping with these problems.

REFERENCES

Aaron, Henry J., and Joseph A. Pechman. eds. 1981. *How Taxes Affect Economic Behavior*. Washington, D.C.: Brookings Institution.

Barry, Brian. 1985. "Does Democracy Cause Inflation? Political Ideas of Some Economists." In Leon N. Lindberg and Charles S. Maier, eds., *The Politics of Inflation and Economic Stagnation: Theoretical Approaches and International Case Studies*. Washington, D.C.: Brookings Institution.

Bator, Francis M. 1982. "Fiscal and Monetary Policy: In Search of a Doctrine," *Economic Choices: Studies in Tax/Fiscal Policy*. Washington, D.C.: Center for National Policy.

Bendick, Marc, Jr. 1982. "Employment, Training, and Economic Development." In John L. Palmer and Isabel V. Sawhill, eds., *The Reagan Experiment: An Examination of Economic and Social Policies under the Reagan Administration*. Washington, D.C.: Urban Institute Press.

Blank, Rebecca M., and Alan S. Blinder. 1986. "Macreconomics, Income Distribution, and Poverty." In Sheldon Danziger and Daniel Weinberg, eds., *Fighting Poverty: What Works and What Doesn't*. Cambridge, Massachusetts: Harvard University Press. Forthcoming.

Blinder, Alan S. 1984. "Reaganomics and Growth: The Message in the Models." In Charles R. Hulten and Isabel V. Sawhill, eds., *The Legacy of Reaganomics: Prospects for Long-term Growth*. Washington, D.C.: Urban Institute Press.

Boskin, Michael. 1985. Testimony before the House Ways and Means Committee. 99 Cong. 1 sess. June 11.

Bosworth, Barry. 1984. *Tax Incentives and Economic Growth*. Washington, D.C.: Brookings Institution.

————. 1985. "Taxes and Investment Recovery," *Brookings Papers on Economic Activity*.1: 1–45.

Bruno, Michael, and Jeffrey Sachs. 1985. *Economics of Worldwide Stagflation*. Cambridge, Massachusetts: Harvard University Press.

Chubb, John E., and Paul E. Peterson. eds. 1985. *The New Direction in American Politics*. Washington, D.C.: Brookings Institution.

Clark, Peter K. 1984. "Productivity and Profits in the 1980s: Are They Really Improving?" *Brookings Papers on Economic Activity* 1: 133–81.

Congressional Budget Office. 1985. *The Economic and Budget Outlook: Fiscal Years 1986–1990: A Report to the Senate and House Committees on the Budget—Part I*. Washington, D.C.: Congressional Budget Office. February.

_____. 1985. *The Economic and Budget Outlook: An Update: A Report to the Senate and House Committees on the Budget.* Washington, D.C.: Congressional Budget Office. August.

Danziger, Sheldon, Robert Haveman, and Robert Plotnick. 1981. "How Income Transfer Programs Affect Work, Savings, and the Income Distribution: A Critical Review." *Journal of Economic Literature* (September) 19(3)975–1028.

Eads, George C., and Michael Fix. 1984. *Relief or Reform? Reagan's Regulatory Dilemma.* Washington, D.C.: Urban Institute Press.

Economic Report of the President. 1954. Washington, D.C.: U.S. Government Printing Office.

Economic Report of the President. 1966. Washington, D.C.: U.S. Government Printing Office.

Economic Report of the President. 1982. Washington, D.C.: U.S. Government Printing Office.

Ellwood, David, and Lawrence Summers. 1986. "Poverty in America: Is Welfare the Answer or the Problem?" In Sheldon Danziger and Daniel Weinberg, eds., *Fighting Poverty: What Works and What Doesn't.* Cambridge, Massachusetts: Harvard University Press. Forthcoming.

Friedman, Milton, with Rose D. Friedman. 1962. "The Role of Government in a Free Society." In *Capitalism and Freedom.* Chicago, Illinois: University of Chicago Press.

Gordon, Robert J. 1984. "Unemployment and Potential Output in the 1980s." *Brookings Papers on Economic Activity.* 2: 537–68.

Gottschalk, Peter, and Sheldon Danziger. 1984. "Macroeconomic Conditions, Income Transfers, and the Trend in Poverty." In D. Lee Bawden, ed., *The Social Contract Revisited.* Washington, D.C.: Urban Institute Press.

Greider, William. 1981. "The Education of David Stockman." *The Atlantic Monthly* (December) 248(6): 27–54.

Haveman, Robert H. 1984. "How Much Have the Reagan Administration's Tax and Spending Policies Increased Work?" In Charles R. Hulten and Isabel V. Sawhill, eds., *The Legacy of Reaganomics: Prospects for Long-term Growth.* Washington, D.C.: Urban Institute Press.

Hibbs, Douglas A., and Heinz Fassbender, eds. 1981. *Contemporary Political Economy.* Amsterdam: North-Holland.

Hirschman, Albert O. 1982. *Shifting Involvements: Private Interest, Public Action.* Princeton, New Jersey: Princeton University Press.

Kiewiet, D. Roderick. 1983. *Macro-Economics and Micro-Politics: The Effects of Economic Issues.* Chicago, Illinois: University of Chicago Press.

Kiewiet, D. Roderick, and Douglas Rivers. 1985. "The Economic Basis of Reagan's Appeal." In John E. Chubb and Paul E. Peterson, eds., *The New Direction in American Politics.* Washington, D.C.: Brookings Institution.

Lipset, Seymour M. 1984. "The Economy, Elections, and Public Opinion." In John H. Moore, ed., *To Promote Prosperity.* Stanford, California: Hoover Institution Press.

Lowi, Theodore J. 1985. "Ronald Reagan—Revolutionary?" In Lester M. Salamon and Michael S. Lund, eds., *The Reagan Presidency and the Governing of America.* Washington, D.C.: Urban Institute Press.

McCallum, Bennett T. 1985. *Monetary vs. Fiscal Policy Effects: A Review of the Debate.* Working Paper 1556. Cambridge, Massachusetts: National Bureau of Economic Research, Inc. February.

Moon, Marilyn, and Isabel V. Sawhill. 1984. "Family Incomes: Gainers and Losers." In John L. Palmer and Isabel V. Sawhill, eds., *The Reagan Record: An Assessment of America's Changing Domestic Priorities.* Cambridge, Massachusetts: Ballinger Publishing Company.

Nichols, Donald A. 1984. "Federal Spending Priorities and Long-term Economic Growth." In Charles R. Hulten and Isabel V. Sawhill, eds., *The Legacy of Reaganomics: Prospects for Long-term Growth.* Washington, D.C.: Urban Institute Press.

Nordhaus, William D. 1983. "Macroconfusion: The Dilemmas of Economic Policy." In James Tobin, ed., *Macroeconomics, Prices, and Quantities.* Washington, D.C.: Brookings Institution.

————. 1975. "The Political Business Cycle." *Review of Economic Studies.* (April) 42: 169–90.

Okun, Arthur M. 1981. *Prices and Quantities: A Macroeconomic Analysis.* Washington, D.C.: Brookings Institution.

Olson, Mancur 1984. "Ideology and Economic Growth." In Charles R. Hulten and Isabel V. Sawhill, eds., *The Legacy of Reaganomics: Prospects for Long-term Growth.* Washington, D.C.: Urban Institute Press.

Perry, George L. 1983. "What Have We Learned about Disinflation?" *Brookings Papers on Economic Activity.* 2: 587–602.

Reeves, Richard. 1985. *The Reagan Detour.* New York: Simon and Schuster.

Salant, Walter S. 1985. "Keynes and the Modern World: A Review Article." *Journal of Economic Literature* (September) 23: 1176–85.

Sawhill, Isabel V. 1982. "Economic Policy." In John L. Palmer and Isabel V. Sawhill, eds., *The Reagan Experiment: An Examination of Economic and Social Policies under the Reagan Administration.* Washington, D.C.: Urban Institute Press.

————. 1981. "Incomes Policies." Washington, D.C.: Urban Institute.

_____.1985. "Unemployment and Poverty: Can We Do Better." Testimony before the Subcommittee on Economic Stabilization of the House Committee on Banking, Finance, and Urban Affairs. 99 Cong. 1. sess. March 19.

Sawhill, Isabel V., and Charles F. Stone. 1984. "The Economy: The Key to Success." In John L. Palmer and Isabel V. Sawhill, eds., *The Reagan Record: An Assessment of America's Changing Domestic Priorities*. Cambridge, Massachusetts: Ballinger Publishing Company.

Schultze, Charles L. 1985. "Microeconomic Efficiency and Nominal Wage Stickiness." *The American Economic Review* (March) 75(1):1–15.

Silk, Leonard. 1984. *Economics in the Real World*. New York: Simon and Schuster.

Stein, Herbert. 1984. *Presidential Economics: The Making of Economic Policy from Roosevelt to Reagan and Beyond*. New York: Simon and Schuster.

Stone, Charles F., and Isabel V. Sawhill. 1984. *Economic Policy in the Reagan Years*. Washington, D.C.: Urban Institute Press.

_____. 1985. "Labor Market Implications of the Monetary/Fiscal Policy Mix." Testimony before a joint hearing held by the Economic Policy and Human Resources Task Forces of the House Budget Committee. November 20.

Thurow, Lester C. 1980. *The Zero-Sum Society: Distribution and the Possibilities for Economic Change*. New York: Basic Books, Inc.

_____. 1985. *The Zero-Sum Solution: Building A World-Class American Economy*. New York: Simon and Schuster.

Tobin, James. 1983. "Okun on Macroeconomic Policy: A Final Comment." In James Tobin, ed., *Macroeconomics, Prices, and Quantities*. Washington, D.C.: Brookings Institution.

Tufte, Edward R. 1978. *Political Control of the Economy*. Princeton, New Jersey: Princeton University Press.

U.S. Department of Labor, Bureau of Labor Statistics. 1983. *Trends in Multifactor Productivity*. Washington, D.C.: U.S. Government Printing Office.

Yankelovich, Daniel, Les Aspin, and Sidney Harman. 1986. *A New Political Framework*. Unpublished document. January.

INSTITUTIONAL CHANGE UNDER REAGAN

Richard P. Nathan

When Franklin Roosevelt was assistant secretary of the Navy, he once complained to Henry Adams about problems he faced. Adams, who lived across the street from the White House, said to F.D.R.,"Young man, I have lived in this house for many years and seen the occupants of that White House across the square come and go, and nothing that you minor officials or the occupants of that house can do will affect the history of the world for long" (Miller 1983, 110).

The question raised by this exchange of whether politicians can "affect the history of the world for long" is hardest to answer in a time period close to the events being observed. The Reagan presidency, as is true of F.D.R.'s, is seen by many observers as marking a watershed for the office in substantive and institutional terms. Both types of changes are important. However, the case can be made that institutional change, to the extent that it occurs, is most likely to be enduring. It is therefore worthwhile when estimating the potentially more lasting effects of a president's tenure to focus attention, as is done in this chapter, on institutional dimensions of the conduct of the office.

At the outset it has to be stipulated that the American political system is fundamentally resistant to change, in large part because of its pluralistic character. As Tocqueville taught us over a century ago, it is the wonderfully animated, competitive, and open character of the American political system that distinguishes it among the democracies of the Western world. The United States has a political system in which everyone can play government and a great many people do. This has always been a striking and strong characteristic of the American political system. If anything, it has become more highly accentuated as technology has advanced and increased specialization has given

121

special interests even more reason to flex their muscles in a political system that enables, indeed encourages, them to do so.[1]

This pluralistic character of the American political system can be viewed as having two dimensions: horizontal and vertical. By horizontal, I refer to the competitive relationships between actors at any given level of the political system—federal, state, or local. But pluralism is not just an important characteristic of the various levels of government; the founding fathers envisaged a new federal form that involves competitive relationships on the "vertical" dimension of polity among the federal, state, and local governments. The organizing structure of this chapter follows along the lines of these horizontal and vertical dimensions.

On the horizontal plane today's president, as a political and governmental leader in a media age that no founding father could have imagined, has the immense challenge of giving direction and expression to a governmental system in which he is the first among equals, though decidedly not sovereign. The president is first among equals in the sense that he is at the center of a churning, interconnected political world in which hundreds of thousands of organizations and individuals see themselves as involved in critical relationships with the president, a person Americans see on the television screen in their homes nearly every day.

On the domestic front, this challenge to give leadership to the nation's governmental system and expression to the office of the president is compounded by the existence of fifty state governments, nearly 40,000 general-purpose local governments, and an even larger number of independent school districts and other types of special districts—many of which participate aggressively in the great game of American government.

Given this political landscape as the baseline, I believe that President Reagan has been decidedly successful in the domestic policy arena, and that his success has enabled him to make skillful use of—and change—American political institutions. The two institutions that I have selected to develop this proposition are the presidency and federalism, both of which relate to the horizontal and vertical dimensions of the American governmental system.

Ronald Reagan was elected at a time when the presidency was in deep trouble. His predecessors, Presidents Johnson and Nixon had left office in disgrace. Both Presidents Ford and Carter were defeated in their bids for reelection; their administrations were not popular. The executive office needed resuscitation, and Ronald Reagan, in a way that surprised many observers,

---

1. John E. Chubb and Paul E. Peterson argue that the American political system has become more highly institutionalized and change resistant over time. See Chubb and Peterson (1985).

has accomplished precisely that. He is the first president in more than twenty-five years to be reelected and to enter a second term with a high level of popular support. His term in office has demonstrated that the presidency can work effectively; he has brought both a leadership style and strategy to bear that are likely to have a strong influence on future practice.

In domestic policy much of the business of the federal government is transacted in the arena of intergovernmental relations. Reagan came to the presidency with a strong and long-standing theory of American federalism, favoring the reduction of the role of the federal government and the enhancement of the role of state governments. In this chapter, I address President Reagan's impact on American federalism. I argue that he has been strikingly successful in achieving his intergovernmental reform aims, and that his efforts to realign American federalism are likely to have a lasting effect. In fact, Reagan's success on this domestic front, which does not tend to be widely appreciated, in my view has been so pronounced that his successful efforts to increase the role of state governments in American federalism have undermined what I believe is his more important objective of social program retrenchment.

THE PRESIDENCY

My discussion of the presidency in this section is divided into two parts, Reagan's style of leadership, and the strategies he has adopted to pursue major policy objectives.

Leadership Style

I use five criteria to assess presidential leadership; each focuses on a different aspect of the role of the president, that is, the president as (1) the representative of the political culture and institutions (the "historical" presidency); (2) a policymaker; (3) a manager of both the policymaking process and the execution of policy; (4) a politician, which involves his role in selecting, motivating, and rewarding and punishing other politicians; and (5) a communicator, as the principal spokesman for his administration.

From the beginning it was conceded that Ronald Reagan is a good communicator, but this concession was not always made in good grace by some observers who stressed Reagan's background as a former movie actor. President watchers now take Reagan much more seriously, however. He is considered to have brought a number of needed and critical qualities to the office. He has a good sense of timing. His presidency has been decidedly ideological, yet he knows when and how to "cut a deal." He is both an ideologue and a pragmatist. He makes the policymaking process come to him. According to one observer, the Reagan presidency stands out for "the chief executive's ideological closure, his propensity to act on his principles" and "his success in doing so" (Greenstein 1983, 4).

Success in a political office also depends on the personality of the office holder and the ability to permeate the public consciousness and engender public trust. This characteristic of the presidency comes closest to the first leadership criterion, the president as the representative of political tradition. President Reagan is perceived by the electorate as genuine, caring, and likable. To a considerable degree his standing as a leader and the acceptance of his ideas is a function of these perceptions, and these public perceptions undoubtedly capture true qualities. Despite the sophistication of modern public relations, the constant visibility of the president makes it hard for him to conceal his personality. Lyndon Johnson, Richard Nixon, and Jimmy Carter all became as familiar to the electorate as their neighbors and co-workers.

Reagan manages people as well as he does issues; by this I refer to his role as a manager of the decison-making process of the presidency. He chooses and deploys his personal aides and subordinates adeptly. To a large degree he has been able to prevent the kind of excesses that critics associate with Kennedy's too academic group of personal advisors, Carter's too instrumental staff, and Nixon's assemblage of like-minded, hardened political advisors who helped destroy his presidency.

Reagan's "troika" (James Baker, III, Edwin Meese, III, and Michael Deaver) in his first term made the White House a smoothly run operation. A look at the background and personality of the principals in that troika is instructive. James Baker, who has roots in the Eastern Establishment, has outstanding political and analytical skills and is an effective manager. Edwin Meese is in many respects a good counter to Baker. He is a Westerner and a longtime Reagan aide and intimate. Meese is a more "rough-and-tumble" politician, known for his skills in rewarding friends and punishing enemies. His origins are in the ideologically more conservative wing of the Republican party, and he was perceived in the first term (and still is) as the keeper of Reagan's ideology in domestic policy. Of the three members of the group, Michael Deaver was the fulcrum in the first term. He has long been a close personal associate of Reagan. Deaver had the role of gatekeeper, with special responsibility for keeping track of Reagan's time and temperament and keeping affairs running smoothly for both Mr. and Mrs. Reagan, in a way that involved substance as well as process.

Not only the president's personal aides, but other components of the Executive Office, have performed well under the Reagan administration. Budgeting has been the central policymaking and coordination mechanism, with Budget Director David Stockman working closely with Baker during Reagan's first term. Stockman's brilliance (and that is the right word for his performance) as both a budget strategist and tactician was a major asset of the Reagan presidency in the early and critical period for policy formulation.

In much the same way that the Office of Management and Budget has been integrated into the Reagan system, another component of the White House staff, the legislative liaison office was tied closely to the Reagan troika in the first term.

Considering the problems, feuds, and frustrations of the inner circle of presidencies of the recent past, the operation of the Reagan White House, especially in the first term, has been a considerable accomplishment. Some important political lessons have been demonstrated by this experience.

An essential element of political leadership is the selection of a balanced set of advisors who bring needed diversity in perspectives and experience to bear so that the leader can be certain of receiving a full range of reactions and advice in addressing critical issues. In addition to assembling a balanced team of advisors to represent the spectrum of the major inputs that should be considered in making decisions, the way a political leader works out relationships with these principal subordinates is also a major element of political leadership. When one considers the immensity of the pressures of the office, Reagan's ability in handling both tasks is impressive. His managerial skill in selecting, deploying, and relating to subordinates is apparent not just in the executive office but also, as discussed below, in his interactions with others in the executive establishment.

Presidential Strategies

Presidents are often depicted as having choices among the strategies they can use to advance their policy preferences. One way of looking at these choices is that they coincide with governmental structure. A president can highlight three types of strategy, for example—a legislative strategy, to advance ideas by enacting legislation that encompasses them; an administrative strategy, to influence the bureaucracy so that federal agencies stress the president's goals in the implementation of laws, or a judicial strategy, to promote both the selection of judges who support his ideas and the involvement of executive branch officials in advancing the administration's goals in judicial processes.

These strategies do not necessarily fit well together. A strong emphasis by the president on any one of them can undercut his ability to win his way with other strategies. For example, Nixon's administrative strategy, pursued in part by aggressively using the budget impoundment powers of the executive office, infuriated the Congress and stalled, if it did not destroy, his legislative program (Nathan 1983, 4). Franklin D. Roosevelt's attempted court packing and Truman's battle with the Supreme Court over seizing the steel industry undercut the power of both presidents to act in other arenas. Similarly, a president who places all of his chips on major legislative achievements is less likely to be able to lean on the bureaucracy (that is, to use an administrative strategy) without undercutting his legislative program.

Against this background, an important characteristic of the Reagan presidency is that he has followed a multiple strategy, while at the same time he has seemed to avoid such a heavy handed approach in any one of the three spheres as to jeopardize his opportunities in the others. I do not mean to imply that other presidents have not attempted and in some cases and periods succeeded in pursuing a multiple strategy. My point is only that President Reagan has adroitly balanced the three strategies, using different emphases as circumstances seemed to warrant for maximum effectiveness. Each of the three basic types of strategy is discussed below.

The Legislative Strategy. Reagan's legislative skills produced important successes in the legislative arena, particularly in the early days of his presidency. The most dramatic evidence of Reagan's achievements in "striking while the iron was hot" was the enactment of two laws during his first six months in office—the Omnibus Budget Reconciliation Act of 1981 and the five-year $737 billion "supply side" tax reduction act, both of which were signed into law on the same day, August 13, 1981.

The 1981 budget act encompassed several major changes in domestic affairs introduced by the Reagan administration. First, and probably most important, the act sent a strong signal that the administration was committed to reducing the size and scope of the federal government's role in domestic affairs. Henceforth, the federal government would do less. The private sector, state and local governments, and voluntary organizations were called upon to do more. Second, President Reagan made fundamental changes in welfare policies in this budget act. Although few observers at the time paid close attention to these changes, the act included welfare policy changes (discussed by Meyer in this volume at greater length) similar to those Reagan had made as governor of California—to focus welfare on the truly needy and in the process prevent working-poor families from falling into the "welfare trap" of long-term dependency.[2] The 1981 budget act also introduced the idea of

---

2. The concepts of "welfare dependency" and the "welfare trap" were developed by Martin Anderson, President Reagan's first domestic policy advisor. See Anderson (1984, 16–17).

workfare, or working for one's welfare payment (which Ronald Reagan pioneered in California during his term as governor), as a new option for state and county governments.

A third major change brought by the 1981 budget act was the advancement of Reagan's objectives of federalism reform. It established six new block grants that reflected Reagan's state-centered theory of American federalism. Although the legislative changes creating these new block grants were important, they fell short of what the president had requested.

All these as well as other changes were contained in a single act. In my view, the budget act of 1981 is the most important piece of domestic legislation since the Social Security Act of 1935. The 1981 budget introduced a marked shift in direction of social spending and fundamental changes in the substance of domestic policy and in American federalism. Its enactment depended heavily on the president's success in convincing Congress to take a single vote on the entire package. One observer describes President Reagan as having used "every opportunity—press conferences, speeches, meetings with members, state of the union messages, and his weekly radio address—to generate congressional support" (Reischauer 1984, 408). He continued to lobby for this act from his hospital bed after the assassination attempt in March 1981.[3]

President Reagan's success in the legislative arena declined sharply after 1981, in part because of the tendency for the luster to wear off a new administration as time passes, and in part because of the steep 1981–82 recession, which reduced the administration's leverage with Congress. Although he proposed a second round of budget cuts in 1981 and similar cuts and changes in domestic policy in his subsequent budgets, he was unsuccessful in maintaining momentum on the legislative front.

President Reagan is not alone among presidents in his ability to take advantage of his opportunities for legislative action as he did in 1981. Former President F.D.R.'s first one hundred days and Johnson's quick action following Kennedy's assassination to enact his Great Society program are examples of successful presidential legislative initiatives that took full advantage of political momentum. A notable point about the Reagan presidency is that he has also used other strategies adroitly to advance his domestic policy objectives. Indeed, the evidence indicates that the different strategies have

---

3. It is interesting that the 1981 budget act probably could not have been passed if Congress had not established new budget procedures seven years earlier under the Congressional Budget and Impoundment Control Act of 1974. That legislation, designed in large measure to prevent abuses of presidential power (former President Nixon's), turned out to be a valuable instrument for executive leadership under President Reagan.

been emphasized with varying intensity according to the changed conditions in different periods of the Reagan presidency. This point can be illustrated by considering the administrative strategy, to which I turn next.

The Administrative Presidency Strategy. Briefly stated, the idea of an administrative presidency strategy is that the president, through his principal cabinet and subcabinet appointees, can influence administrative processes in a way that enables him to move forward on important policy objectives. In the following paragraphs I consider both the rationale for, and some of the background of, this approach to presidential leadership.

Government in modern industrial societies has become so pervasive and complex that the legislative process is increasingly forced to operate at a high level of generalization. This often means enacting new policies in broad terms and then assigning to the responsible bureaucratic organizations and experts the task of developing and implementing guidelines and regulations to carry them out. One result is that the responsible agency officials often exercise considerable policy discretion.

Both the pluralism and the formal structure of the American political system often put presidents in a position to use their appointment powers in the implementation process in order to emphasize the values and central purposes of their administration. Drawing on recent experience, President Reagan and his principal aides have been energetic and skillful in pursuing this strategy on a basis that, I believe, strengthens the nation's political system.

Important differences exist between the United States and other Western parliamentary political systems that facilitate this kind of an administrative role for the president. The fact that political appointees constitute a large group (approximately 2,500 persons) at the national level in the United States enables the president to use administrative tactics to greater advantage than is the case in most other political systems.

Richard M. Nixon stands out among recent presidents for his systematic effort at the beginning of his second term to select and deploy new cabinet, subcabinet, and other appointed officials on a basis that explicitly and publicly called for their involvement in administrative processes. Eight years later, President Reagan, in a much less obtrusive way, took office with a similar idea about taking on the bureaucracy.

The most significant difference between Presidents Nixon and Reagan in these terms is that Nixon did not decide on this plan until the end of his first term, whereas Reagan and his chief aides started out with this strategy. Nixon had to retool midstream. Even without Watergate, one can question whether he could have done so successfully. Reagan, by contrast, adopted an administrative approach in domestic affairs from the outset. His system for choosing the original cadre of cabinet and subcabinet officials, and the way they were prepared for their new tasks, is distinctive among recent presidents.

In past administrations the customary practice after winning an election has been for the president to pick a broadly balanced and often diverse cabinet—one that can heal wounds and bring the country and the party together. However, cabinet members were frequently portrayed as becoming adversaries, rather than agents, of the president. This, for example, was President Kennedy's experience. Theodore G. Sorenson wrote in 1963 that cabinet officers are "bounded by inherent limitations." Sorenson complained that they cannot and do not ignore their standing in their department and their "relations with the powerful interest groups and Congressmen who consider it partly their own" (Sorenson 1963, 11).

The White House under President Reagan did not operate this way in 1981. Edwin Meese, III, assisted by an experienced hand, E. Pendleton James (President Reagan's first personnel chief, who had held a similar position under former President Nixon), carefully selected both cabinet and subcabinet officials on a basis that first and foremost involved ideological harmony with the goals of the new administration.

Although the appointment process was a slow one, when it was completed the new Reagan administration turned quickly to the serious business of revising the budget that had been sent to Congress on January 15, 1981 by Jimmy Carter for fiscal 1982. Cabinet nominees were closeted with Budget Director-designate David Stockman and long-time Reagan aides and told what was expected of them. They were not allowed to bring agency staff members to these meetings, were assigned policy changes, and were told to "hit the ground running."

It was not only at the cabinet level that policy discipline was sought and obtained. Although it may not even have been fully appreciated within the Reagan administration at the time, Reagan's next levels of policy officials (subcabinet officials, such as undersecretaries, assistant secretaries, and their deputies and aides) tended to be even stronger ideologues than their cabinet superiors. Subcabinet officials were also hand-picked by the White House, and it was made clear to those officials that this was the case—that is, that they were the president's appointees. Policy guidance for the officials who addressed domestic issues was the responsibility of Meese of the White House troika.[4]

---

4. Meese, now Attorney General, has a related assignment in the second term of the Reagan administration as head of a new cabinet-level Domestic Policy Council.

The Reagan system for selecting, deploying, and relating to subcabinet officials is particularly interesting. Subcabinet officials are less visible publicly than their cabinet superiors; they operate outside the glare of the media spotlights of Washington. In a number of domestic agencies, they changed agency operations by using administrative strategies to pursue objectives that reflected more the pure Reagan conservative ideology than the views of their generally more conciliatory cabinet chiefs. This was especially the case for the agencies responsible for big-spending domestic programs that the Reagan administration has opposed, particularly the social programs of the departments of health and human services, labor, and education.

It was probably a wise strategy to select subcabinet appointees who were more strongly ideological than their cabinet chiefs. In a number of instances in which strong ideologues were in positions of power as cabinet secretaries and agency heads in President Reagan's first term, as in the case of Department of the Interior James Watt, the administrative strategy backfired and become a major public embarrassment. Secretary Watt's heavy-handed efforts to advance a very conservative agenda in the administrative processes of the Department of the Interior were highly visible and controversial. The same thing was true at the Environmental Protection Agency under administrator Anne Burford Gorsuch. Both appointees resigned under fire.

Although the comings and goings of lower-level appointed officials receive less attention in the national news media, there have been notable cases under President Reagan in which this administrative strategy ran into problems and some officials had to be jettisoned or later resigned amidst controversy. Two most prominent cases involved Senate confirmation proceedings. Donald Devine, director of the Office of Personnel Management and one of the chief architects of Reagan's administrative strategy, withdrew his nomination for a second four-year term in the face of stiff opposition to his policies. The other case was the rejection by the Senate of the promotion of Assistant Attorney General William Bradford Reynolds to associate attorney general. Reynolds was the Justice Department's principal official responsible for civil rights enforcement.[5]

It is my view that Reagan's administrative strategy could not have avoided some of these kinds of incidents. However, in the larger context, the benefits

---

5. Several other examples also attracted some, though less prominent, media attention. In the Department of Education at the beginning of Reagan's second term two appointees who had made intemperate comments about the problems of handicapped students were forced to step aside even before they could take office. A similar incident involving the removal of a subcabinet official under fire occurred at the beginning of Reagan's second term in the Occupational Safety and Health Administration when William Brock took over as the new secretary of labor in 1985.

of pushing Reagan's ideas into the bureaucracy through this administrative appointment process outweigh the costs in terms of the tempests they cause. The kinds of cases just described are inevitable in any administration. Talented appointees are hard to find and attract to government. Often the people chosen have had limited governmental and political experience. American government is characterized by short tenure and high turnover for these appointees. Ours is a system of "government by amateurs" (or, at least, the extensive reliance on governmental short-term appointed officials). It is bound to produce mistakes when new appointees are learning; in some cases they simply are not able to do so.

It is hard to draw a balance sheet on the success of the Reagan administration's use of political appointees to push its major domestic policy objectives into administrative processes. How does one establish the counterfactual? What would have happened in a particular policy area if Reagan's appointee had not been a committed policy partisan? A presumption is made here, which research suggests is valid, that members of the permanent government (career officials with tenure rights) are likely to disagree with Reagan's conservative goals in many areas of domestic policy, and that, without the administrative strategy they would have been much more successful in preventing Reagan from achieving his domestic policy goals. The conclusions of a study of the beliefs and attitudes of federal officials in domestic policy areas during the Nixon administration are relevant to this point: "Our findings document a career bureaucracy with very little Republican representation but even more pointedly portray a social service bureaucracy dominated by administrators hostile to many of the directions pursued by the Nixon administration in the realm of social policy" (Aberbach and Rockman 1976, 466–67).

Besides appointment power, three other principal elements of the administrative strategy are regulation writing, personnel deployment, and budgeting. Reagan's appointees have used all three. They have changed regulations, have slowed or shifted grants to political advantage, have delayed new appointments in the career service, and have reassigned senior officials.[6]

When the iron got cold on the legislative front, the Reagan administration put more emphasis on other avenues, both administrative and judicial, for advancing its domestic policy goals. During the second and third years of Reagan's first term, subcabinet appointees in the domestic policy areas pushed for greater involvement in administrative processes. This probably reflected the time they needed to become familiar with their respective agencies, but

---

6. Ironically, Carter's widely hailed civil service reform, which includes assignment of officials in the Senior Executive Service so that they can be moved around more easily, gives the Reaganites an added opportunity for administrative action.

it also may have indicated a deliberate (or at least fairly clear) shift from the use of a legislative strategy to a greater reliance on the administrative and judicial strategies as opportunities and conditions changed.

Some experts in public administration argue that Reagan and his principal aides for domestic affairs overplayed their hand in the administrative arena. The cost of doing this is that aggressive policy officials alienate the career staff and the affected interest groups. When this happens, the appointed officials can become caught in a congressional pincer action or a media blitz that ends up undercutting the policy changes they are seeking to make. According to this line of argument, a set of understandings—often subtle— exists between policy and career officials. The dexterity required to identify and adhere to these understandings is seen as not having been clearly demonstrated by the Reagan administration.

The principal issue I raise is the effect of this kind of administrative strategy on the character and morale of the career service. Values associated with the importance of the role of professional employees in the career service are juxtaposed with arguments in support of an administrative strategy for political executives; the trade-off is one between the political process and professional expertise. No definitive conclusion can be reached on this issue. Career officials perceive themselves as being threatened (and they are threatened) by the approach described here. This perceived threat not only has a negative impact on the existing staff—weakening morale and in some cases causing early exits of capable career officials—but it also tends to have a dampening effect on the recruitment of new government employees.

In more basic terms, political scientists argue that the president should not control, or even try to control, the bureaucracy. They contend that the bureaucracy is and should be subject to many influences from Congress, the media, interest groups, and the courts. To give an example of this point of view, one observer from this school of thought maintains that the bureaucracy is a "representative institution" in and of itself and that the president's role is not analogous to that of the chief executive in more hierarchical structures (Long 1952).

Although some Reagan appointees may have overstepped the bounds of good practice in their dealings with the bureaucracy, my conclusion is that American national government at high levels is not a subtle business. I believe the administrative strategy of the presidency is a valid and valuable instrument of presidential leadership. I give the Reagan administration high marks for developing and sticking with the administrative strategy as a way to press forward its goals by penetrating, and in this way influencing, administrative processes. In my view it is notable that the Reagan administration manages to stay this course without getting so bloodied (the James Watt and Anne

Burford Gorsuch cases are obvious exceptions) that administrative failures threaten its ability to make headway in the application of other presidential leadership approaches.

This argument is grounded in the pluralism theme of this chapter. In the dynamic and competitive American political system, leadership is hard to exercise. The price paid for pluralism is the rough-and-tumble, or jagged, quality of our political system. Policy changes are not easy to achieve, yet are often needed. I believe that the use of administrative levers is thus justified as a presidential leadership strategy. Indeed, a good part of the public confidence in Ronald Reagan, even on the part of some of his ideological opponents, is a function of the respect of the public for his sense of direction and strength of purpose in pursuing his goals. When the mood shifts again, as it will, and liberal social values are on the upswing, I believe that this administrative strategy of the presidency will be just as important then as it has been for Reagan as a way to shift gears in the field of domestic policy.

The Judicial Strategy. The third strategy for presidential policy leadership in domestic affairs is judicial. The opportunities are twofold: an administration can push its policy objectives by intervening (or deciding not to intervene) in judicial processes. In some cases the strategy is to activate government lawyers; in other cases, to restrain them. In civil rights, antitrust, and environmental litigation, for example, holding back government lawyers often has been the course of action most in line with the Reagan administration's aims.

Some readers may find this idea is objectionable. There is a tendency for people who are ideologically opposed to Reagan's goals to regard "intrusions" into judicial processes as violations of moral imperatives. My view is that what in essence is involved here are policy decisions about the use of governmental powers to deal with value issues, and wide differences of opinion frequently exist on those policies. Presidential power can be—and is—balanced and checked in our political system in many ways. The need for leadership to respond to what politicians believe are important values leads me to the conclusion that both judicial and administrative strategies on the part of a national administration are a legitimate and appropriate use of presidential powers to advance policy objectives.

I have not studied judicial strategy as closely as the other two types of strategy. Nathan Glazer in this volume discusses judicial policies and strategies in two domestic policy areas where they are especially important, civil rights and civil liberties. In civil rights, for example, the Department of Justice has vigorously opposed the application of the affirmative action concept in the courts. The department is reported to have sought to eliminate numerical goals and quotas in employment from court decrees in more than fifty cases (Pear

1985b). In much the same way, the Department of Justice has opposed in the courts the use of busing to achieve racial balance or has refused to intercede in instances where this was the issue.[7]

Two political scientists who studied the effects of judicial actions on environmental issues during the Reagan presidency conclude that the administration set policy on a new course largely because of policy changes made in the judicial arena.[8]

Another part of the judicial strategy is more conventional. Court appointees are recruited who can be expected to make decisions favoring the purposes and ideas of the president. The Reagan administration made notable progress on this front in the lower courts during its first term, and may yet fundamentally change the majority pattern of the U.S. Supreme Court in the second term.

Just as administrative and legislative strategies have been emphasized at different times in Reagan's first term, the legislative and judicial strategies have been interwoven in an interesting pattern, as the chapters in this volume suggest. Nathan Glazer points out in his chapter that the Reagan administration at the outset did not make much headway and, in fact, did not push hard to bring change in civil rights issues. This, he notes, surprised many observers. Yet Glazer goes on to state that in the second half of Reagan's first term, the situation changed. The administration took a much more aggressive stance in litigation on civil rights. This shift, as I noted earlier, coincides with the attenuation of the legislative strategy after the 1981 successes and the stepping up of the administrative strategy in the second and third years of President Reagan's first term.

REAGAN'S IMPACT ON AMERICAN FEDERALISM

I turn next to the vertical dimension of American government in domestic affairs. No one can accuse Ronald Reagan of being a wallflower on the subject of American federalism. Beginning well before he was president, Reagan consistently has advanced a state-centered theory of federalism. Twice he prominently has advanced broad-gauged and radical proposals to rearrange

---

7. The case cited above of the rejected appointment of William Bradford Reynolds is pertinent here. The rejection was reportedly a result of charges that he had held back government lawyers in cases addressing the enforcement of civil rights policies. An account of the Senate vote against Reynolds' confirmation referred to the assertion by one senator that Reynolds "failed to enforce laws he disliked." (See Pear 1985a).

8. The study notes that a drop of 84 percent occurred in the number of cases referred by the Environmental Protection Agency to the Justice Department between June 1981 and July 1982. See Kraft and Vig (1984).

functional responsibilities in American federalism, and on both occasions he has been burned. The first such effort was the plan Reagan proposed in his campaign against Gerald Ford for the Republican presidential nomination in 1976 when he called for the "systematic transfer of authority and resources to the states" (Cannon 1982, 202). This proposed plan, which affected $90 billion in federal programs, aroused widespread criticism because of the inability of Reagan and his advisors to spell out the details and explain the consequences. It became known as "the $90 billion misunderstanding." But it did accurately reflect the candidate's basic position.

These views had not changed by 1980 when Ronald Reagan was elected president. In his inaugural address in 1981, President Reagan made a second effort to advance his theory of federalism when he promised to curb federal powers and to "demand recognition of the distinction" between federal powers and "those reserved to the states." News accounts at the time noted that Reagan's comments on federalism brought a cheer from the section where the governors were seated at the inauguration.

The Reagan Approach to Decentralization

President Reagan's approach to decentralization can be distinguished from that of his immediate Republican predecessors, Nixon and Ford, in the emphasis Reagan has placed on the transfer of federal authority to the states. In 1981 Reagan told a group of governors that "the ideal situation" would require turning back to the states "tax sources that more properly belong there and which would then help fund responsibilities that also properly belong at the state level instead of the federal level" (*Congressional Quarterly* 1981, 177). This concept lay behind both his 1976 campaign proposal and his 1982 "swap and turn back" recommendations.

These recommendations were described at length in Reagan's January 1982 State-of-the-Union message. Programs with total 1982 appropriations of $46.6 billion were to be realigned between 1984 and 1991. The federal government was to assume responsibility for Medicaid, which is administered by state and county governments. In exchange, the states were to assume responsibility for the Aid to Families with Dependent Children (AFDC) and food stamp programs. The plan also called for establishing a trust fund to finance turnbacks, that is, programs turned over to the states. Certain federal taxes were to be relinquished to the states to help finance these programs.

Although both of Reagan's grand designs for federalism were unsuccessful, the basic goal of shifting spending and taxing authority to the states is clearly evident in steps he has taken as president to change domestic policies and programs. In short, I believe Reagan has achieved notable success in the pursuit of his goals for federalism reform, although he has done so more indirectly and incrementally than he did in his 1976 and 1982 comprehensive reform proposals. The three types of measures taken together—the cuts in domestic spending, the changes made in federal programs designed to turn authority over to the states, and the massive federal tax reductions enacted in 1981—can be viewed as a federalism reform strategy. All three measures challenge the states to take on greater responsibility.

This push to decentralize is not a new theme or purpose for a modern president. Indeed, it has deep roots in U.S. history. Ronald Reagan, like many Republican politicians, is a traditionalist on federalism issues. He has been a strong supporter of decentralization and is a proponent of a two-level (federal-state) concept of American federalism. His approach can be contrasted to the more dynamic, three-level (federal-state-local) view of American federalism associated with liberal politicians and scholars and with the Democratic party. It is ironic that this view, which is widely identified with the writings of Morton Grodzins, emerged in its most dramatic form during the Eisenhower administration. Grodzins' famous description of American federalism as a marble cake (juxtaposed to the traditional layer cake) was published as a chapter in the report of a presidential commission on national goals that Eisenhower established.[9]

An important dimension to this analysis is what emerged in the 1960s as a new form of "technocratic federalism," characterized by the rise of new and politically powerful groups of professional specialists in major domestic program fields. As one analyst states, "In the 1960s and on into the 1970s, new federal programs draw heavily upon the 'professional specialisms' in the field of health, housing, urban renewal, transportation, welfare, education, the environment, energy and poverty" (Beer 1982, xviii). According to this analyst, the result was that social programs typically followed a services strategy, which was aided and abetted by categorical grants-in-aid from the federal government to state and local governments. These particularistic intergovernmental payments were often used to stimulate the creation of programs favored by what Beer calls "professional specialisms."

How did the Reagan administration regard these professional minipolities of social service? The answer is simple: Reagan has long opposed the paternalism and social engineering values associated with many of the political subsystems of technocratic federalism in the urban and social policy

---

9. Grodzins' marble cake model depicted governmental functions and responsibilities in U.S. federalism as intermixed in "vertical and diagonal strands and unexpected whirls." See Grodzins (1960, 265).

fields. A more difficult question is, how has Reagan's program as president affected these political subsystems?

The Results of President Reagan's Policies

During the Reagan administration many of the program areas in which domestic budget cuts have been made or devolutionary objectives have been advanced through block grants and related decentralization policies are the same program areas in which the new social service technocracy is strong and active. One must also consider how pull-backs and devolution at the federal level affected the providers of services at the state and local levels.

Research conducted at Princeton University based on fourteen states and forty local governments shows that the cuts and changes in domestic grants-in-aid programs made in President Reagan's 1981 budget act had more adverse effects on people (notably the "working poor") than on state and local governments. See Nathan, Doolittle, and Associates (1983). The states were affected by several important changes, especially the creation of new block grants,[10] and the passage of provisions that gave states authority to reshape the large and expensive Medicaid program; these changes shifted responsibility from the federal government to the states.

After 1981 the momentum of President Reagan's retrenchment policies in domestic affairs was dissipated as Congress rejected most of the administration's proposals for further cuts and adopted new domestic spending measures to stimulate the economy and reduce unemployment (see Nathan and Doolittle 1984). Some policy shifts that enhanced the role of states did take place, however, even after 1981. The most notable was the 1982 passage of the Job Training Partnership Act, which gave state governments the lead role in setting policy for job training programs.

Even though Reagan's early cuts were large, the Princeton researchers observed a tendency by both politicians and scholars to exaggerate them and

10. Four new block grants in the health field were created in the 1981 budget act. They are for alcohol, drug abuse, and mental health (replacing three categorical grants); maternal and child health (replacing seven categorical grants); preventive health services (combining eight separate grants); and primary health care. A block grant for elementary and secondary education was also established consolidating twenty-nine categorical grants. Revisions were made in the existing community development block grant giving states new authority to allocate funds among small cities. States were also given new authority under the community services block grant to allocate funds to community action agencies for services to low-income persons. Other existing broad grants were changed in less important ways and described as new block grants by the administration, notably those for social services and energy assistance to low-income homeowners. A total of fifty-four previous grants with total funding of $7.2 billion were affected by these changes.

in turn to downplay the institutional effects of the administration's policies.[11] One of the major conclusions of the Princeton research on the effects of the Reagan administration's cuts and changes in federal grants-in-aids is that even though his grand federalism redesign never got off the ground, these changes significantly advanced Reagan's federalism reform objectives, reflecting his state-centered devolutionary theory of American federalism.

The role of most of the fourteen state governments in the Princeton sample was found to have increased in response to the Reagan program, although the character of this response varied according to the political ideology and fiscal condition of the state.[12] In general, the healthier was the fiscal position of the jurisdiction and the greater was the popular support for the particular service, the stronger was the response.[13] Five state governments are classified as having made the most pronounced response to the Reagan changes. All five replaced substantial amounts of the federal aid cuts and increased state spending in the areas in which the federal government was pulling back. (Although in most cases it was not an across-the-board response; it was limited to particular areas of public spending.) Eight states are classified in an intermediate response group. In some cases, they replaced federal aid and in all cases were found to have made institutional responses to the Reagan program that enhanced the role of the state government. Only one state government in the sample is classified as having made little or no response to the Reagan program.

The influence of economic conditions on the behavior of state and local governments in response to the cuts and changes in federally funded domestic programs developed in a particularly interesting way. The largest cuts were made in 1981. Shortly after the 1981 budget act was adopted, the nation entered a sharp recession. Typically in a recession state and local governments overreact. Fearing the worst, they cut spending, increase taxes, and in general "batten down the hatches." This behavior was clearly manifest in the 1981–82 period because the recession came on so suddenly and hit so hard. As it

---

11. This tendency to exaggerate the 1981 domestic budget cuts is both interesting and understandable. Both liberals and conservatives had good reasons to do this. Conservatives wanted to take credit for the change in direction on domestic spending by the federal government. Liberals, by contrast, were unhappy about the cuts; they tended to overstate their magnitude in order to alert their supporters to the need to fight further cuts and in some areas reverse the policy changes made in 1981.

12. The sample for this study also includes forty local governments (urban, suburban, and rural) within the fourteen states.

13. In a few instances, total public spending for some services actually rose, as state and local governments increased expenditures out of own-source revenues in response either to proposed federal cuts that never materialized or to cuts whose impact was delayed due to forward funding.

turned out, however, the recession was short-lived. When the recovery came, many state and local governments were relatively flush. Moreover, because policy changes made in Washington always take time to play out through the system, it was not until the economic recovery was well under way that many of the cuts in federal programs made in 1981 (to the extent federal aid was reduced) began to be felt. The timing of the impact of the cuts was fortuitous from the point of view of those who support domestic social programs.

This volatile pattern of state and local spending produced full coffers at the state level and for many localities at just the time they began to feel the effects of Reagan's 1981 federal aid cuts. Even though these cuts were not that large for state and local operating and capital programs (the cuts hit much harder for entitlement, or welfare-type, programs), many states and localities were in a good position to consider claims from groups that either experienced federal aid cuts or feared them.

An important behavioral observation needs to be added at this juncture. Retrenchment involves more than money: *It sends a signal*. Reagan sent a signal to the domestic public sector that the federal government should and would do less, and that states and localities and nonprofit institutions that provide social services should do more. It is not surprising that the politics of social programs changed to reflect the seriousness that service providers attributed to Reagan's policies. Increasingly, the proponents of social programs—health, education, welfare, day care, employment and training, community development, the environment—turned to others for succor. In particular, claims were made at the state level at just the time that many states could respond to them.

It will take a while before census and other data on state and local government finances can be analyzed to determine the magnitude of state responses to these new and stronger claims. Moreover, such analysis is never easy because of the large number of factors that influence governmental finance. The evidence from the available data and from the Princeton research suggests that even in states regarded as politically moderate (and in some cases even conservative) efforts were made to have states take a more active part in fiscal, programmatic, and institutional affairs than they had previously taken in response to Reagan's policies.

Thirty-eight states raised taxes in 1983. According to the U.S. Bureau of the Census, the tax revenues of state governments in 1984 showed a dramatic 14.8 percent increase in 1984. Focusing on the condition of state finances in 1984, Steven D. Gold and Corina L. Eckl note a marked improvement: "State finances are in much better shape today than they have been in the past several years, but the improvement is not universal and it follows an extended period of severe fiscal stress. The upturn is the result of the unexpectedly vigorous economic recovery, large tax increases in 1983, and restraint in spending. Many states took advantage of their stronger financial position in 1984 to increase spending, satisfying some of the pent-up demands which had been frustrated during the fiscal crises of earlier years'' (Gold and Eckl 1984, 1). Writing in the fall of 1984, Gold and Eckl expect the increase in state revenue to carry over to expenditures, with education being the major area of increased spending.

To summarize the issues considered in this section, it appears that no decided change has occurred in the overall level of domestic public spending. Rather, there has been a plateau in this spending. This plateau, assuming it continues, is of considerable importance. In the fiscal 1985 budget, which was sent to Congress at the beginning of Reagan's reelection year, budget director David Stockman included a new chapter entitled ''Budget Program and Trends.'' Although it is long, it is worth quoting here what Stockman had to say about how the Reagan administration saw itself as reversing the tide of domestic spending: (*Budget* 1985, 3-2).

> After three budget rounds, the explosive domestic budget growth of the three decades prior to 1980 has clearly been contained. Constant dollar domestic spending doubled between 1954 and 1961; doubled again by 1971; and nearly doubled again by 1981. But after completion of most congressional action on the 1984 budget, real domestic spending now stands lower than in 1981. And if the policies proposed in the President's 1985 budget are adhered to, there will be essentially *no growth* in real terms through 1989. Thus, after an era in which the real cost of government *doubled three times* in less than three decades, the shift in national policy inaugurated by the Reagan administration will result in a *decade long domestic real spending freeze*.
>
> Moreover, this abrupt halt to the runaway momentum of domestic government is now built into the structure of the budget—even if the modest additional savings proposed for 1985 and out-years are not fully implemented by Congress.

Summary of Effects of Federalism

Institutional changes take time to become manifest. Nevertheless, I believe that when one looks back at this period it will be seen as one in which state governments have taken on a larger role in the domestic public sector. Ample historical precedent supports this prediction. In earlier conservative periods, such as the 1880s and the 1920s, it was the states that took on new and additional social responsibilities in circumstances in which the federal government was not active or even was retrenching. Not all states took this lead, but it was the case for many of them.

Research by political scientists shows that historically the more affluent, older states, which also tend to be the most politically competitive and progressive ones, have been the major innovators.[14] In the current period these generalizations apply in the case of the states in the Princeton study. But there is also increasing evidence that other states, which are becoming politically more progressive or moderate in the current period, are also changing because the state government is playing a more active role in major program areas.

A SUMMING UP

The authors of the chapters in this volume are very close to the events we seek to interpret. Nonetheless, I believe that, barring some earthshaking development, the Reagan presidency has now set in place changes in the nation's political institutions that are likely to have lasting effects.

President Reagan's main contribution is in demonstrating that the executive office can work. He came to the office during a period in which the legacies of Vietnam and Watergate, and the defeat of two successive incumbents who stood for reelection (Ford and Carter), had raised serious doubts about the ability of a president to deal with the steadily increasing pressures.

It is difficult in retrospect to generalize regarding the public's expectations about Reagan's likely prospects in this setting. My recollection is that many close observers of the Washington scene and system saw Reagan as a media success who would be overwhelmed by the immense substantive and managerial demands of the presidency. It is therefore surprising, at least to this observer, that Reagan's abilities—to seize important opportunities, to hold the initiative, to select and motivate his principal subordinates, and to win the confidence and respect (indeed affection) of the public—have restored a belief that an extraordinary, but mortal, person can give leadership and a sense of direction to the American national government from the office of the presidency.

Looking more specifically at the approach that President Reagan has taken to organize and operate the executive office, I note several aspects of his approach that should in my opinion influence future practice. The artful combination of skills of the members of Reagan's first-term troika indicates a need for balancing different qualities among the president's top advisors, that is critical to the maintenance of judgment and perspective in the White House. Had Nixon surrounded himself with a similarly balanced group of senior advisors, Watergate very likely would not have happened. The dispersal, but retention, of the members of this troika (Deaver on a part-time başis) after Reagan's reelection and the centralization of White House au-

---

14. See Walker (1969) and Gary (1973).

thority under Donald Regan seemed to me to produce problems at the beginning of the second term, suggesting that the organizing principle of the initial White House troika group has considerable validity.

Reagan has used the budget process and has blended the three main strategies discussed in this chapter (legislative, administrative, and judicial) and in so doing has avoided rigidities. This is very important. It reflects a sense of timing and of what the president can readily control (contrasted to the more intellectual Carter and Nixon approaches) that demonstrate how necessary political skills are to the effective operation of the presidency. In particular, President Reagan and his principal lieutenants, in a fairly quiet (but emphatic) way, have taken advantage of the appointive powers of the presidency in the administrative sphere to implement the policies of the federal government; this effective strategy highlights the conservative values and principal objectives of the Reagan administration's policies in domestic affairs. This is an underutilized, and in my view, appropriate leadership strategy for the presidency. When the favored ideology shifts back to a more liberal stance on domestic issues, liberals will do well to take a leaf from this page of the Reagan presidency manual.

I have noticed a tendency for people who do not agree with President Reagan's policies to give grudging respect to his standing with the public and to the effectiveness of his administration, but then to say that it is President Reagan's subordinates, not Reagan himself, who deserve the credit. My view is that this is wrong. No one can do the job of the president for him; the presidency cannot be delegated.

One has to be impressed, I believe, by Ronald Reagan's handling of the presidency, not because everything has worked like a charm, but because the office is so immensely difficult. In these terms, I believe that Reagan's performance should be given high marks; whether one agrees or disagrees with his policies, we should be grateful for his resuscitation of the office of the presidency. This does not mean that successors in the office will do as well or better than he has done. The American political system does not have a long memory. Events change. Personality and personal characteristics, which are so important to the conduct of high office, cannot be taught or predicted. President Reagan has changed attitudes toward the executive office and has demonstrated skills and tactics that are likely to be useful to future incumbents, but this is not the same as having made a fundamental structural change that will influence future presidents. The transmission process of what appears to have worked for Reagan is a subtle one, but there is such a thing as learning from experience, and in the case of the Reagan presidency, that is desirable in the institutional framework of this analysis.

The review in this chapter of Ronald Reagan's effects on American federalism also indicates that a major shift has occurred. Yet an irony is revealed in the analysis. On the one hand, Reagan's effectiveness in office has produced a decided shift in spending priorities as defense spending has risen and federal domestic spending (much of it in the form of grants-in-aid) has plateaued and in some areas fallen off. On the other hand, evidence also indicates that the administration's retrenchment and devolutionary policies, in the way that they have come together, have had a stimulative effect on spending at the state and local levels, particularly at the state level. The equilibrating tendency revealed here between these retrenchment and devolutionary goals shows how hard it is to make changes in the American political system. Ronald Reagan has been an effective leader in Washington in putting his stamp on the domestic policies of the U.S. national government, but in a real sense his stamp appears to have been canceled—not fully but partially— by state and local policies and actions.

REFERENCES

Aberbach, Joel D., and Bert A. Rockman. 1976. "Clashing Beliefs within the Executive Branch: The Nixon Administration Bureaucracy," *American Political Science Review*. 70:466–67.

Anderson, Martin. 1984. "The Objectives of the Reagan Administration's Social Welfare Policy." In D. Lee Bawdin, ed., *The Social Contract Revisited*. Washington, D.C.: Urban Institute Press.

Beer, Samuel H. 1982. "Forword." In John William Ellwood, ed., *Reductions in U.S. Domestic Spending*. New Brunswick, New Jersey: Transaction Books.

Budget of the United States Government, Fiscal Year 1986. 1985. Washington, D.C.: U.S. Government Printing Office.

Cannon, Lou. 1982. *Reagan*. New York: G.P. Putnam.

Chubb, John E., and Paul E. Peterson. 1985. "Realignment and Institutionalization." In John E. Chubb and Paul E. Peterson, eds., *New Directions in American Politics*. Washington, D.C.: Brookings Institution.

Congressional Quarterly. 1981. February 23: 177.

Gold, Steven D., and Corina L. Eckl. 1984. "State Budget Actions in 1984." Fiscal Affairs Program, National Conference of State Legislatures. Legislative paper 5. September.

Gray, Virginia. 1973. "Innovation in the States: A Diffusion Study." *American Political Science Review* 67: 1174–85.

Greenstein, Fred I. 1983. "The Need for an Early Appraisal of the Reagan Presidency." In Fred I. Greenstein, ed., *The Reagan Presidency, An Early Assessment*. Baltimore, Maryland: Johns Hopkins University Press.

Grodzins, Morton. 1960. "The Federal System." In President's Commission on National Goals. *Goals for Americans*. New York: Columbia University Press.

Kraft, Michael E., and Norman J. Vig. 1984. "Environmental Policy in the Reagan Presidency." *Political Science Quarterly* 99(3): 429.

Long, Norton. 1952. "Bureaucracy and Constitutionalism," *American Political Science Review* 46(3): 808–18.

Miller, Nathan. 1983. *FDR: An Intimate History*. New York: Doubleday.

Nathan, Richard. 1983. *The Administrative Presidency*. New York: Wiley. Chaps. 1–4.

Nathan, Richard P., and Fred C. Doolittle. 1984. "Overview: Effects of the Reagan Domestic Program on States and Localities." Unpublished document. Princeton, New Jersey: Princeton Urban and Regional Research Center. June 7.

Nathan, Richard P., Fred C. Doolittle, and Associates. 1983. *The Consequences of Cuts*. Princeton, New Jersey: available through Princeton University Press.

Pear, Robert. 1985a. "Senate Committee Rejects Reynolds for Justice Post." *New York Times*. June 28.

Pear, Robert, 1985b. "U.S. and San Diego Get Hiring Change." *New York Times*. May 9.

Reischauer, Robert D. 1984. "The Congressional Budget Process." In Gregory B. Mills and John L. Palmer, eds., *Federal Budget Policy in the 1980s*. Washington, D.C.: Urban Institute Press.

Sorenson, Theodore C. 1963. *Decision-Making in the White House: The Olive Branch or the Olives?* New York: Random House.

Walker, Jack L. 1969. "The Diffusion of Innovation among the American States." *American Political Science Review* 63: 880–99.

THE EUROPEAN WELFARE STATE IN TRANSITION

Robert Haveman, Barbara Wolfe, and Victor Halberstadt

This chapter focuses on the industrialized economies of Western Europe and their performance in the years since 1975. The specific focus here is on the interaction of these economies and the structure and operation of the welfare states that have come to characterize many of them. The patterns are complex and confusing. Western Europe policymakers have neither a clear, common understanding of the nature of the interaction between the welfare state and economic performance nor a clear, common vision of how to improve economic performance while maintaining the gains in security and equity that the welfare state yields.

There is little doubt that the existing structure of the welfare state in these countries has contributed to their current economic problems but there is little agreement about the precise ways in which the welfare state has inhibited economic performance. Moreover, the poor economic performance has at least a dozen other contributors including the OPEC oil crisis, increased competition from newly industrialized countries, stricter environmental regulations, and expectations based on previous full-employment policies that encouraged trade unions to act as if they could not price themselves out of the market (see Lindbeck 1985). Similarly, there is no agreement on corrective policies.

The authors wish to thank many persons who provided data and comments on this paper: A. Atkinson, I. Byatt, J. Dekkers, G. Eliasson, C. Gillion, K. Goudswaard, B. Hofman, J. LeGrand, A. Lindbeck, J. Martin, J. Palmer, D. Ramparkash, G. Reid, T. Smeeding, E. Wadensjo, R. Walker, T. Wilson, and H. van der Kar.

We do not seek here to settle the question of how and to what extent one factor—the welfare state—has contributed to poor economic performance. Rather, we seek only to clarify the issues in the debate.

In the first section, we describe both the post–World War II growth of Western European welfare states and the post–1975 decline in economic performance. These facts are easily set down. We focus our discussion on three European states that span the range of economic performance, the magnitude of the welfare state relative to the economy, and the nature of recent policy responses: the Netherlands, Sweden, and the United Kingdom. Although these three countries illustrate the trends that can be observed in nearly all industrialized countries, they cannot be said to represent the complex and diverse "Western European picture."

In the second section, we characterize the dominant perspectives encountered today in these three Western European states regarding the welfare state and its impact on economic performance. In most cases, economic analysis at some level supports these perspectives. We indicate some of the linkages that are identified in each case, and offer a historically based perspective on the effectiveness of the current welfare state.

In the third section, we attempt to characterize the main remedies that present themselves. We then discuss the welfare state policies that have been implemented over the past several years in the three countries. This is more easily said than done. For example, although "retrenchment" of the welfare state in the interests of economic performance rolls off the tongues of policymakers in the Netherlands, Sweden, and the United Kingdom, to date relatively little "retrenchment" can be found.

Finally, we summarize our findings and speculate on the future of welfare state policies in Western Europe.

WELFARE STATES AND ECONOMIC PERFORMANCE: GROWTH AND DECLINE

The commitment to the welfare state in most Western European countries is far more fundamental and comprehensive than it is in the United States. It includes a view that the measure of a civilized society is its success in securing an above-subsistence standard of living for all its citizens, regardless of their circumstances, misfortunes, or even imprudence. In this view, a society should be judged by the extent to which it has eliminated poverty. A minimum income guarantee along with a child benefit (payable for all children under a particular age) characterizes most of these systems. Equality of opportunity is generally extended through all levels of schooling, with (nearly) free tuition for everyone at all levels, including universities. In addition, many countries provide a grant to students for living expenses while they are attending universities. Private financing of health care is more restricted than in the United States, and full public coverage is generally available for persons with limited resources. Employment, once provided, is frequently protected by regulations that make it difficult and costly to fire a worker.

In Sweden, a wage policy has been implemented to narrow pay differentials. Housing benefits ensure that a decent standard of housing can be financed; sickness benefits ensure income during illness that lasts more than a few days; maternity benefits provide income when a parent takes leave from work to care for an infant; one-parent benefits provide extra funds for single persons raising a child alone; generous pensions are paid to the retired and disabled. In addition, health and safety standards in the workplace, safety regulations on mass transit and private automobiles, and extensive environmental controls protect people from externalities caused by market failures.

These measures have both economic and equity rationales. Public regulation and expenditures to improve environmental quality are required because environmental services are not privately appropriable and exchangeable for a price in the market. Provision and regulation of health care are required because families have insufficient income to purchase minimally accepted levels of care, because health problems have spillover effects, because private insurance may be unavailable for certain groups or insufficient to induce appropriate levels of care, and because individuals have insufficient information to judge the appropriateness of care. Large income differences generated by inequality in ability, education, and training, in combination with unregulated market rewards, are viewed as leading to conflict between social groups. Hence, the true "solidarity" is often cited as the underlying basis for the welfare state. The welfare state is thus viewed as contributing to reducing uncertainty and income differences; increasing economic stability and social cohesion; facilitating technological change; and increasing human capital via education, health care, nutrition, housing, environmental quality, and occupational health and safety.

As defined, this concept of the welfare state is a broad one and incorporates everything from social security to education, health, and housing; welfare and progressive taxation; direct job creation and manpower policies; regulations constraining the firing of employees; and subsidies to troubled enterprises, sectors, and regions. In the remainder of this chapter, we discuss primarily expenditure programs that are designed to directly affect individual and social welfare.

The appendix table to the chapter shows how welfare state expenditure programs for the Netherlands, the United Kingdom, and Sweden have grown absolutely and relatively since the early postwar period. The growth of the nonspending components of the welfare state is more difficult to document, but these components are also an integral part of the welfare state, especially in the Netherlands and Sweden.

If the figures for the three countries are averaged, the welfare state programs grew from about 11 percent of gross domestic product (GDP) in 1950 to more than 26 percent in 1970 (the increase in the Netherlands and Sweden, however, was much greater than that in the United Kingdom). This period was one of optimism in Western Europe: economies were recovering from the war and growing rapidly; employment was high, unemployment low. The public spending required to build the welfare state could and was largely financed out of the dividends of economic growth. Citizens enjoyed both the increasing disposable income and the benefits of expanding social programs.

Even though labor productivity expanded by 5 percent per year in Western Europe from 1960 into the mid–1970s—reflecting the adoption of new technologies already used elsewhere, low energy costs, falling trade barriers, and a rapid flow of rural labor into urban manufacturing—clouds began to appear on the horizon. Newly industrializing countries became more competitive, inflation rose, and investment opportunities became less profitable. Because governments had accepted responsibility for maintaining full employment, labor unions began to seek and firms to grant wage increases beyond the limits of productivity increases. In addition, employers began bearing increased nonwage labor costs in the form of social insurance contributions. Employment growth faltered.

The years from 1973 to 1975 marked a turning point. Fourfold oil price increases as well as higher prices for other raw materials raised production costs, upset trade balances, and made a capital stock constructed for a cheap energy regime obsolete. Profits fell, and instead of seeking to offset the lost demands through fiscal and monetary measures, governments waged an uncoordinated fight against inflation through tight monetary policy, thereby further reducing demand, employment, and productivity growth. Although public spending rose dramatically after 1973, much of the increase resulted from citizen claims for the unemployment, disability, and retirement benefits to which they were entitled if these contingencies struck. Some of the increase stemmed from the failure of the Western Europe states to recognize the passing of the old regime; instead, benefits in welfare state programs were made more generous, coverage of the population more comprehensive, and the regulations governing benefit awards more lenient.

The budgetary problem was also exacerbated by the interaction of demographic and economic changes that increased the nonactive relative to the active population. As life expectancy increased, the population over age sixty-five grew rapidly relative to the working population, and so did the demands for health care, retirement pensions, and independent living arrangements.[1] As employers sought to contain rising labor costs, they released older workers more rapidly than they hired young ones. Demands for disability, early retirement, extended schooling, and unemployment benefits rose rapidly. Women joined the labor force in unpredicted and unprecedented numbers, both as full-time and part-time workers, and with this change the demands for day care for children and home care for the elderly expanded rapidly.[2] All along the line, the demands for welfare state benefits increased; at the same time the governments increased the supply of benefits to accommodate the increased demand as if nothing had changed in the ability of the economies to support this growth. By 1980, welfare state programs accounted for about 35 percent of the combined economy represented by the three countries, having doubled since 1960. By contrast, the comparable figure for the United States was 21 percent, although this figure also represented a near doubling of social program expenditures since 1960.

It is important to distinguish between the different sources of welfare state growth before and after 1973. Before 1973, the growing economic base generated an increased supply of welfare state services that created its own demand; after 1973, an increased supply was required to meet the growing demand for benefits caused in part by an economic base that had ceased to grow, in part by demographic changes, and in part by an illusion that poor economic performance was only a temporary phenomenon that did not imply the need for welfare state retrenchment. This crucial distinction was not recognized until well after it occurred; the lag in recognition—and the continuation of welfare state business-as-usual until the early 1980s—is now widely viewed as a major source of the current problems.

Only after 1980 did realism set in, and then it was combined with disillusionment. With the United States and Western Europe locked in stagflation set off by another round of oil price increases in the late–1970s, economic developments were largely beyond the control of any single country. Hence, the disillusionment. The realization also grew that the trend toward lower employment and a larger inactive and dependent population could not continue indefinitely. Welfare state policies would have to be bent toward

---

1. From 1962 to 1982 the population 65 years old or older increased from 9.3 to 11.7 percent in the Netherlands; from 12.1 to 16.6 in Sweden; and from 11.7 to 15.0 in the United Kingdom, respectively.

2. Women's labor force participation reached 76 percent in Sweden, 39 percent in the Netherlands, and 59 percent in the United Kingdom as of 1982, up from 62, 31, and 52 percent, respectively, in 1972.

increasing productive employment and the ratio of active to inactive population, or welfare state benefits would simply have to be cut back. Without such adjustments, the inexorable cycle in which poor economic performance leads to increased demand for benefits, which requires increased taxes, which further retards economic performance could not be avoided. Although the post–1980 rhetoric in Sweden tended to emphasize increasing productive employment, some government leaders in the Netherlands and the United Kingdom spoke of reducing the options for inactivity and making the options that remained less attractive. Whatever the official rhetoric, the welfare state's role in the economic growth process—as well as the Keynesian view that welfare state measures would act as automatic stabilizers—was being increasingly questioned by the end of the 1970s.

This questioning continued into the next decade, and by 1985, many Western Europeans were ready to rethink the goals and components of the welfare state. At one extreme was the increasing—and increasingly vocal—population which saw the welfare state and its dependents to be the main culprits in the lagging economic performance. This group saw the welfare state as breeding a new generation of weak people—people who were largely devoid of drive, the desire to pursue excellence, and the willingness to roll up their sleeves and contribute to the national enterprise, people who were content to remain dependent on cumulated government benefits and the security of the welfare state.

Analysts began to question both the incentives incorporated into the welfare state—which discouraged hard work, saving, enterprise, and risk taking—and the taxes required to finance it. Others charged that the increased bureaucratic and administrative costs and regulations associated with the growth of the welfare state had to be lifted from the backs of citizens and enterprises if economic vitality was to be restored. Still others mainly questioned the inflexibilities and increased costs of labor market policies, some of which had been designed to foster full employment but which now seemed to breed unemployment.

A few analysts and many policymakers advocated a continuation of generous welfare state interventions to achieve the goals of reduced uncertainty, poverty, and inequality. Some people denied that the welfare state had generated adverse side effects, others believed that the benefits of welfare state programs simply outweighed the costs. Although many commentators, analysts, and policymakers have eventually concluded that the structure and growth of the welfare state could be inhibiting economic progress, the policy debate has not been carried out in such explicit terms. It is to that debate that we now turn.

SORTING OUT PERSPECTIVES

The welfare state in Western Europe is an important concept, principle, and symbol. Until the early 1980s, policymakers in Western Europe could not voice the view that continued welfare state growth might interfere with economic performance without risking a loss of political support. Although that was no longer the case after the mid–1980s, most citizens in the three countries on which we have focused appear to persist in viewing the welfare state as a strongly rooted, unique, humane, and civilized accomplishment. There appears to be little erosion of support in these countries for the reduction of poverty and inequality, reduction in income uncertainty, and increased insulation from the vagaries of the market, disease, ignorance, and chance—at least as objectives to be sought after. Indeed, many people believe that some reduction in economic performance is a small price to pay to achieve these goals; still others do not believe there is a negative link between these programs and economic performance, but only that poor economic performance increases the importance of these programs.

In the Western European context, criticism of the welfare state is muted. Numerous linkages between the welfare state and economic performance are alluded to, perhaps most directly in terms of constraints on labor market demand, but quantitative research on the magnitude of these linkages is relatively rare, and those who speak or write about labor supply and saving incentives rely almost exclusively on U.S. research and studies.[3] Nevertheless, we attempt in this section to summarize the range of viewpoints that have been expressed and the economic arguments that support them.

The Welfare State: Problems of Efficiency and Equity

There are several variants of the overall view that because the welfare state has developed a variety of efficiency and equity problems, reforms are in order. One such variant focuses on adverse incentives. Advocates of this perspective emphasize that the welfare state and the taxes required to finance it have exposed the highest and lowest income groups to high marginal tax rates that have eroded initiative and work effort. This situation is seen as the result of a combination of numerous factors: income-conditioned benefits, multiple and overlapping programs targeted on the low-income population,

3. For a rare exception see Wolfe et al. (1984). Indeed, in a recent book evaluating the case for the privatization of welfare state measures in Western Europe, LeGrand and Robinson state, "the impact of the welfare state on incentives is an empirical question that cannot be solved a priori. The available evidence [is] mostly American." See LeGrand and Robinson (1984, 10–11).

highly progressive income taxation, high replacement rates in the social insurance programs, lenient application of eligibility criteria, and extended
duration of coverage (for instance, in unemployment programs). As a result
of these incentives, an excessive demand for benefits exists and, hence,
excessive levels of benefit recipiency and welfare state expenditures. Workers
once out of the active population (unemployed or disabled) and receiving
transfers are reluctant to move back into employment if jobs are available.

In a related view, the welfare state is seen as having become unwieldy,
bureaucratized, and administratively inefficient. The multiplication of programs and the taxes required to finance them have led to an enormous amount
of "income cross-hauling"; representative households in all classes pay a
high proportion of their income in taxes and receive extensive transfers and
publically provided services. The administration of the *gross* flows absorbs
some of their potential equalizing effect, while the reduction in *net* income
differences is far smaller than the gross flows imply. Moreover, the direct
provision of services to people has reduced freedom of choice in the delivery
of these services and has constrained the search for alternative approaches to
help people entitled to benefits. Direct provision by government agencies not
only reduces the incentives for service provision to be efficient and innovative,
but also reduces the ability of consumers to convey their preferences regarding
the character and quantity of the services they want.

Related to these views is yet another line of criticism: the welfare state
provides a wide variety of programs with overlapping objectives. These programs, it is argued, are uncoordinated, unintegrated, and sometimes inconsistent. As a result, programs and their constituencies compete for funds,
driving up aggregate spending. Moreover, people must deal with several
administrative bureaucracies, each with its own income and household definitions and means tests. Because benefits can be cumulated, are means tested,
and may be highly taxed if other income is received, some families may
receive high benefits without working; a "poverty trap" is created, and
program and budget costs are excessive. Given the enormous money flows
involved, it is argued that the objectives of reducing poverty and inequality
could be accomplished with far less budgetary cost.

Another inefficiency view of the welfare state argues that social policy
measures are excessively costly because they supply benefits or subsidies to
people who could well afford to pay for them. Because of this lack of targeting,
the reduction of poverty and inequality obtained for any level of budgetary
outlay is less than it could be. This perspective, it should be noted, poses a
direct challenge to the principle of "universality" as well as to the principle
of income-graduated benefits, which have guided the evolution of much of
the welfare state in Western Europe.

Other critics focus on the labor market-profit squeeze—the linkage of growing welfare state benefits; their financing through employer-based, non-wage labor impositions; and inflexible bargained wages. The argument is that the financing of the welfare state—largely through payroll taxes and employer-borne contributions—raises the cost of labor and hence reduces the quantity of it that is demanded.[4] Moreover, when money wages do not adjust to market forces and product price adjustment is constrained (because international markets dominate sales for these open economies), profits will be squeezed by the increased employer levies. Investment, output, and labor demand will then be reduced. The resulting unemployment and economic slowdown will simultaneously increase the demand for benefits, lead to higher levies to pay for them, and thus increase the nonwage labor costs associated with the employment of the remaining workers.

A "consequence" of these high taxes is an increased incentive to avoid paying them. Thus critics of welfare state policy point to the potential linkage between the welfare state and the growth of the underground economy.[5] High income taxes and employee-based social security contributions cause a large gap between gross and net incomes for workers. As a result workers have an incentive to work informally, not reporting the income and not paying the taxes on it. The price of services in the underground economy is lower than the price in the formal economy, benefiting buyers; simultaneously, the providers of services receive increased net income. At the same time, workers in the formal economy pay the "full cost" of unemployment and other benefits—and the costs are higher on the smaller base. This dynamic carries its own incentive to go "black"— to enter the unreported (and untaxed) sector. The implied erosion of the formal economy also has adverse effects on economic reporting and the accuracy of statistics on economic performance; and the misinformation that these statistics then yield can bias the formation of economic policymaking.

The Welfare State, A Source of Alienation

A different but related viewpoint is the alienation perspective. Because of a large and generous welfare state, it is argued, alienation between the active and inactive population grows. Some of the people who work and are independent of the welfare state have come to view themselves as fools when

---

4. These are particularly high in the Netherlands and Sweden, where the employer's social security contributions were 16.2 and 21.3 percent of the employee compensation in 1982 (OECD 1984).

5. Fase (1984) and Feige and McGee (1982) estimate that the unreported economy in the Netherlands is some 10 to 20 percent of GDP; Dilnot and Morris (1981) suggest it is 7.5 percent of GDP in the United Kingdom. For a more general discussion, see Frey and Weck (1983).

they see other people similar to themselves living at about the same level without working, depending instead on welfare-state benefits. The resentment is reinforced when the same active population is required to pay higher taxes, and those taxes are used to support the inactive population.

This alienation can be augmented further if the behavior of the inactive, dependent group is viewed as antisocial or immoral. The receipt of publicly provided benefits by squatters, youths with no experience or interest in labor market attachment and with unconventional interests and life-styles, and people viewed as consciously "working the system" erodes general support for welfare state measures.

The Welfare State: Just Fine, Thank You

A quite different perspective is the view that nothing—or almost nothing—is wrong with the welfare state. A few changes might improve the system—some involving spending reductions and others involving increases—but the basic structure of welfare state programs should be maintained. These programs, it is believed, are *not* the principal cause of economic problems, but even if they were, the shortfall in economic performance is a small price to pay for the elimination of poverty and the "solidarity" that the welfare state creates. Advocates of this view maintain that the growth in welfare state spending is caused by poor economic performance, especially the lack of employment, and not the other way around. Thus unemployment, disability, and early retirement benefits rolls grow because the economies are failing to provide jobs—*not* because benefits induce workers to drop out of the labor force voluntarily. The beneficiaries are victims of the economic system and, as is appropriate in any civilized society, have the right to receive benefits to allow them to maintain a decent standard of living.

To advocates of this position, the benefits of welfare state programs clearly outweigh the costs. Minor retrenchments aimed at middle-class beneficiaries— for example, taxing benefits on consumption benefits such as housing—or changes to reflect the increased labor force participation of women in recent years may be acceptable. At the same time, advocates of this perspective argue for other reforms that would increase welfare state expenditures—for example, improved child support for single-parent or single-earner families.[6]

---

6. Advocates of this view include Bradshaw (1985) and Townsend (1984), both of the United Kingdom, who suggest improving targeting of benefits via eliminating special married women's tax allowances and setting limits on tax relief for mortgages and on contributions to private pension plans. Townsend argues that post-tax incomes are too unequal (in the United Kingdom) and that if the richest 20 percent were taxed more heavily, the disposable income of the poorest 20 percent could be doubled.

A number of these defenders of the welfare state are critical of politicians who support retrenchment policies. The cutbacks that are proposed or enacted, they believe, have been determined primarily on the grounds of political expediency. As a result, the cuts have not been tied to careful analyses of benefits and costs in relation to the goals of the welfare state, but rather to the ease with which the cuts could be made. Because universal benefits are less politically vulnerable than means-tested or otherwise targeted programs, the former are the least likely to be cut, despite their relative ineffectiveness.[7] Thus, the persons most in need of transfers tend to face the greatest cuts.[8]

Welfare state defenders also maintain that public sector efforts to align and improve the structure of transfer programs have been hampered by public and parliamentary opposition. As proposed selective program reforms that may be economically justified, especially those affecting private sector workers, have encountered strong opposition, legislatures under pressure to reduce expenditures have responded by enacting across-the-board reductions.[9] Again, benefits to the most vulnerable groups are reduced, thereby undermining the fundamental goals of the welfare state.

The requirement of equal treatment (by sex) in social security imposed by the European Community on all its members (the "Third Directive" adopted in December 1978 to be implemented by December 1984) has also caused changes that are not necessarily in keeping with the fundamental goals of the welfare state. The directive requires the elimination of discrimination between men and women in terms of eligibility for benefits; obligation to contribute to the financing of the benefits; level and duration of benefits; and insurance of dependents in social security coverage of sickness, incapacity, unemployment, and old age. Some people believe that politicians have taken advantage of this requirement in order to modify benefit schedules and, in

---

7. LeGrand (1984) provides evidence that in the United Kingdom welfare state spending cuts have occurred in programs that both benefit low-income persons and are supplied by low-income persons (such as public housing and personal social services). He argues that those programs benefiting or provided by middle-income persons (such as national health services, education, old age pensions) are largely untouched. He provides evidence that, from 1979–80 to 1983–84, real expenditures on public housing were cut by 58 percent, education expenditures remained constant, and medical and social services increased by 13 percent.

8. An even more jaundiced view of negative consequences of the unequal distribution of cuts in social benefits is termed the "Matthew effect" (the Gospel of Matthew, chapter 13, verse 12: "Because to those who possess will be given and they will have in abundance; but those who do not possess will even be deprived of the little they have.") According to this view, cutbacks are the result of a political decision-making process whereby the more strongly organized groups succeed in maintaining (or creating) social services that are in the interest of its members, at the expense of those less powerful or organized. See DeLeeck (1984).

9. See Halberstadt, Goudswaard, and LeBlanc (1984) for a fuller discussion and evidence on these across-the-board cuts. See also Wolfe et al. (1984).

the process, to cloak benefit cuts (in the Netherlands) or to camouflage benefit increases (in the United Kingdom).

The Modern Welfare State: Out of Date

Our own view might be termed the "need for modernization" perspective. Although this view is implicit in many of the other perspectives on the problems of the welfare state, we suggest it as an independent and coherent one. The issues that are raised by it are fundamental to understanding the basic reforms that have been proposed.

Essentially, we suggest that the current welfare state is out of date; that the demographic, labor market, family-household, and economic conditions that existed when the welfare states were designed in the early postwar period no longer exist; and that the welfare state needs to be modernized to reflect these new and changed conditions. Consider, first, a little history.

The Beveridge Report in the United Kingdom in the 1940s (Beveridge 1942), as well as Germany's social insurance system legislated under Bismarck in the 1880s, substantially influenced the thinking that underlay the formation of all of the Western European welfare states. Whereas prewar welfare policies focused on helping destitute people, the Beveridge Report emphasized the *prevention* of destitution. The state was to provide merit goods considered essential for growth in economic productivity—education and medical care—to people as a matter of right, in the belief that, individually, people could or would not purchase or produce enough of these. Similarly, a state role was viewed as essential in guaranteeing protection against income losses from events that were judged to be out of the individual's control— unemployment, sickness, disability, or retirement. Following Bismarck, cash transfers were designed to eliminate poverty defined in absolute rather than relative terms.

In implementing this approach, the early welfare state measures were geared to the traditional family unit. The breadwinner and his dependent wife and children were viewed as a stable unit over time. The worker—the male family head—was either employed or not, and if employed, worked full time, year round. He was employed in the formal economy, and earnings were therefore subject to taxation and social benefit contributions.

The benefits that welfare state programs provided for specified types of income losses were to be "legally claimed" by means of an insurance contribution paid by the employee or the employer, or both. This was the insurance principle stressed by Beveridge.

This vision of the welfare state presumed that the risks of unemployment, sickness, disability, and retirement were exogenous to the economy and society and that the level of risk would be steady over time. The social security systems were designed for economies in which there would be sporadic, but not massive, unemployment. Similarly, sickness, disability, and retirement were not viewed as subject to individual choice. It was presumed that there would be no behavioral responses to availability of transfers in the form of early retirement, reduced labor supply, or prolonged unemployment. Hence, the social insurance contributions required of employers were viewed as indirect wage levies, not as expenses affecting producer costs, prices and international competitiveness.

The costs of rearing children were viewed as unavoidable risks—analogous to income losses from health problems, retirement, or unemployment. The notion that people made choices regarding the number and spacing of children in response to financial incentives was not generally reflected in the design of welfare state programs, although some countries viewed child benefits as a profertility policy.

Because provision of benefits in the form of the dole carried stigma, the primary burden of support was to be through social insurance rather than public assistance.

In view of these common presumptions, it is not surprising that the early systems in each of the three countries under discussion shared certain characteristics. In all of them, for example, benefits for income losses from unemployment, disability, and retirement were flat rate rather than earnings related, and the level of benefits received was not tied to or conditioned on the worker's or spouse's income. Wives were not eligible for certain benefits, even if they worked and established a contribution record of their own. Children's allowances were provided with no consideration of incentives. There was, however, no special program to support single-parent families. The replacement rate of social insurance was a relatively high proportion of the national median wage. Social insurance premiums were paid by both employee and employer, and education, housing, and medical care benefits were financed out of the general fund and provided at very low user cost.

Today, some forty years later, the world looks quite different, and the common presumptions that guided the formation of the welfare state may no longer hold. As women entered the labor force in record numbers, the traditional one-earner family was no longer the dominant arrangement. Both young and old people established independent living arrangements, and state programs contributed much to the units' financial support.

The fall in fertility rates over the period complemented the increased work of women and, as a result of this work and rapid economic growth, family discretionary income increased. At the same time, life expectancy increased rapidly. Divorce rates climbed rapidly, and single-parent families became an increasing proportion of the total.

Economic changes accompanied these demographic trends. Although welfare state programs were designed to handle unemployment associated with normal business cycles, the massive, long-term unemployment that developed after 1973 could not be easily accommodated. Wage-setting arrangements had become revolutionized, powerful trade unions or tripartite (employer, union, government) bargaining arrangements kept wages from being reduced and often forced wage increases in excess of productivity gains. The availability of generous unemployment, disability, and pension benefits has induced reductions in labor supply and work effort, and has seriously eroded the incentive of persons receiving benefits to return to work when jobs become available. Because business bore the costs for welfare state measures through payroll-based levies, the substitution of capital for labor was encouraged; although productivity grew, employment did not. Profits became squeezed as increased costs could not be passed along in price increases; this was especially true for producers operating in world markets. And, as both income and payroll taxes rose, individuals and enterprises found it advantageous to operate outside normal economic channels, and the underground economy grew.

Finally, as the size of programs grew within each of the main welfare state areas of activity—education, health care, and housing—interest groups and their respective bureaucracies accumulated influence and power. These interests gained if benefits and services—and, hence, expenditures—could be expanded. These incentives interacted with the development of new and expensive technologies (especially in health care) and the provision of services at a zero price to generate enormous demand for increased public expenditures on welfare state programs.

In a variety of dimensions then—demographic, social, economic, and technological—the world for which the early welfare state had been designed had changed dramatically. To be sure, some modifications in policy had been implemented to accommodate these changes—early retirement, more accessible disability transfers, extended unemployment, day care, subsidization for independent elderly living, and provision for extended schooling. Yet, at its core, the welfare state designed in the 1940s represented an outmoded approach to new problems in a new environment. And although it eased the costs of transition and reduced the hurts of change, its structure contributed to the very problems it was designed to alleviate. Thus, reform—and some retrenchment—is required.

PROPOSED CHANGES IN THE WELFARE STATE

Associated with this cacophony of views of the welfare state and its interaction with the economy are an equally large number of strategies for its reform and overhaul. Each proposal has some underlying rationale and some view of the problem that motivates it; often but certainly not always, the analysis motivates the proposal.

It is difficult to identify and rank the large number of proposals that have been offered. They do not fit into neat categories; nor do related proposals rest on any single view of the root nature of the problem. Each is based on some combination of analysis and ideology. As with the perspectives, we attempt to impose some order on a debate in which there is no agreement on the nature of the problem or on the approach to be pursued.

Perhaps only one motivatation lies behind the plethora of proposed— but largely not enacted—strategies now on the political agenda in Western Europe: the view that high unemployment, low economic growth, and unprecedented deficits make budgetary—and, hence, welfare state—business-as-usual impossible. Because tax rates are already high, efforts to reduce the deficit through tax increases seem infeasible. Given the domination of the budget by welfare state programs, some retrenchment, reorganization, or reform of these measures seems to be an important option. Throughout the Western European debate, then, there is a consensus on only two points: that the aggregate budgetary costs of the welfare state need to be reduced and that, to the extent possible, the objectives and the basic nature of the welfare state need to be maintained. Because of differences in ideological commitment, the latter point has played a dominant role in Sweden and the Netherlands, whereas the former has dominated in the United Kingdom.

Decisiveness surely has not characterized this debate; no coherent philosophy, analysis, or ideology has guided the proposing or making of policy in this area in any of the countries studied. Indeed, the tentativeness of the steps taken or proposals made there has often been contrasted with the apparent decisiveness in U.S. policymaking in the 1980s. Many people admire the U.S. decisiveness while rejecting as "ruthless" the vision that has motivated U.S. policy measures; others admire both. A few disdain both the vision and the decisive measures.

The strategies that have been put forth in Western Europe span a wide range. Some virtually reduce the welfare state to a social insurance scheme, others actually expand it; some retain the current structure, others substitute a new (typically, simpler) structure for the existing mélange of programs;

some are concerned with incentives, others are not. Each proposal reflects multiple objectives, somehow but mysteriously weighted.

Improving Incentives for Work and Enterprise

A number of proposals, often made by economists, have suggested reforms designed to improve the incentive structure implicit in welfare state programs. These proposals typically involve some combination of measures that (1) reduce the replacement rates in unemployment, disability, and retirement pensions for workers with relatively high earnings; (2) tighten the criteria for eligibility for disability pensions and reduce the role of vocational characteristics or labor market conditions in gaining eligibility; (3) reduce the period of eligibility for unemployment benefits and accelerate the pace at which benefits fall to social minimum income levels; (4) reduce social minimum income in order to reduce the base level of social benefits; (5) replace separate benefit programs targeted on low-income persons with a simpler structure avoiding excessive cumulative tax rates; (6) increase categorization to focus benefits on groups not expected to work, as opposed to those who either are working or are expected to work; and (7) increase the flexibility of industry to hire and fire workers at competitively set rates.

The Simplification Strategy

In response to complaints about multiple and overlapping programs, complex administration, inconsistent definitions of income and family units among programs, and complex tax laws financing the welfare state, many plans have emphasized simplicity through program integration or substitution of a single program—a low-guarantee negative income tax or a "guaranteed bottom income"—for the multiple programs now in place. These proposals claim to alleviate poverty and to improve incentives, as well as to cut costs by reducing administrative needs. The single program to be substituted for others may well come with some reduced benefits, thus saving costs while potentially improving targeting.[10]

The Privatization Strategy

The move to privatize welfare state benefits is gaining support in the three countries under discussion here, especially in the United Kingdom and

---

10. See Parker (1983) for a proposal of this sort from the "right," Dilnot, Kay, and Morris (1984) for one from the "left."

to a lesser extent in the Netherlands. No simple characterization is possible, however, as the nature of the privatization proposed varies widely. The basic strategy, however, reflects the view that efficiency in provision improves when individuals have a more decisive role regarding the level and composition of their benefits and when private and competitive sources of supply are substituted for public provision. It also reflects the view that people today have more discretionary income, so governments have less need to be concerned about providing too little. The proposals involve a shift in provision (but not financing) such as the contracting out to private enterprises various welfare state activities—in particular, housing, education, home care, training, and health care—and a shift away from public toward private financing in other areas such as private insurance against income losses due to retirement and disability above some social minimum income level.[11]

The Alternative Financing Strategy

Opposition to the welfare state comes from employer groups who deplore the effects of financing welfare state benefits through mandatory levies placed on employers, especially in the context of inflexible bargained wages. Their typical solution is to seek alternative financial bases, such as spreading the employer-borne payroll taxes over other tax bases, for example, by increasing value-added taxes. An alternative approach involves the diversion of unemployment benefits into employment subsidies or public service employment, but this policy has little impact on budget costs. A stronger variant of this approach would be to reduce the constraints of those institutional arrangements with which the welfare state and its financing interact (namely, the rigid collective bargaining arrangements and high minimum wages).[12]

Often, changes in the welfare state are proposed in combination with other measures designed to improve economic performance. These include income policies (a traditional short-term suggestion to reduce wage demands), reduction of working hours (to reduce measured unemployment and labor costs),[13] relaxation of labor market constraints (to increase wage flexibility,

---

11. This latter idea—to publicly provide a minimum pension tied to a socially defined benefit level that guarantees at least a subsistence level and then facilitate private insurance—is part of a number of proposals but to date the idea has evoked little popular support. For an example of such a proposal, see the recent policy paper of the Netherlands Scientific Council for Government Policy (1985).

12. For example, the Netherlands has a tripartite collective bargaining arrangement under which the public sector, unions, and employers are all represented in the process by which terms of employment and reimbursement are determined.

13. One proposal advanced by a commission of the Dutch Labor Party chaired by Professor Joseph Ritzen argues for swiftly reducing the work week to twenty-five hours.

part-time work options, and to reduce the constraints on the ability of firms to reduce the work force), tax reform (to reduce work disincentives associated with high tax rates and to shrink the underground economy), general across-the-board budget cuts, import restrictions or export promotion or subsidization, and improved targeting and elimination of benefits to certain upper-income groups.

Clearly, little consensus exists regarding the interaction of the welfare state and the economy. The varied proposals obviously reflect the confused perspectives—not to mention the hunches, self-interests, and ideologies—on which they are based.

WHAT CHANGES HAVE OCCURRED IN THE WELFARE STATE

It would be surprising if the changes in the welfare state that had been implemented in recent years were more coherent than the perspectives and proposals that dominate the national debate. If anything, the changes that have been made have been less coherent than the perspectives and proposals are. The disparity between the official claims of retrenchment—which imply a concerted effort to control welfare state costs, improve incentives, and reduce benefits—and the policies actually implemented is considerable. In fact, few retrenchment policies with teeth have been implemented, even in the United Kingdom, where such discussion is most virulent. In this section, we seek to point out the changes actually in progress, and to explain why change—in particular, retrenchment—is so difficult.

Reindexing

Probably the most common form of retrenchment has been the reindexing of government transfer programs,[14] effectively decoupling these benefits from real wages. In the United Kingdom, pensions and long-term sickness benefits have been reindexed to prices rather than to the greater of prices and wages, while supplementary benefits (to working-age recipients) have been reindexed to exclude housing costs from the index. In Sweden, the base used for the index has been changed and the frequency of increases dropped from three times a year to once a year. In the Netherlands, the link between the net level of minimum guaranteed income and the minimum wage has been broken, so that the living standard of retired persons on pensions and the nonactive

---

14. See Wartonick and Packard (1983) for a discussion of reindexing in five industrialized countries.

working-age population supported by transfers will tend to erode relative to the standard of active labor force participants. As increases in wages outpace increases in prices, workers' relative position in the income distribution will tend to improve.

Privatization

A limited amount of privatization has occurred, particularly in the United Kingdom. The measures include the provision of ancillary services of the national health service, deregulation of public transport workers, closing of residential homes, and cuts in home help services. The first three of these were decisions of the central United Kingdom government; the last was a response by local government to pressure from the central government to cut total expenditures. All these measures have fallen heavily on the most disadvantaged service recipients and providers—those with the least political power. Little progress has been made in privatizing pensions, although substantial discussion has occurred.

"Individualizing" Benefits

In response to the mandate that men and women must be treated equally, both in terms of benefits received and taxes contributed, benefits have been "individualized" in the Netherlands and throughout Western Europe. In the Netherlands, there is now a social minimum for single persons, which serves as the basic safety net, as well as an individualized earnings-related employment benefit and an individualized retirement benefit. This change was carried out in a way to be budgetarily neutral, with little analysis or discussion of the redistribution consequences of these changes.

Modification of Benefits

Cuts in particular benefits have often led to budgetary increases elsewhere. The complexity and interdependence of income-conditioned benefits have, in fact, largely prevented real *net* budget cuts; attempts to cut benefits have generated only a change in type of benefits paid. Thus, a 10 percent cut in housing expenditure (including the selling off of council houses in the United Kingdom) led to an increase in rents paid and thus an increase in eligibility for means-tested assistance programs such as rent rebates and other social welfare programs. In the Netherlands, cuts in the social minimum benefit led to annual payments of a flat amount to persons below the social minimum income.

The official goal, often stated as the basis for considering changes in policies, is that such changes should not increase the inequality of the final income distribution. However, even with this official goal, proposals to cut benefits for politically powerful groups—the elderly or people represented by unions—generate substantial political opposition. Only policies that directly violate this objective—those aimed at weak groups such as the long-term unemployed, single-parent families, and people who have never worked—appear politically acceptable. An example is the benefit reductions for unemployed youths in the Netherlands in 1984; never-employed youths under age nineteen are no longer eligible for unemployment benefits (although they are eligible for the lower social minimum payment). Similarly, in Sweden, eighteen- and nineteen-year-olds now receive no government assistance unless they participate in team-based required work.

Reduction of Job Creation Policies

In most of Western Europe, job creation (or saving) policies are generally viewed as ineffective, having been tarred with the same brush as the failed subsidies to faltering firms. The Netherlands and the United Kingdom have reviewed these expensive "lame-duck subsidies" and found them generally to be ineffective and inefficient. As a result, these countries have become skeptical of employment subsidization—job creation programs—also and have cut them back. Generally, the earlier commitment to the goal of maintaining high employment—the commitment to the "right to a job"—is no longer actively pursued. In addition, unemployment has been redefined; for example, in the Netherlands, former workers older than age fifty-seven are officially classified as "retired" rather than "unemployed." Such a change symbolizes policymakers' loss of confidence in their ability to maintain full employment.

Although the policies actually pursued have harmed certain groups, the overall reduction in the growth of the welfare state has been small. This is true both in the United Kingdom, where the lowest income group has been the hardest hit, and in Sweden where pensioners have had some reduction in benefits. Although some benefits have been cut, the numbers of recipients are up. Moreover, although recent welfare state policies differ across countries, there has been little exchange of information among them on the effect of the policy changes. This is not surprising—indeed, there has been little if any evaluation of the cumulative effects of policy changes. Although defense of the basic objectives of the welfare state—eliminating poverty and reducing inequality and insecurity—should not be used to foreclose welfare state reform and modifications, in many cases it appears to have done so.

LIKELY OUTCOMES

The lesson from this chapter is unsatisfying. It might be expected that the highly industrialized democracies of Western Europe would agree on the effect of the welfare state on economic performance, but no such consensus exists. It might be expected that the debate over social policy would be based on more than hunch and ideology, but it is not. It might be hoped that the official statements of governments would match their policies, and that both would have a rational basis, but they do not. And, as if all this is not bad enough, the three countries we have studied are barely attempting to learn systematically either about the interaction of the welfare state with economic performance or about the remedial effects of the policies they are discussing or undertaking. In the Netherlands and Sweden, less so in the United Kingdom, express or implied criticisms of the welfare state are not taken lightly. Although actions may be taken to rein in the system or to constrain its growth, the rationale for such policies tends to be stated obliquely. Direct criticism of the welfare state's adverse effects on economic performance still comes with high political costs. Finally, even though debate and ferment on these issues exists in all three countries, the cross-national communication necessary for rational and objective changes in welfare state policies does not exist.

Given the near-absence of systematic discussion and policymaking on welfare state issues in Western Europe, it is difficult to predict the likely policy shifts over the next decade. Nevertheless, from our discussion, several themes seem clear.

First, the view that society is better off with an extensive welfare state—that income security and minimal inequality are preferable to a more unequal distribution of a bigger pot—will continue to dominate. Eliminating poverty is viewed as a requirement of a civilized society. Reorientation or reform may take place, but there will be no serious dismantling of the welfare state.

Second, the long-term slowdown in economic growth and the high unemployment rates and public deficits that plague Western Europe will continue to influence the welfare state debate. The discussions will increasingly focus on ways to reduce the public sector or to restructure it without growth in welfare state expenditures as a percentage of the GDP. Social-democratic and labor interests will find it increasingly difficult to advocate increases in public social spending, or at least they will condition such proposals on economic growth. Debate on the welfare state will continue to center on which programs to cut or restructure, how to reduce inflexibilities in the labor market, and how to distribute the taxes required for the support of welfare state measures.

Our third conclusion concerns the role that ideology and the commitment to the goals of the welfare state will play in future policy changes. Those countries that are ideologically committed to the welfare state (for instance, Sweden and the Netherlands) are likely to cut aggregate social spending the least and, when retrenching, will target cuts on nonpoor beneficiaries or use cuts to correct program inefficiencies. Retrenchment will, in effect, be from the top down. In those countries with less ideological commitment to welfare state principles (for instance, the United Kingdom), the broad-based programs that benefit the middle class will continue to be largely immune from retrenchment, and benefit cuts or privatization will fall more heavily on the poor. Recent cuts in the United Kingdom in housing and home health benefits and public transport, and the privatization of certain largely unskilled service jobs, are likely to portend future bottom-up targeting of cuts on the low-income population possessing less political power.

A fourth element in understanding the future public debate in Western Europe could perhaps be the continuing fallout of recent changes in the socialist countries—from China, with its slow move away from collectivism to private initiative, to the Gorbachev-led renewed Soviet efforts to reignite growth by restructuring incentives, to changes in Comecon countries designed to increase the potential from private enterprise. All these could increase Western Europe's skepticism regarding the ability of centralized, large government simultaneously to reduce inequality and stimulate a growing economic pie. This skepticism has been reinforced by the increased recognition that their own countries have faltered in maintaining growth and reducing inequalities as public spending and the welfare state grew at the expense of economic performance.

What does all this imply about the future welfare state in the countries we have studied?

1. Expansion of the welfare state seems highly unlikely unless growth were to speed up and unemployment to fall again—phenomena that are unlikely both in the short and medium run.

2. Retrenchment of welfare state spending will be proposed by governments and opposed by trade unions, by groups that would be affected, and by persons motivated by a commitment to reduction of inequality. What retrenchment does come may be camouflaged in efforts to achieve other, more widely held, objectives (for example, reduction in inflation or deficits or increases in investment), to respond to more general mandates (such as the EEC directives to individualize benefits), or to reduce inefficiencies or incentives in existing programs.

3. The growing proportion of the population that is above retirement age, combined with the perception that the economic status of this group is relatively high, will generate pressure to restructure the health care sector to

reduce costs, to privatize the earnings-related portion of public retirement pensions, and in the longer run to raise the current retirement age.

4. Increased female labor force participation will conflict with the pressures for welfare state retrenchment by stimulating political opposition to retrenchment in countries with relatively heavy female employment in social service programs, by increasing the demand for child care and elderly care services, and by increasing the demand for disability and early retirement benefits as women compete with older men for newly created jobs.

5. Governments are likely to levy user and beneficiary charges in health, higher education, day care, and housing in order to decrease the burden on taxpayers for the public provision of such services.

6. Employment and wage subsidies are likely to be viewed as plausible instruments for increasing employment, relieving high private nonwage labor costs, and offsetting the inefficiencies from high minimum wages and trade union power.

In sum, the welfare state will no longer be a "growth industry," but neither is its dismantling in the offing. Indeed, political leaders who endorse either extreme view have little standing in any of the countries we have studied. The benefits of the welfare state—reduced uncertainty and inequality, increased human capital and social cohesion—are still appreciated and desired. However, the costs associated with these gains—reduced work effort, savings, profits, and initiative; increased unreported activities; and excessive use of zero-priced or highly subsidized services—seem to be increasingly recognized.[15] As a result, policymakers will seek to reduce inefficiencies, improve incentives, and reduce the aggregate tax burden. We hope that these changes will not work to the disadvantage of those people who are least well off.

---

15. See Haveman (1985) for an examination of the gains and losses attributable to the welfare state.

REFERENCES

Beveridge, Sir William. 1942. *Social Insurance and Allied Services*. Cmnd. 6404. London, England: Her Majesty's Stationery Office.

Bradshaw, J. 1985. "In Defense of Social Security." In P. Bean, J. Ferris, and D. Whytes, eds., *In Defense of the Welfare State*. London: Tavistock.

DeLeeck, H. 1984. "The Matthew Effect. On the Unequal Distribution of Social Benefits." Unpublished document. Belgium: University of Antwerp.

Dilnot, A. W., J. A. Kay, and C. N. Morris. 1984. *The Reform of Social Security*. Oxford: Institute for Fiscal Studies.

Dilnot, A. W., and C. N. Morris. 1981. "What Do We Know about the Black Economy?" *Fiscal Studies* (March) 2(1).

Fase, M.M.G. 1984. "Informele Economie en Geldloop: Emige Aspecten van Meting en Interpretatie vanuit Monetair Gezichtspunt" ("The Informal Economy and Money Flows: Some Aspects Regarding the Measurement and Interpretation from a Monetary Viewpoint"). In *De Informele Economie*. Leiden, Netherlands: Stenfert Kroese.

Feige, E. L.,and R. T. McGee. 1982. "Aanbodeconomie en het Zwart Circuit: de Nederlandse Laffer-Curve" ("Supply-side Economics and the Black Circuit: The Dutch Laffer Curve"). *Economisch Statistische Berichten* (November 24), 67: 1248–33.

Frey, B. S., and H. Weck. 1983. "Estimating the Shadow Economy: A 'Naive' Approach." *Oxford Economic Papers* 35: 23–44.

Halberstadt, V., K. Goudswaard, and B. LeBlanc. 1984. "Current Control Problems with Public Expenditure in Five European Countries." In M. Emerson, ed., *Europe's Stagflation*. Oxford: Clarendon Press.

Haveman, R. 1985. *Does the Welfare State Increase Welfare? Reflections on Hidden Negatives and Observed Positives*. Leiden, Netherlands: Stenfert Kroese.

LeGrand, J., and R. Robinson, eds. 1984. *Privatization and the Welfare State*. London, England: George Allen & Unwin.

Lindbeck, A. 1985. "What Is Wrong with the Western European Economies?" *The World Economy* (June) 8: 153–70.

Netherlands Scientific Council for Government Policy. 1985. *Safeguarding Social Security*. The Hague, Netherlands: NSCGP.

Organization for Economic Cooperation and Development. 1984. *Economic Outlook*. Paris: OECD.

Parker, H. 1983. *The Moral Hazard of Social Security Benefits*. London, England: Institute of Economic Affairs.

Townsend, P. 1984. *Fewer Children, More Poverty: An Incomes Plan*. Bristol, England: University of Bristol.

Wartonick, David, and M. Packard. 1983. "Slowing Down Pension Index: The Foreign Experience." *Social Security Bulletin* (June) 46(6): 9–15.

Wolfe, B., D. de Jong, R. Haveman, V. Halberstadt, and K. Goudswaard. 1984. "Income Transfers and Work Effort: The Netherlands and the United States in the 1970's." *Kyklos* 37(4): 609–37.

APPENDIX TABLE

Selected Welfare State Programs, 1950–80
(Percentage of Gross Domestic Product)[a]

Programs	1950[b] United Kingdom	1950[b] Netherlands	1950[b] Sweden	1960 United Kingdom	1960 Netherlands	1960 Sweden	1970 United Kingdom	1970 Netherlands	1970 Sweden	1980 United Kingdom	1980 Netherlands	1980 Sweden
Education	2.9	3.5	1.9	4.2	5.2	3.9	6.1	8.2	3.5*	6.3	8.5	5.4
National health	4.0	1.0*	n.a.	3.9	1.4[c]	2.4	4.8	5.3	5.3*	6.2	5.7	5.9
Personal social service[d]	0.3	...	...	0.2	n.a.	...	0.6	n.a.	...	1.2	n.a.	...
School meals/welfare fund	0.5	...	n.a.	0.4	...	0.3	0.4	...	0.1	0.3	...	0.3
Social security[e]	5.9	6.2	5.2	6.7	9.3	9.1	9.0	15.2	13.5	12.1	23.1	25.1
National insurance retirement	2.2	1.0	0.9	3.1	2.8	4.1	4.2	5.1	5.2	5.6	6.4	6.4
Widows/guardians	0.2	...	...	0.3	0.5	n.a.	0.4	0.7	n.a.	0.3	0.8	n.a.
Unemployment	0.1	0.1	0.1	0.2	0.3	0.2	0.4	0.7	0.3	0.7	2.0	0.4
Sickness	0.6	1.1	0.7	0.6	1.3	1.8	0.9	2.7	3.2	0.3	3.5	4.4
Invalidity	...	...	...	...	...	0.0	...	1.5	0.1	0.6	4.6	0.5
Injury/disablement	0.1	0.9	0.3	0.2	0.7	0.2	0.2	0.2	0.1	0.2	0.1	0.3
War pensions	0.7	0.1	...	0.5	0.1	...	0.3	0.1	...	0.2	0.2	...
Family allowances	0.6	2.1	1.4	0.6	2.1	1.9	0.8	2.5	2.2	1.6	2.3	3.4

Supplement benefits	0.8	0.1	0.7	0.9	0.8	0.2*	1.3	0.7	1.1	1.5	1.5	3.7
Other[f]	0.6	...	1.2	0.5	...	0.4	0.4	0.3	1.1	0.9	0.9	1.7
Administration	g	0.8	...	g	0.6	0.1	g	0.6	0.1	g	0.8	0.3
Housing	2.9	...	0.2	1.7	n.a.	0.9*	3.1	3.9	0.8*	3.6	1.2	3.2
Total programs	16.2	10.7	7.4	17.2	15.8	16.3	23.9	31.8	23.1	29.7	38.5	39.6
GDP (millions of national currency)	11,447	15,776	29,780	22,780	38,630	62,656	43,574	103,551	151,289	193,488	302,900	519,189

SOURCES: United Kingdom—*Annual Abstract of Statistics* for the years shown, London: Her Majesty's Stationery Office; Sweden—*Statistic Årsbok,* various years, Stockholm, Sweden: Statisticha Central Byren; and "Fact Sheets on Sweden," various years, Stockholm: Swedish Institute; Netherlands—T. Braakman, M.P.C. van Schendelen, and K. P. Scholten, 1984. *Sociale Zekerheid in Nederland,* Antwerpen: Spectrum; and Central Bureau of Statistics, *Statistisch Zakboek* (statistical fact book) and *Miljoenennota* (budget document), various years, Den Haag, Netherlands: Staatsuitgeverij. Some of the data for 1950 are estimated.

n.a.   Not available.
*   Estimated.
a.   Includes capital expenditures, which differ from OECD estimates.
b.   The figures for 1950 are less reliable than those for other years shown.
c.   Not comparable with other countries.
d.   For Sweden, some services are included in family allowances; for the Netherlands, some services are combined.
e.   Totals may not add because of rounding.
f.   Not comprising the same categories. Sweden includes unemployment/disabled rescheduling programs (education, public works).
g.   Administration included in several items.

PHILOSOPHY, POLICY, AND POLITICS: INTEGRATING THEMES

John L. Palmer

Taken at face value, the views of the authors of this volume give disparate readings of the extent to which the Reagan years constitute a radical reorientation of the American political course. Glazer looks at the ''social issues''— that grab bag of value-laden concerns (abortion, school prayer, and the like) that have occupied such a prominent place in public dialogue under this administration—and concludes that America is experiencing a significant change in public values, not just a particularly adroit exploitation of political ephemera by an especially talented politician. Heclo, in contrast, looks at our ''public philosophy''—the weighing of public values with political realities, past and present—and concludes, more or less, *plus ça change*. He finds that the Reagan administration has served to consolidate the philosophy behind the American version of the welfare state. Meyer winds up in some harmony with Heclo, observing that we have undergone an (overdue) tightening of the social support system, with probably more to come in response to deficit reduction pressures, but that we have yet to address adequately the underlying problem of poverty. In other words, the Reagan administration has validated the New Deal by solving some part of the ''welfare mess''—that is, the administration halted the mindless expansion of benefits—without coming up with any constructive approaches to persistent social problems. Sawhill reaches harsher conclusions about the implications of the past several years for our economy: she observes that the administration has not only failed to address the fundamental problems—the ongoing standoff between inflation and economic growth—but has both obscured the dialogue over these issues and created new problems (mainly, huge trade and budget deficits) that render any future resolution of these old problems still more problematic. Finally,

175

Nathan argues that Reagan has been remarkably effective in revitalizing both the institution of the presidency and the spirit of federalism (without, albeit, ensuring any shrinkage in the overall size or influence of government in American life). Haveman, Wolfe, and Halberstadt supply the garnish for this strangely assembled dish with their suggestion that, from "over there," it may look as though we Americans know exactly what we are doing. That is, compared with the vacillation and confusion prevailing in Western European policymaking, we at least give the appearance of operating under clearly articulated principles.

How is the reader to digest this mélange of optimism and pessimism? Are some of the foregoing conclusions simply "right" and some "wrong"? Guidance on the first question is offered in the remainder of this chapter. On the second, I suggest, in summary here and with only minor qualification, the answer is no. We are undergoing a serious conflict—crisis would not be too strong a word—of values in this country. We have reached no agreement on the federal role in resolving this conflict (hence, no real change in public philosophy). We have, in our confusion, agreed to stop moving forward in the welfare state direction (hence, the arresting of growth in social program spending). We have also, in our confusion, securely hitched our political fortunes to an economic star, about the movements of which we are little wiser than a decade or so ago. And we have, in our indigenous distaste for any "can't do" philosophy, taken to our hearts a charismatic president who has, at least temporarily, persuaded us "not to worry." Small wonder the Europeans may be awed by our optimism.

In the remainder of this chapter, I present my own digestion of the disparate conclusions in this volume in three groupings that correspond to commonly accepted categories of discourse about public life: philosophy, policy, and politics. I make no effort to systematically summarize the chapters, although I draw on them liberally, and I assume that readers will absorb the volume as a whole. Although I do not think my interpretations are seriously at odds with those of the other authors, my conclusions are—without qualification—my own.

PHILOSOPHY

It is often said that the one clear service the Reagan administration has rendered this country is to focus public debate on "the real issues": the ideological or value conflicts that have percolated through our public dialogue over the past several decades, but that have too often sunk into debate over the technicalities of federal policies. It is certainly true that the value-laden issues—particularly the role of religion in our public life, our moral obligation for the economic well-being of our fellow citizens, and the function of the federal government in the formation of public values—have attained a new visibility under the Reagan administration. But it is not at all clear whether the current ideological ferment represents just another of our periodic bouts of moral rejuvenation, akin to the populist crusades of earlier years, or whether it represents a more lasting turn toward the ideological in our public discourse.

In this section, I argue the latter proposition. In particular I argue that our current political disagreements are rooted in the ambiguities of our religious tradition and that the long evolution of that tradition has reached a critical phase. From being a largely centripetal force through most of our history, religion is now poised to become a centrifugal one—with real implications for our social cohesion. In pursuing this undoubtedly unpopular line of argument, I am not trying to assert that religious factors alone explain the current situation in America, and will shape the future, but only that they have exercised, and will exercise, a much more significant influence on American public life than most political analysts of today are inclined to acknowledge.

Because this contention will not meet with ready acceptance, let me return to one that will. I began this discussion by observing that the Reagan administration can rightfully be credited with clarifying the value dimensions of our public policy debates. Ironically, however, I suspect that the administration's contribution to clarifying the debate will end by illuminating much less consensus on public purposes than the administration believes there to be. Also ironically, I suspect that the most immediate result will be a kind of reinforcement of the "procedural liberalism" discussed in the Heclo chapter and deplored by so many modern conservatives.

Under pressure, for example, from the Meese-led Justice Department, the courts are far more likely to defend their historically validated prerogatives for deciding certain kinds of issues than they are to embark on a wholesale abdication of judicial tradition in favor of the social values espoused by the administration. Similarly, state and local governments are much more likely to respond to constituent pressures to provide services—as the Nathan chapter indicates they are already doing—and to quarrel with the federal government over the allocation of resources to support the services, than they are to engage in a thoroughgoing—and electorally expensive—sorting out of value questions at their level. State governments have evidenced a much-diminished appetite for states' rights in recent years, and even local jurisdictions have often revealed themselves as eager to yield "moral authority" to the federal executive or judiciary. (Witness, for example, the self-proclaimed powerlessness of many big city mayors in the fight over school busing.) The political price of coming between environmentalist and developer, prochoicer and prolifer, black community and white community simply appears to be higher than many state and local politicians feel they can afford.

The point is that the value conflicts are both real and pervasive—a point that President Carter came to appreciate (and acknowledged in his remarkable "malaise" speech) but that President Reagan has yet to grasp. (Ignorance of this particular point proves itself to be not only bliss but also political wisdom.) President Reagan's vision of an America made up of myriad communities, bound together by common moral values and commitment to the "American way" of economic competition, has had obvious political appeal, but it obscures both the contemporary reality of our extraordinarily pluralistic society and the historic reality of our ongoing disagreements over the compatibility of "moral values" and "economic competition."

Apropos of the historic reality, Heclo, in his chapter, notes the dualism of the American philosophic heritage: "In one corner stands a rights-based individualism founded on the claim that society should be conceived as composed of separate, unique individuals with conceptions of what is good. . . . In the other corner . . . [the] communitarian interpretation . . . [that] calls for fuller recognition of the claims of collective membership in an ongoing social enterprise."

Behind these two strands of thought lies a long history of debate over values, the rehashing of which is not necessary here. Suffice it to note that the Founding Fathers spent considerable energy juggling the philosophical conflicts between economic liberty and "civic virtue" (the latter never clearly defined in their writings, but referring to any principles by which private interests could be subordinated to the public good). They were apparently well versed in the work of European thinkers on these subjects, and they seem to have clearly understood the formidable nature of the task confronting them: to wit, how to ensure the political viability of the republic against economic greed and factionalism—historically, the bane of democracies—without falling back on a European-style reliance on central authority and civic obligation. That they failed to achieve any consensus is testified to by their own writings and by the ongoing disputes among scholars over the "real meaning" of the American Revolution and Constitution. That they plunked down on the side of economic liberty and moral skepticism is, I think, incontestable: the elaborate system of checks and balances embodied in the Constitution that emerged from their debates attests to an absence of agreement on any higher notion of "virtue" than that, whatever virtue may be, no one idea of it should be permitted to dominate. As the historian Richard Hofstadter summed it up, "Modern humanist thinkers who seek for a means by which society may transcend eternal conflict and rigid adherence to property rights as its integrating principles can expect no answer in the philosophy of balanced government as it was set down by the Constitution-makers of 1787'' (Hofstadter 1957, 16–17).

But if the Constitution really does provide no ''means by which society can transcend eternal conflict,'' Americans might well wonder why we, compared with most other countries, have been so little scarred by ideological antagonisms. Until the 1960s, the United States had been, by almost everyone's account, both remarkably unideological in its politics and remarkably moralistic in its public dialogue. We talked as if we each had a clear conception of peculiarly American values,[1] but when it came to empowering the federal government to act, we were as skeptical and pragmatic, as voters, as any of the Founding Fathers. Rarely have purely moralistic or ideological causes gained national constituencies (the abolition and prohibition movements being the two conspicuous exceptions). Why, then, have such basic value questions come to the fore with such force at the federal level right now?

Glazer's chapter suggests a number of answers to this question. First, the judicial activism of the past thirty years or so has extended the federal arm into domains hitherto the province of state and local governments, thus transforming moral matters of community concern into constitutional issues of national concern. Second, widespread concern over indications of moral dissipation—the proliferation of pornography, school discipline problems, crime, drug abuse, and the like—has politicized segments of the population previously unmoved by moralistic appeals. And, finally, the most vociferous group of ''political moralizers,'' the religious fundamentalists, are better organized, better funded, and less obviously tainted by bigotry than in times past; consequently, they cast a wider political net.

I accept Glazer's conclusions, but I suggest that they point to a phenomenon larger, older, and ultimately much more problematic for our public philosophy than simply an ongoing conflict over ''social issues'' at the federal level. (About the likelihood of ongoing conflict, Glazer and I are in complete agreement.) This phenomenon—which one recent writer identified as ''the lost soul of American politics'' (Diggins 1984) and which religious fundamentalists simply label, with venom, ''secular humanism''—is the dissolution of the mainstream Protestant religious conviction that animated the writing of the Declaration of Independence and that has placed its particular stamp so forcefully on American history. Of course, the Protestant religion never was a monolithic force in American history, but for most of our history it

---

1. See, for example, Bercovitch (1981).

retained sufficient coherence in the public consciousness to serve as a kind of political center of gravity. Its dissolution, long in the making, is only now coming to have acute political consequences.

To many secular humanists of today, the idea that religion—one particular brand of religion—might be the sine qua non of the American experiment will not meet with ready acceptance. Bemused and bewildered as they are (and as Glazer notes) by the passions aroused by the social issues, they are inclined to think of religion as an historical accident of the American experience: an accidental byproduct of the fact that the country was founded by Anglo-Saxon malcontents, imbued with a Calvinistic disposition for capitalism but disaffected by the European religious strife of the seventeenth century. That such a people would take the principle of religious freedom very seriously seems logical to the humanist; that they would also endow their political and economic experiment with a vague sense of religious mission also seems logical. But that religious conviction provided the *confidence* to undertake the experiment in the first place—and that loss of that conviction could imperil the will to continue—does not seem at all logical to the beneficiaries of three centuries of materialistic/democratic progress.[2]

Yet consider George Washington's farewell observation: "Of all the dispositions and habits which lead to political prosperity, religion and morality are indispensable supports." Consider also the admonition of that inexhaustible interpreter of American life, de Tocqueville (1945, 6–7):

> It must never be forgotten that religion gave birth to Anglo-American society. In the United States, religion is therefore mingled with all the habits of the nation and all the feelings of patriotism, whence it derives a peculiar force. . . . [In America] religion has, as it were, laid down its own limits. Religious institutions have remained wholly distinct from political institutions, so that former laws have been easily changed while former belief has remained unshaken. Christianity has therefore retained a strong hold on the public mind in America; and I would more particularly remark that its sway is not only that of a philosophical doctrine which has been adopted upon inquiry, but of a religion which is believed without discussion. . . . The Americans, having admitted the principal doctrines of the Christian religion without inquiry, are obliged to accept in like manner a great number of moral truths originating in it and connected with it. Hence the activity of individual analysis is restrained within narrow limits, and many of the most important of human opinions are removed from its influence.

The assumption of shared values "believed without discussion" is, of course, one of the hallmarks of President Reagan's rhetoric. But I did not quote de Tocqueville at such length just to underline the anachronistic element in the president's vision. Rather, I want to suggest that

---

2. Several readers, better versed than I in American religious history, called my attention to other recent works that support or extend my argument about the centrality of Protestant religion to American political life. Particularly relevant is Neuhaus (1984).

- The historic commonality of religious outlook in the United States, coupled with the strict separation of church and state, goes a long way toward explaining the oft-remarked "pragmatic" orientation of Americans in political affairs: we could change laws, as de Tocqueville noted, with minimal ideological fuss because we satisfied our need for agreement on "the meaning of life" outside the political sphere.

- At least in part because American moral strictures were so unquestioningly linked to our religious faith, we never made a separate enterprise of inculcating civic virtue and hence we have a very weak sense of civic obligation (compared to most European countries). As one recent writer put it, in America, "government does not make demands on people; they make demands on it" (Mead 1986, 5).

- Because the United States has never experienced a strenuous political sorting of public and private values, we developed no tradition (again, comparable to the Europeans) of social solidarity; we have remained a preeminently pluralistic society.

I will return to these observations later in this chapter, but here I want to stay with de Tocqueville. I am not going to argue at length that "times have changed" since he wrote. They have, President Reagan notwithstanding. What religious historians called "mainline Protestantism"—the denominations primarily involved in the founding and settling of this country—has been steadily losing ground through much of this century, but with particular speed after the 1960s. My point is not that America is becoming "less religious" (although on the whole I think it is),[3] but that the particular brand of religion that enabled us to unfetter our individual economic interests while maintaining a kind of collective conscience no longer serves this function.

Religion, like the rest of our society, has become increasingly pluralized, and the current keeper of the American "flame"—the flame being a faith in the complete compatibility of economic interests and moral values—is a group long regarded (and still regarded) by the majority of the population as a "radical fringe." The "evangelical moralists" (Daniel Bell's term) are the one significant segment of the population that shares *all* of President Reagan's vision. Although mainstream Protestants (and Catholics and Jews, for that

---

3. Although large numbers of Americans continue to profess religious belief—eight out of ten, for example, consider themselves Christians, according to a recent poll—it is not clear what practical significance the profession of faith has for their personal and political lives. In 1985, George Gallup (1985) noted that the "widespread appeal or popularity of religion" went hand in hand with "glaring lack of knowledge; inconsistencies in belief; superficiality of faith; and in part, the failure of organized religion . . . to make a difference in our society."

matter) may support the president for a variety of reasons but wring their hands over the abandonment of *their* American dream of social justice, and although the corporations and the Yuppies more often than not *do* support the president without any particular reference to religious convictions, the evangelical moralists stand alone with the president in asserting God's blessing over American free enterprise.

I find this situation deeply disturbing. I think the president and his religious fundamentalist supporters are on solid ground in their linking of religious convictions to faith in the American way of democratic capitalism, but I do not see them as pointing in any direction that the country can (or should) go. The problem they are addressing—the absence of any widely accepted secular basis for morality—has bedeviled liberal thinkers for years. Writing almost forty years ago (about philosophical issues several centuries old), the Princeton philosopher W. T. Stace observed:[4]

> No civilization can live without ideals, or to put it in another way, without a firm faith in moral ideas. Our ideals and moral ideas have in the past been rooted in religion. But the religious basis of our ideals has been undermined, and the superstructure of ideals is plainly tottering. . . . Of course we know that it is perfectly possible for individual men, very highly educated men, . . . to live moral lives without any religious convictions. But the question is whether a whole civilization, a whole family of peoples, composed almost entirely of relatively uneducated men and women, can do this. . . . Perhaps in a few hundred years most of the population will, at the present rate, be sufficiently highly educated and civilized to combine high ideals with an absence of religion. But long before we reach any such stage, the collapse of our civilization may have come about.

Stace's difficulty is the difficulty of the nuclear-age secular humanist; having faith in his secular ideals, he is skeptical that they can be transmitted to the mass of the population in time to ''save the world.'' But to the religious fundamentalists, the crusading spirit of secular humanism serves only to undermine the religious values that have, thus far, in fact saved the world. Stace would have to acknowledge that they have a point. They may even succeed in their efforts to evangelize the mainstream population, but I doubt it. I incline toward the view that Glazer expressed elsewhere in this volume: that where conservative religious values survive, they may deserve judicial or legislative protection from the advance of secular humanism, but that they are unlikely to spread spontaneously to—and should not and cannot be forced upon—the mainstream population.

---

4. Stace (1966), p. 548. For more recent discussion of this subject, see Reichley (1985).

In any event, we do not need to determine here the future of religion in this country to be able to conclude that, for the moment, the new political organizations of the conservative religious movement have simply added to the cacophony of values on the American political stage. I have gone into the value conflicts at such length not because I was striving for some definitive prognostication—I know these issues are much too complex to be dealt with adequately here—but because I think that the conflicts will bear more significantly on our political future than they have on our past, and I think that they have been too lightly dismissed by most analysts of the Reagan years.

Reagan himself may in fact be, as so many have concluded, an idealogue on the surface and a Rooseveltian pragmatist under the skin, but this does not mean that the Americans to whom he speaks are Roosevelt's Americans (or, as Reagan might prefer, de Tocqueville's Americans). American culture has changed appreciably in the last 50, not to mention 150, years. For all that President Reagan talks as if Americans are still together, dreaming the same American dream, fundamentalist and secular humanist alike agree that the spiritual bottom has dropped out—and it seems unlikely that presidential rhetoric alone will bring it back. Although the president can incarnate nostalgia for that dream, he is fundamentally—in this realm, at least—an anachronism, acknowledged as such by an electorate that routinely separates his person from his policies and denies his party a working majority in the Congress.

What, then, remains, in this analysis, of the widely touted Reagan "mandate"? Only what remained after the constitutional debates of 1786–87: moral skepticism and agreement on the primacy of the value of economic liberty. This is not to argue, as some of Walter Mondale's supporters would have it, that in Reagan's overwhelming reelection "naked self-interest" triumphed over communitarian values: from the point of view sketched here, there was no real engagement. The fact that the Yuppie now lies down with the lamb (the Christian fundamentalist) may be some testament to Reagan's political acuity and the Democrats' philosophic disarray, but it is mostly testament to the absolute incoherence of our public dialogue about values. The only thing that most of us seem to be able to agree about right now is that every American has a right to enrich himself as best he can, within the rules of the game— and that, toward the end of enrichment, there should be fewer rules. It is the abandonment of any effort to make coherent sense of principles that is so troubling to the president's critics within the conservative wing of his own party.

All this failure to sort out values underlies, I think, Heclo's conclusion that the Reagan administration has thus far served primarily to consolidate the public philosophy that emerged in the New Deal and post–New Deal years. Insofar as Americans have sorted out the role of the government in the formation and maintenance of our public values, it has been done only to reinforce the middle-class value of economic security. That is, we have accepted the idea that the government owes an assurance of economic stability to the middle class and, somewhat more doubtfully, we have validated the notion of a "safety net" for the most dependent of our people. Meyer's chapter, incidentally, raises the question of how, when deficit push comes to deficit shove, we may further refine the trade-off between these two values. But Heclo's main point holds: that behind all the sound and fury about values, all Americans have managed to agree on is just what we agreed on in the Depression—that is, arguments about political principles must bow to economic expediency. For an understanding of what that "bow" has involved, I turn now to the sphere of social and economic policy.

POLICY

Over the past 200 years, the value conflict discussed above—the historic tension between the American public's clear appreciation of the role of economic liberty in political affairs and the much less clear appreciation of the need for some sort of civic virtue—has rooted itself in distinctively conservative and liberal outlooks on the role of the federal government in economic and social affairs. Academic literature has made much of the subtleties of the distinction, but here a simplification should suffice. The conservative outlook embraces the least possible federal regulation of the economic sphere and the most necessary regulation of the social sphere, both consistent with the maintenance of public *order*. In contrast, the liberal outlook embraces the most necessary regulation of the economic sphere and the least possible regulation of the social sphere, both consistent with the public *good*. Conservatives, viewing the pursuit of the good as an individual matter, emphasize personal responsibility for economic well-being and define individual rights as *against* the state. Liberals, viewing the pursuit of the good as a more communitarian enterprise, emphasize collective responsibility for economic well-being and define individual rights as from the state and against the marketplace. Both points of view are united by a peculiarly American mistrust of central authority in domestic affairs, but divided on how that authority should be used: the conservative says, "to foster the pursuit of economic opportunity"; and the liberal says, "to promote the achievement of economic equality." Conservatives, in sum, would make social policy the servant of an economic vision, and liberals, the reverse.

Whatever violence I may have done to political philosophy in my characterization of polarity of these outlooks, the polarity itself is a commonplace of our political life. As numerous other writers have observed, much of the history of American domestic politics can be viewed as vacillations between the liberal and conservative poles of thought. Thus the 1920s and 1950s appear as decades in which conservative business values dominated and concerns for political and social equality receded, whereas in the 1930s and 1960s, the national social conscience resurged, producing major expansions in the role of the federal government.

These changes in national mood may be cyclical, but there is a marked asymmetry in the swings. Movements in the conservative direction have increasingly turned out to be little more than holding actions that have temporarily halted a long-term trend toward expanded federal involvement in the economic and social spheres, whereas swings in the liberal direction have tended to produce enduring changes in American life. Thus, little of the New Deal was repudiated during the Eisenhower administration. And the Nixon and Ford administrations both maintained a strong federal role in antidiscrimination efforts and actually presided over the largest growth in federal social spending in the post–World War II era. As McClosky and Zeller summed it up in *The American Ethos*, "the long-term result of this asymmetry is that norms relating to such democratic values as freedom of expression, due process of law, and equality of rights and opportunities are now more firmly entrenched and substantially broader in scope than they were in the nineteenth century, while the norms relating to the values of capitalism are more qualified and circumscribed" (McClosky and Zeller 1984, 293).

These observations would seem to suggest that the "Reagan Revolution" may in reality be no more than the "Reagan Respite." To some extent, I think this is true. Although many conservatives, including the president, have talked as though they were embarked on a major dismantling of federal domestic programs, they have clearly not succeeded, as Heclo and Meyer observe in this volume and as an earlier Urban Institute volume documented (Palmer and Sawhill 1984). In fact, what is really remarkable is how large the federal domestic role remains, given the president's popularity, the generally artful orchestration of his administration's pursuit of its policy agenda, and the ensuing fiscal pressures for retrenchment.

Consider federal responsibilities for managing the economy, protecting the environment, preventing discrimination, and alleviating economic insecurity in general and poverty in particular. None of these were generally accepted roles for the federal government before the 1930s, and many were not before the 1960s. Yet, the vast array of programs and policies that have arisen to address these ends over the past fifty years are largely intact well into Reagan's second term. Only in areas that, before the 1960s, were left primarily or exclusively to state and local governments—such as education, social services, and community development—has the administration effected very major retrenchment. And even here, we have not witnessed the major restructuring or sorting out of federal, state, and local roles to the pre–New Deal status that the president and most strong conservatives favored. Thus, although the New Deal political coalition may no longer be intact, the basic New Deal policy legacy has emerged largely unscathed, as has much (though not all, by any means, as I will discuss later) of the Great Society policy legacy.[5]

One can conclude from all this that the conservative challenge of the past decade has served to clarify and consolidate a substantial consensus regarding the role of the federal government as it has evolved over the past fifty years and that, as a result, a broad scale reversal of that role appears even less likely now than it might have appeared before the advent of the Reagan administration. But it would be a mistake to let that conclusion validate the "respite" interpretation of the Reagan years. The conservative critique of liberal social and economic policies, which gained intellectual force throughout the 1970s, has simply proved too telling and, through the personality and rhetorical skills of Ronald Reagan, it has acquired popular credibility.

To put the argument in bolder and more philosophical terms, the liberal effort to promote a sense of social solidarity and to formulate a more egalitarian rationale for social and economic policies has failed. Americans are not buying it (although, to the dismay of many conservatives, they seem perfectly willing to go on accepting welfare state "freebies," shorn of the liberal philosophical trappings). Insofar as American liberalism continues to partake of collectivist notions of the public good, it will continue to fail to capture the popular political imagination. Many lines of thought support this contention, but here I will just draw on three for which some foundation has been laid in the earlier chapters of this volume.

Social and Economic History

Many Americans on the far left of our (admittedly narrow) political spectrum have a penchant for viewing the train of American social and economic history as simply a retarded version of the European one—that is, we are headed eastward down a track with a destination in some version of the Western European welfare state. The fact that our public sector has always been significantly smaller than the public sectors of countries on the Continent

---

5. In the chapter on "Social Policy" in Palmer and Sawhill (1984), D. Lee Bawden and I document that although Ronald Reagan might have rhetorically called into question certain aspects of the New Deal, he primarily attacked the hallmarks of the Great Society and the 1960s elaborations on New Deal programs in his policy and budget prescriptions. This is where he had his greatest successes.

is attributed, in this view, to our later embarkation from the capitalist point of origin; being a newer country, we have simply been slower to understand the inevitability of market failure and of the need for state intervention to promote economic and social welfare. From the left, then, the Reagan phenomenon is regarded as just the Neanderthal, American equivalent of what Haveman, Wolfe, and Halberstadt point to as underlying public sector retrenchment throughout Europe. That is, with the slowdown in economic growth experienced by all Western countries in the 1970s, the affordability of the welfare state has become a matter of concern, but this concern need not entail any backing off from principles; with the resumption of any reasonable level of growth, the train will proceed on its course.

The extent to which this view misvalues the difference between American and European *political* experience can be appreciated by simplifying that experience into models of political life—here borrowed from two open advocates of the welfare state, Furniss and Tilton (1977). In their vision, Western democracies may be divided into three general types: the positive state, the social security state, and the social welfare state. The primary aim of the positive state is to protect the property holders from the difficulties of unregulated markets and from potential redistributive demands. The economic policy orientation is toward government-business collaboration for economic growth (although not such full employment as to strengthen labor's hand unduly and lead to wage inflation). The social orientation is toward social insurance programs that equalize income over a person's life cycle, spread the risks of unemployment and sickness from the individual to the general population, and encourage a strong, consistent attachment to the labor force—in short, proefficiency and antiegalitarian. A social security state goes well beyond the positive state in pursuing a maximalist full-employment policy, with government-business collaboration, public ownership of many industries, and extensive public employment. A minimum of income and many important services are guaranteed to every citizen as a matter of right, but substantial incentives are preserved for voluntary action by individuals to provide more for themselves and family.

Despite their differences, both the positive and social security states are marked by considerable economic inequality and differential access to social services and by a relatively large and independent private sector. In contrast, a "true" social welfare state pursues a much more thoroughgoing egalitarianism grounded in the notion of "solidarity" among socioeconomic classes. Its goals include guaranteed full employment (1.5 to 2.0 percent unemployment), a guaranteed minimum income and adequate housing as a fundamental right of citizenship, the replacement of private pensions with a public program providing full income security for all retirees, a national health service, highly progressive taxation of incomes and capital (sufficient to eliminate vast discrepancies among citizens' personal resources), centralized community planning and land use regulation, and the "termination of capitalist hegemony in the cultural sphere."

From this brief characterization, it is evident that of the three countries Haveman and his coauthors focus on, Sweden and the Netherlands both approach "true" social welfare states, whereas England is more appropriately characterized as a social security state. But the fact that not *one* of Furniss and Tipton's welfare state goals has *ever* been an accepted item on the American political agenda— and the tepid variants that have surfaced (for example, a negative income tax) have generally proved to be more political millstones than milestones—suggests that, regardless of the commonality of social and economic problems experienced by Western capitalistic societies, the uniqueness of the American political experience will continue to shape our response to those problems in ways that will set America apart from Europe. For the United States, the outer limit of the range of politically acceptable policy choices clearly lies to the "right" of the social security state; and, as the Reagan administration has demonstrated, the center of gravity, despite lurches to the left, continues to lie closer to the positive state than to the social security one.

This observation is borne out by the extreme popularity of President Reagan's rhetoric, quite independent of his policies. He can strongly criticize even such widely accepted public "goods" as public education, minimum-wage laws, and welfare programs and can propose more private sector and market-oriented approaches to all three at no great political cost—and perhaps net political gain. In contrast, presidential candidates who have espoused the values of a social security state—socialized medicine, large-scale public employment, and a guaranteed minimum income—have suffered quite different fates. George McGovern, of course, springs to mind here, but it also must be remembered that Franklin Roosevelt was initially elected (with substantial support from American business) not on a platform to launch the American welfare state, but, rather, to balance the federal budget. Because Roosevelt is widely credited with having done the former while failing at the latter, and because we are here crediting Reagan with something similar (with consolidating whatever there is to the American welfare state while further unbalancing the budget), it seems worthwhile to briefly review the political foundations for the New Deal economic and social consensus, as they constitute the foundations for whatever economic and social consensus we currently have.[6]

---

6. I am indebted to Skocpol (forthcoming) for much of the argument in the remainder of this subsection.

The social insurance programs initiated under the New Deal were originally designed to be a right "earned" only through long-term attachment to the labor force, just as means-tested public assistance programs were never intended to be a substantial, permanent federal function (Roosevelt himself termed them a dangerous "narcotic") but were expected to wither away with the restoration of a healthy economy and the maturation of the social insurance system. Interestingly, though, the report of President Roosevelt's Committee on Economic Security, which provided the blueprint for the Social Security Act of 1935, argued that the approach to social policy imbedded in this act would work only if the federal government ensured full employment. Later, many liberal New Dealers also became "social Keynesians," adopting the view, which eventually predominated in many Western European welfare states, that permanently high levels of federal social spending should be coordinated with macroeconomic stimulation and sector-oriented policies to ensure steady growth with full employment. This line of thought fed directly into what I suspect is the one truly welfare-statist piece of legislation ever to attain serious consideration in the American political process—the Full Employment Bill of 1945. This bill would have reorganized and greatly strengthened federal budgeting and economic planning capacities and unequivocally committed the federal government to ensuring full employment by whatever means.

But such an institutionalized interventionist role for the federal government and subordination of economic policy to social goals could not survive the scrutiny of a pluralist Congress. Reflecting the historic American skepticism of centralized power and collectivist visions of the social good, the legislative process diluted the Full Employment Bill of 1945 into the Employment Act of 1946, which enshrined the expectation of federal responsibility for the national economic health, but did little to add to federal powers for actually discharging such responsibility. Commercial, and not social, Keynesianism became the order of the day. Thus, we came to rely on the "fine-tuning" of fiscal and monetary policies within relatively limited parameters for both our economic and social well-being.

Lest it be thought that the welfare state vision died only because F.D.R. did, we should note that, although Truman actually presided over the working out of the legislation, the outcome was presaged by Rooseveltian rhetoric. In justifying the New Deal economic and social activism of the federal government, Roosevelt initially relied heavily on images of social cooperation over selfish individualism and constantly stressed the experimental nature of federal efforts. As time went on, however, the official line became simultaneously more populist—for example, the attacks on the "economic royalists"—but also more conservative (in keeping with the innate conservatism of the populist

movement). Collective solidarity as an antidote to excessive individualism
gave way to populist reform as a better means for safeguarding traditional
American values of liberty, individualism, and "getting ahead."

Given President Roosevelt's charisma and the depth of social unrest and
economic insecurity during the Depression, it is possible that, had Roosevelt
advocated principles for government intervention that were more consistent
with those of a social welfare state, these principles might today have more
respectability. But I doubt it. From the late 1930s to the 1970s politicians
appear to have recognized that the pragmatic approach to legitimizing federal
intervention in economic and social activities was the surest way to stabilize
and moderately extend the federal role in U.S. domestic politics. Even during
the liberal 1960s, successful political leaders eschewed collectivist visions of
a welfare state in favor of instrumental arguments that social policies would
help every individual and group to get ahead in a growing economy.

What I have been arguing here is that the peculiarities of the American
public philosophy discussed in the preceding section of this chapter historically
have had very real implications for American social and economic policymaking and that, far from being an anomaly in our political history, President
Reagan bears out this observation. But philosophy and history do not suffice
to explain the president's political popularity. Given the American proclivity
for pragmatic politics, policies will generally and quite quickly be tested
against results; those policies that lived by instrumental justification will,
when socioeconomic realities fail to conform to expectations, die by instrumental justification. Thus, the fiscal and economic problems of the late 1970s
served to discredit the liberal policies of the 1960s and set the stage for the
new conservative pragmatism of the 1980s. And, as argued later, the conservative policies of the 1980s have so shaped fiscal and economic conditions
as to preclude, for pragmatic reasons, any sudden federal about-face in the
socioeconomic sphere.

Economic and Fiscal Constraints

The rapid growth of the economy and the great expansion of federal
responsibility and spending for social welfare between World War II and the
early 1970s were mutually reinforcing. On the one hand, there can be little
doubt that the former facilitated the latter. Americans felt more able and
willing to spend a rising share of their incomes for various public purposes
when the purchasing power of what remained for their private purposes also
grew strongly. On the other hand, the relatively strong performance of the
economy appeared to validate the Keynesian policies, which relied in part on

the massive increase in social spending to augment and stabilize the demand side of the economy.

This harmony of economic and social policies was shattered by the mid-1970s, as stagflation set in and the entry of baby boomers into the labor market increased job competition and further depressed real wage growth. As Meyer notes, in the absence of strong economic growth to reconcile competing national objectives, the historically high levels of social spending in the 1970s were increasingly "financed" by a decline in defense spending, growing federal deficits, and rising tax burdens, which, along with increases in earnings that barely kept pace with inflation, effectively halted growth in private purchasing power. By 1980, despite a stabilizing of social spending as a percentage of GNP in the second half of the 1970s, even the outgoing Democratic president was advocating more restraint in social spending in order to accommodate a modest tax cut and defense buildup. In other words, given other national priorities, the country perceived that it could no longer afford to support the levels of social spending to which it had become accustomed.

Further undermining the Keynesian harmony of social and economic policies was a strong resurgence of the peculiarly American mistrust of "big government," fed by—among other things—conservative arguments that government itself was the cause of the economic woes of the 1970s. Mainstream economic thinkers had long speculated about the consequences for economic efficiency of the pursuit of social goals—in particular, speculated about the presumed trade-off between higher levels of government regulation, taxation, and social spending and the healthy functioning of the economy. In the late 1970s, the more extreme of these speculations blossomed together with public mistrust of government into the doctrine of "supply-side economics." Despite the lack of supporting evidence, proponents of supply-side economics argued that the costs to long-term economic growth of even modest expansions in public spending, taxation and regulation were high—as would be the benefits of shrinking all three.[7] The doctrine found its policy expression in President Reagan's "Program for Economic Recovery," and a new har-

---

7. In her chapter in this volume, Sawhill notes that "the empirical evidence suggests that any such effects are small" and places the primary blame for stagflation on oil price shocks and other factors. Economist Robert Lampman, who recently undertook a comprehensive review of the evidence on the consequences of increased social spending and the taxes to pay for it, reaches an even stronger conclusion: "On many of the key questions about the relationship of social spending and the economy there is so little evidence and theory is so inconclusive that no firm conclusions can be drawn about whether change in social spending [and the taxes to support it] harms or helps economic performance. Economists simply do not know" (Lampman1985, 7).

mony between economic goals and social spending policies was proclaimed, this time requiring reduction rather than expansion of social spending.

Of course, as Sawhill documents, nearly all the results of supply side-monetarist economic policies pursued in the early 1980s were disappointing. The initial promise of the Reagan administration was for an immediately revitalized economy, the painless elimination of inflation, and a budget surplus by mid-decade—all fueled primarily by the strong incentives to work, save, and invest produced by the large tax cut. Instead the United States had the deepest recession since World War II and an explosion in the federal budget and trade deficits. More than three years into the recovery there is still no sign of any improvement in underlying rates of savings, investment, and worker productivity relative to those of the 1970s. The big bright spot, of course, has been the sharp deceleration in inflation, but this deceleration can be traced to the recession and falling worldwide commodity prices, not supply-side policies per se.

Beyond these immediate consequences, the persistence of large budget and trade deficits casts a long shadow over our long-term economic prospects. The total national debt has already more than doubled in the 1980s and will probably triple before the decade is out. And the large flow of foreign loans helping to finance this deficit will soon result in a shift in our international economic status from the world's largest creditor nation to the world's largest debtor. Since the initial recovery from the 1982 recession, the supply side of the economy has been sputtering, while the country has indulged in a binge of borrowing and overconsumption that is unparalleled in our history. The recent fall in oil prices and interest rates and improvements in the deficit outlook are encouraging signs for the near term. But just as the country had to pay a severe price in short-term economic growth for the double-digit inflation that was the legacy of the 1970s, so will it probably pay a price in long-term economic growth as a result of the large budget and trade deficits.

There is little doubt what all this means for federal social spending. Social programs face tough sledding for the foreseeable future. The notion that social spending and taxes are detrimental to the economy seems to have passed from the realm of an appealing argument to conventional wisdom over the past decade, in no small part because it has been consistently and persuasively advanced by President Reagan and his administration. (It does seem ironic that the United States is reacting so strongly to this argument at relatively low levels of public expenditures as a percentage of the U.S. GNP while, as Haveman, Wolfe, and Halberstadt argue, Western European countries may not be taking it sufficiently seriously at much higher levels of public expenditures as a proportion of their GNPs.) A growing public perception of the failure of supply-side macroeconomic policies or a future president who argues otherwise undoubtedly could moderate this shift. But advocates of social spending will still face a much greater burden of proof than in the past.

More concretely though, the dramatically different fiscal dynamic and budgetary outlook of the country relative to the situation in the past promises to keep inexorable restraining pressure on federal spending for all purposes. The budget deficits of the 1980s are a manifestation of a situation that is qualitatively as well as quantitatively different. The deficits of the 1960s and 1970s were not only far smaller relative to the economy than today's are, they were also more cyclical in nature (that is, primarily a result of recession and temporarily high unemployment). Thus, they declined rapidly with only moderate economic growth and no change in tax and spending policies. Moreover, the effect of inflation through "bracket creep" reinforced this tendency and always ensured projected budget surpluses, though at the expense of higher personal tax burdens.

In contrast, primarily because of the changes in the tax law, including an end to "bracket creep," and the defense buildup initiated in 1981—and despite the concomitant cutbacks in domestic spending—the deficits of the 1980s are predominantly structural, reflecting a fundamental imbalance between tax and spending policies. (Tax indexation—a feature of the 1981 tax bill which adjusts personal income tax brackets to inflation—now precludes an increase in tax burdens without an explicit change in policy.) Congress has taken several steps to redress this imbalance since 1981 by passing some modest tax increases, scaling back the planned defense buildup, and further trimming domestic program spending. The result has been a major improvement in the deficit outlook. Even under relatively optimistic assumptions about the future performance of the economy, however, restoration of budgetary balance will still require some combination of major tax increases and spending cuts. Under these changed conditions, it is likely to be a long time before the American public feels the fiscal largesse for much increase in domestic spending.

Knowledge and Institutional Limits

So far I have argued that the evolution of America's public philosophy, our experience in the realms of social and economic policymaking, and the current realities of our economic and fiscal situation all portend a more limited role for the federal government in domestic affairs than might have been anticipated either from a study of the Western European experience or from observation of the growth of the post–New Deal American "welfare state." But there is yet another reason—suggested in the volume and elsewhere—why we should not regard the recent rise of the conservative outlook and the demise of the liberal one as merely a transitory or cyclical phenomenon. Conservative skepticism about what the federal government *should* do appears to have been translated into popular skepticism about what the federal government *can* do.

During the 1970s, conservative thinkers argued with increasing plausibility that, regardless of our differences over values, we should share a skepticism about our institutional capacity for effecting desired social outcomes through central government action. The president articulated this skepticism in connection with the original intentions of the Founding Fathers who, in his view, "knew well that if too much power and authority were vested in the central government, even if intended for a noble purpose, not only would liberty be threatened, but *it just wouldn't work*. . . . I think during the last decade and before, we've gotten a taste of just what [they were] warning us about" (Reagan 1984, emphasis added). These concerns have buttressed the administration's overriding efforts at simplifying the policy agenda—focusing on a few major issues with clear priorities and a strong grounding in easily understood principles—which critics both decry and acknowledge to be a major source of the administration's early successes.

In practice, as I discuss later, simplification has had three major policy themes: a refusal to mount new federal programs, an effort to curtail existing ineffective programs, and the devolution of responsibility for as many programs as feasible to state and local governments. And, as I conclude later, although the administration has had only mixed success in all three areas, what success has been achieved is likely to reinforce public acceptance of conservative arguments about the practical limitations of the federal role in domestic affairs.

The refusal to mount new federal programs has been characterized by political scientist James Ceaser as "an attack on the policy-making state" (Ceaser 1984, 81). That is, a rejection of the liberal effort to "rationalize" both society and the process of governing by subjecting more areas of societal activity to scrutiny, with the goal of developing a general public policy to better conditions. As Ceaser observes, contemporary liberals have argued that, even where there is no explicitly legislated general federal policy for a particular sphere of activity, a (presumably inferior) policy of sorts may be said to exist de facto, since the sphere of activity is influenced by the federal government in one way or another (for example, through the tax code, regulation, loan guarantees, or direct spending). Where inadvertent policy prevails, it was argued, advertent policy would be preferable. This mentality seemed to reach its apotheosis under the Carter administration, with its energy policy, urban policy, and family policy.

The Reagan administration's counterargument was sometimes grounded in a dismissal of alleged "problems"—for example, reports of widespread homelessness were said to be greatly exaggerated. More often, however, the counterargument was grounded on the probable counterproductiveness of federal intervention—for example, any sort of "industrial policy" would simply further erode our international economic position by helping the wrong industries. In short, the market works, so don't mess with it.

These arguments gained public credence in the recession of 1981–82, when unemployment rose to double-digit levels for the first time since the Depression and yet Congress (reluctantly) and the president (enthusiastically) "stayed the course," avoiding any fine-tuning of fiscal policy. The result was the strongest one-and-a-half year economic recovery since World War II, which brought unemployment rates back down to the levels that had prevailed before the recession, with even further gains against inflation beyond its major decline during the recession.

Sawhill argues that, when one considers the tax cuts and defense buildup already in place in 1981 and declining world oil prices, this outcome is perfectly consistent with Keynesian views of the world, and she is right. But to the public, unschooled in economic argument, the outcome is more likely to validate the case against interventionist policies. Similarly, attention to the quality of public education appears to be on the rise with only federal exhortation—not dollars—to buoy it. These sorts of developments bolster the anti-interventionist cause.

The administration's arguments for eliminating or curtailing existing federal programs appear to have met with less public acceptance than the arguments for not mounting new programs. Nevertheless, we have witnessed a reduction of more than ten percent in federal social spending (relative to GNP) and a redesign of many programs, both concentrated in those areas most under attack by the administration. In general, the administration argued that social programs should be subjected to much tougher tests of effectiveness and that efforts at "social engineering" should be abandoned because we do not know how to do it. In line with these arguments, the ax fell heaviest on what Meyer terms the "front-end" efforts, such as education, job training, social services, and community development, intended to help disadvantaged populations enter the mainstream of economic and political activity. The benefits of these "front-end" efforts are much harder to demonstrate than those "back-end" safety-net efforts, which largely provide income maintenance and health care financing and were pruned far less.

The absence of clearly demonstrable benefits may provide much of the explanation for public acceptance of the cutbacks and curtailments, the potential harm of which cannot be clearly demonstrated either. But in some areas where harm could have been demonstrated—and was predicted by the administration's opponents—it has not materialized. For example, when one of the hallmarks of social engineering—the work-incentive features of AFDC— was eliminated, welfare recipients by and large did not quit working but chose instead to give up their benefits. Also, despite the achievement of fairly substantial savings in means-tested programs in general, maximum benefit levels (the levels provided to recipients without private sources of income) adjusted for inflation ceased to decline as they had done in the late 1970s and turned upward. Of course, here I am talking only about public acceptance of a line of argument, and not about larger issues of equity—and in the public perception of these larger issues may lie the germ of a liberal backlash. But for the time being, the administration's arguments about the ineffectiveness of many social programs seem to hold considerable sway with the public.

Finally, the nature of the state and local governments' response to the federal retrenchment increases the credibility of the administration's arguments for decentralization. In brief, these lower levels of government have demonstrated a considerable capacity for commitment to the equitable and innovative provision of a wide range of public services deemed in the national interest. See Nathan, Doolittle, and Associates (1983), and Peterson (1984 and 1986). As Nathan notes in his chapter of this book, "Even in states regarded as politically moderate (and in some cases even conservative) efforts were made to have states take a more active part in fiscal, programmatic, and institutional affairs than they had previously. . . ." Concern that this would not be the case was a major factor inhibiting efforts throughout the 1970s to simplify and streamline the federal grant-in-aid structure, even though the desirability of such simplification was widely recognized at the time.

It can be argued—indeed I read Heclo to be arguing—that the policy changes resulting from the administration's three-pronged effort at simplification, discussed earlier, could easily be reversed with the advent of an administration of opposing viewpoint, with the perceived failure of the new policy regime, or with the return to fiscal health. I grant that either of the latter two would make a big difference, because the primary basis for the public support that has both underlain and limited Ronald Reagan's successes in these areas appears to be pragmatic, not ideological. However, this pragmatism seems strongly grounded in a growing public appreciation (arising from the experience of the 1960s and 1970s) of the limitations of public action—that is, an appreciation of the argument of doing less, with a clearer sense of priorities; doing it better; and doing it more at the state and local levels. On balance, the experience of the 1980s is more likely to reinforce than to erode that appreciation.

GOVERNANCE

It is one of the many paradoxes of the Reagan administration that, just as the president seems to have succeeded in convincing the American public of the incapacity of the federal government for leadership in many spheres of domestic concern, he has simultaneously convinced us (or at least many political scientists among us—Richard Nathan, in this volume, included) of the capacity of the presidency for leadership of the federal government. Gone from the current political discourse is the picture of the hobbled chief executive, ineffectually battling the forces of "paralysis, stagnation, and drift" (Carter's words). In its place, Americans have the image of a confident leader, enjoying broad-based public support and using the too-long-neglected tools of his office to effect major changes in the American political landscape. The presidency, according to Nathan and others, has undergone a much-needed resuscitation.

It is a welcome thought. Much as I want to believe it, however—and persuasive though I find Nathan's arguments about the president's political skills—the paradox still bothers me. I feel obliged to voice my mounting disquietude over what seems to be a widening gap between "popular leadership"—what works on the six-o'clock news—and genuine political leadership—what works in the consensus-forming institutions of government. If the president can present himself as the powerful captain of the ship of state and earn the American public's grateful confidence, surely he cannot go on indefinitely pointing out that the ship is, in fact, a very leaky boat and we would be wise to hold tight to whatever nongovernmental life raft—family, community, and so on—we have at hand. Of course, while the president has been belittling the domestic capabilities of the federal government, he has been working diligently to restore what he sees as overriding values—our confidence in ourselves as Americans and in our national purpose—and for this we may have reason to feel thankful. But I am not sure that he has succeeded, as Nathan argues he has, in better equipping his office to cope with future problems on the domestic front. In short, I see a real tension between the president's interpretation of his role as a popular leader, appealing to what Heclo has termed our "anti-government nationalism," and his role as a political leader, forging our inevitably conflicting values into an enduring political consensus.

The chapters in this volume provide some grist for my doubts. Heclo, for example, observes that the president's primary aim—to reduce the domestic presence of the federal government—may be frustrated by "the inadvertent but continued nationalization of politics under the Reagan administration." The president's own popularity, among other things, has served to rivet public attention ever more firmly on Washington, while public opinion polls continue to provide scant evidence of any emerging consensus on the desirability of further reductions of the federal domestic role. The president's criticisms of the government have clearly struck a popular chord, but it is not clear that this popularity translates any longer into usable chips in the policy sphere.

Further evidence of the tension between popular and political leadership is afforded by Sawhill's chapter on the economy. Although virtually all political commentators argue that the president's popularity derives in large measure from his ability to "communicate" with the public—that is, to translate the complexities of policymaking into simple and upbeat messages—Sawhill's observations suggest that simplicity and upbeatness will not serve well the cause of political consensus on the resolution of our economic problems. As she concludes:

> Economics cannot deliver what politics requires. Although . . . there is a critical need for better economic mousetraps, there is also a need for public understanding of the limits of existing policies. The person in the best position to educate the public is the president of the United States. In this sense, what President Reagan has said—and not said—to the American public about the complexity of the issues and the hard choices that must be made may be as important as the policies he has pursued.

I return to the question of the problematic legacy of Reagan's communication skills later, but here I want to stay with the issue of political leadership. The foundation of President Reagan's reputation as a political leader was laid within the first six months of his taking office, in the stunning success of his 1981 budget and tax cut proposals. The president's masterly handling of a politically divided Congress in the passage of the Omnibus Budget Reconciliation Act and the Economic Recovery Tax Act contrasted so glaringly with Carter's inability to move a legislature dominated by his own party that political pundits were moved to say "of such stuff are political legends made." Yet in the months and years that followed, the administration found itself more and more at odds with even its own party in both houses of Congress. Far from providing legislative leadership, the president has increasingly ended up being cornered by congressionally engineered consensus over major pieces of legislation. Nowhere is this more evident than in the area of the budget where, since 1981, Congress has consistently rejected the president's proposals, which have relied solely upon further cuts in domestic programs (coupled with highly optimistic economic projections) to reduce the deficit, and has developed its own budgets, relying much more on a series of modest tax increases and slowdown in the defense buildup.

Finally, I think that this "fiscalization" of the policy debate—a direct result of the president's initial policy successes—bodes ill for the policy-making process. The fact that the deficit in general, and the possibility that the controversial new budget control act (Gramm-Rudman-Hollings) in particular, will shape decision making on domestic programs for the foreseeable future may signal a presidential victory of some sort for the long run (as Meyer notes, by "pulling the revenue plug" the president has effectively halted the "seemingly inexorable trend" of social program growth), but it surely also signals a defeat for the political process in the short run. Furthermore, meaningful public participation in that process is virtually precluded by the arcana of Gramm-Rudman-Hollings, which are ill-understood even by many congressional supporters of the legislation. In sum, what the country has developed to deal with the deficit is a piece of legislation of dubious constitutionality that, in the words of one congressman, "substitutes process for guts." The act is acknowledged by many in Congress to be an abdication of their political responsibility, but it was enacted because of perceived popular pressure to "do something" about the deficit. This, it seems, is the unhappy effect of popular, as opposed to political, leadership.

All these considerations lead me to a more equivocal assessment of President Reagan's impact on "governance" than that offered by the Nathan chapter. But two obvious questions remain:

- Given the ebb of public morale in the 1970s and the general disaffection with our political institutions, was an injection of what I have been calling "popular leadership" necessary to prevent further erosion of public trust? That is, is Reagan's role in fact comparable to Franklin D. Roosevelt's—as Reagan himself has asserted—in restoring our confidence to "get moving" again?

- Are the costs of popular leadership as I have outlined them—excessive reliance on the persuasive powers of the presidency at the expense of an appreciation of the real problems of governance, inflated and overly simplistic expectations of the performance of the economy, and preoccupation with the legerdemains of federal budgeting in preference to coming to grips with the deficit—are these merely a temporary price of a necessary shift in political direction, or are they harbingers of worse problems?

Clearly the answers to such questions as these at this time must be highly speculative. That said, I would tender to the first question a very cautious "yes, but . . . ." Americans did need a dose of Reaganesque confidence and good humor, but it would have been better for our health had the dose been diluted by more realism. Indeed, the cause of conservatism would have been better served by more realism. I say this—fully aware that realism is often not conducive to confidence and good humor—for two reasons. First, because I think we have been promised the moon when a minor meteor would have sufficed. Much of this volume attests to the ripeness of the country—philosophically, economically, socially, and politically—for a shift in the conservative direction. But, by so inflating our expectations of the results of that shift, the president has let his conservative followers in for some unnecessary political grief. We will undoubtedly, for reasons argued earlier, continue to proceed along a more conservative path in the next several years than in the 1960s and 1970s, but conservative politicians will be penalized more than they otherwise might have been by disappointed expectations.

Second, I think that the president has permitted his relentless optimism to blind him to a unique opportunity. The American people apparently found President Reagan's personality so appealing that they would have swallowed some painful truths from him (of the sort, for example, that Sawhill has to tell) which they were unwilling to swallow from his predecessors. Compared with other occupants of the Oval Office over the past quarter-century, President Reagan exhibits a remarkably healthy perspective on power—he is neither preoccupied with getting it nor tormented about using it—and this perspective probably accounts in no small measure for the public trust he has earned and maintained. In this regard, he provides an excellent object lesson for any successor. But, as I suggested earlier, the political benefits of his personality have accrued too much to the man and too little to the office. This adds up to a missed opportunity for political consensus building. The president, of course, will not see it that way, but I am willing to bet that his successor (along with many members of his own party) will.

This brings me to the longer-term legacy of the president's popular leadership. Other writers have noted "The Rise of the Rhetorical Presidency" and documented its pitfalls,[8] among which must be numbered: lack of realism in public discourse; mounting public appetite for style and drama in political life, accompanied by an ever-shorter political attention span; declining tolerance for long-term solutions to complex problems—the list goes on. President Reagan has certainly furthered the rise of this kind of presidency, and he will, in history, certainly be assigned his share of responsibility for the pitfalls. But it is also worth noting that rhetorical presidents—the other two modern ones being Roosevelt and Kennedy—cast long and sometimes dark shadows over their own office. Truman observed himself to suffer from his

---

8. For example, see Ceasar, Thurow, Tulis, and Bessette (1981).

want of F.D.R.'s eloquence; Johnson's anguish over the Kennedy glamor has been amply (and painfully) documented; and, I think it could be argued, both the Nixon and Carter administrations were severely troubled by the preoccupation of both presidents with the Kennedy myth. Being "a hard act to follow" may be a good thing in Hollywood, but not so in the White House.

The long-term costs to governance of the two other problems noted earlier—the oversimplification of economic issues and the fiscalization of the policy debate—are harder to assess, both because their consequences are so highly interactive (oversimplified economics produced an unanticipated deficit, which in turn produces obstacles to economic growth, which in turn prompts a simplistic—albeit arcane—solution, which in turn postpones the search for a real solution, and so on) and because our present fiscal and economic situation is so unprecedented. Just at the time when, for reasons independent of our current policies, we have arrived at an historically unprecedented turning point in our economic insularity (the internationalization of the economy and our declining productivity and competitiveness would pose, as Sawhill suggests, problems enough for any administration), we are also confronted with an unprecedented constraint—the gargantuan trade and budget deficits—in our flexibility for dealing with the economy. Predicting the ultimate outcome of the combined phenomena is clearly impossible, but it is not hard to foresee a serious erosion of the public trust if the present unhealthy interaction of the economy and the deficits continues much longer.

CONCLUDING THOUGHTS

Where we go from here is anybody's guess. The most I have been able to conclude thus far is that we are not going back to the older and simpler America of the conservative vision and we are not going forward to the egalitarian society of the liberal vision. President Reagan has been extremely successful in forcing a hard look at the liberal navigational tools, in consequence of which we have trimmed our domestic sails and dumped what many have agreed was some needless federal ballast. But he has not come up with new tools for handling persistent social and economic problems—chiefly poverty, the trade-off between inflation and economic growth, and the evermore problematic deficits. Furthermore, although President Reagan may have temporarily restored our faith in free market solutions to these problems, this volume finds little foundation for building a political consensus around that faith. Thus, I think that when the next socioeconomic crisis rolls around, both political parties are going to find themselves in a fair state of confusion.

The root of the confusion, as I have diagnosed it in this chapter, lies in the failure of both liberal and conservative outlooks to address the tension among what I have termed the philosophical, practical, and political strands of American public life. The liberals, having enjoyed a protracted period of dominance along all three dimensions, have lost their political and socioeconomic nerve–that is, have had their toolbox discredited—but have yet to relinquish their philosophical nerve. They still cling, however discordantly, to notions of "civic virtue" and "collective good" and refuse to admit the possibility that virtue and good might sometimes be incompatible with economic prosperity (not to mention politically unsalable to their own diverse constituency).

The conservatives, in contrast, after long years of keeping a philosophical flame alive in exile, have recovered their political and socioeconomic nerve and may be about to lose their philosophical one. (Richard Reeves, in *The Reagan Detour*, has a wonderful discussion of the incipient cracks in the Republican philosophy, in the course of which he quotes a Republican congressional staffer observing the 1984 Republican convention as saying, "The only thing they're sure of out there is that they love Ronald Reagan. Well, first we win the election, and then we get to the business of tearing each other apart—and maybe the country too" (Reeves 1985, 71). The conservative Republicans cling to the notion of economic liberty and do not want to admit the possibility that liberty alone leaves Americans with no basis whatsoever for public agreement on moral values. We are back to the Founding Fathers, but with a difference: the glue—the religious conviction that gave the confidence—is gone.

And so, for purposes of this discussion, we are back to de Tocqueville. As I suggested at the outset of the discussion, his observations about the role of religion in shaping our society go a long way toward explaining our current situation. In particular, they shed light on why our political discourse has taken its present turn to the ideological; why we are still, at such a late date, embroiled in such fundamental questions of public responsibility and individual obligations; and why, despite our pride in our American identity, we have remained such a pluralistic society.

President Reagan has served us well by insisting on the value dimension of political discourse, but by harkening back to a no-longer-prevailing commonality of religious outlook, he has not helped us develop a vocabulary that might transform ideological differences into political consensus. He has also served us well by reminding us of the limits of public responsibility, but without clarifying the obligation of individuals to anything but themselves. And, finally, he has restored some sense of our national purpose, but by grounding that purpose in individual economic interests, he has done little to further (and, indeed, may retard) our sense of social unity. Withall, I think that both political parties must contemplate a mixed legacy from the 1980s.

If my assessment of this legacy rings somewhat sombre, it is not because of any strong political bias I can detect in myself. It may simply be that the objective of this volume—in effect, to approximate the writing of history without the historian's perspective of time—predisposes me to be more conscious of how far we have to go than of how far we already have come. Daniel Bell, I believe, evidenced a similar consciousness some dozen years ago, when he surveyed the legacy of the 1960s. Writing in the neoconservative journal, *The Public Interest*, Bell (1974, 68) observed:

> In the heyday of the imperial republic, the quiet sense of destiny and the harsh creed of personal conduct [that characterized the Founding Fathers] were replaced by a virulent "Americanism," a manifest destiny that took us overseas, and a materialist hedonism which provided the incentives to work. Today that manifest destiny is shattered and the Americanism has worn thin, and only the hedonism remains. It is a poor recipe for national unity and purpose.
>
> Yet in the trial and defeat—and there has been defeat—a virtue emerges: the possibility of a self-conscious maturity that dispenses with charismatic leaders, ideological doctrines, and manifest destinies. . . .

Whatever Bell might conclude about the legacy of the 1980s, I think he would agree with me that "the possibility of a self-conscious maturity" has not been advanced.

REFERENCES

Bawden, D. Lee, and John L. Palmer. 1984. "Social Policy." In John L. Palmer and Isabel V. Sawhill, eds., *The Reagan Record: An Assessment of America's Changing Domestic Priorities*. Cambridge, Massachusetts: Ballinger.

Bell, Daniel. 1974. "The Public Household—on 'Fiscal Sociology' and the Liberal Society." *The Public Interest* (Fall) 37: 68.

Bercovitch, Sacvan. 1981. "The Rites of Assent: Rhetoric, Ritual and the Ideology of American Consensus." In Sam B. Girus, ed., *The American Self*. Albuquerque, New Mexico: University of New Mexico Press.

Ceasar, James W. 1984. "The Theory of Governance of the Reagan Administration." In Lester M. Salamon and Michael S. Lund, eds., *The Reagan Presidency and the Governing of America*. Washington, D.C.: The Urban Institute Press.

Ceasar, James, Glen E. Thurow, Jeffrey Tulis, and Joseph M. Bessette. 1981. "The Rise of the Rhetorical Presidency." *Presidential Studies Quarterly* (Spring).

de Tocqueville, Alexis. 1945. "Philosophical Method of the Americans." In *Democracy in America*. Vol. 2. New York: Alfred A. Knopf.

Diggins, John Patrick. 1984. *The Lost Soul of American Politics*. New York: Basic Books.

Furniss, Norman, and Timothy Tilton. 1977. *The Case for the Welfare State*. Bloomington, Indiana: Indiana University Press.

Gallup, George Jr. 1985. "Religion in America." In *Religion in America Today, The Annals of the American Academy of Political and Social Science* (July) 480: 169.

Hofstadter, Richard. 1957. *The American Political Tradition and the Men Who Made It*. New York: Vintage Books.

Lampman, Robert J. 1985. *Balancing the Books: Social Spending and the American Economy*. Washington, D.C.: National Conference on Social Welfare.

McClosky, Herbert, and John Zeller. 1984. *The American Ethos: Public Attitudes Toward Capitalism and Democracy*. Cambridge, Massachusetts: Harvard University Press.

Mead, Lawrence M. 1986. *Beyond Entitlement*. New York: The Free Press.

Nathan, Richard P., Fred C. Doolittle, and Associates. 1983. *The Consequences of the Cuts: The Effects of the Reagan Domestic Program on State and Local Governments*. Princeton, New Jersey: Princeton University Press.

Neuhaus, Richard John. 1984. *The Naked Public Square*. Grand Rapids, Michigan; William B. Erdmen Publishing Company.

Palmer, John L., and Isabel V. Sawhill, eds. 1984. *The Reagan Record: An Assessment of America's Changing Domestic Priorities*. Cambridge, Massachusetts: Ballinger.

Peterson, George. 1984. "Federalism and the States: An Experiment in Decentralization." In John L. Palmer and Isabel V. Sawhill, eds., *The Reagan Record: An Assessment of America's Changing Domestic Priorities*. Cambridge, Massachusetts: Ballinger.

————. 1986. "The Reagan Block Grants: What Have We Learned?" Washington, D.C.: Urban Institute Press. Forthcoming.

Reagan, Ronald. 1984. "Prayer in School," Radio Address to the Nation. February 25. *Weekly Compilation of Presidential Documents*. 20:9. March 5.

Reeves, Richard. 1985. *The Reagan Detour*. New York: Simon and Schuster.

Reichley, A. James. 1985. *Religion in American Public Life*. Washington, D.C.: Brookings Institution.

Skocpol, Theda. n.d. "America's Incomplete Welfare State: The Limits of New Deal Reforms and the Origins of the Present Crisis." In Gosta Esping-Andersen, Lee Rainwater, and Martin Rein, eds., *Stagnation and Renewal in Social Policy*. Armonk, New York: M. E. Sharpe. Forthcoming.

Stace, W. T. 1966. "Man Against Darkness." In *The Borzoi College Reader*. New York: Alfred A. Knopf.

ABOUT THE AUTHORS

Nathan Glazer is professor of education and sociology at Harvard University and coeditor of *The Public Interest*. His most recent book is *Ethnic Dilemmas, 1964–1982* (1983).

Victor Halberstadt is professor of public finance at the University of Leiden, The Netherlands. He is chairman of the Social Economics Council of the Dutch government, and has written widely on economic policy and social security in the Western European context. He is a coauthor of *Public Policy toward Disabled Workers: Cross National Analysis of Economic Impacts* (1985).

Robert Haveman is the John Bascom Professor of Economics at the University of Wisconsin, Madison, and Research Associate at the Institute for Research on Poverty. His research is in the economics of poverty and income distribution, cost-benefit analysis, and the incentive effects of government taxes and transfers. He is a coauthor of *Public Policies toward Disabled Workers: Cross National Analysis of Economic Impacts* (1985).

Hugh Heclo is professor of government at Harvard University and a former senior fellow at The Brookings Institution in Washington, D.C. His most recent works are *Policy and Politics in Sweden* (1986) and *Thinking Institutionally* (forthcoming, 1987).

Jack A. Meyer is the president of New Directions for Policy, a firm specializing in social science research and public policy evaluation. He is also a resident fellow in economics at the American Enterprise Institute. He has published extensively in the field of social policy and health-care cost management.

Richard P. Nathan is professor of public and international affairs at the Woodrow Wilson School of Public and International Affairs, Princeton University. He has conducted research and written extensively on a wide range of U.S. domestic topics. His most recent book is *The Consequences of the Cuts* (1983).

John L. Palmer is codirector of The Urban Institute's Changing Domestic Priorities project. His current research interests are federal budgeting and social policy. He has been an assistant professor of economics at Stanford University, a senior fellow in the Economic Studies Program of the Brookings Institution, and an assistant secretary for the U.S. Department of Health and Human Services. He is coauthor of *The Deficit Dilemma* (1983) and *The Reagan Record* (1984).

Isabel V. Sawhill is codirector of The Urban Institute's Changing Domestic Priorities project. Her areas of research include human resources and economic policy. She has directed several of the Institute's research programs and held a number of government positions, including that of director of the National Commission for Employment Policy. She is coauthor of *The Reagan Record* (1984) and *Economic Policy in the Reagan Years* (1984).

Barbara Wolfe is an associate professor of economics at the University of Wisconsin, Madison, a Research Associate at the Institute for Research on Poverty, and executive chair of the Center for Health Policy and Program Evaluation. Her research is in the areas of health economics and human resources. She has published in numerous journals including *American Economic Review*, *Journal of Public Economics*, *Journal of Political Economy*, and *Journal of Human Resources*.

INDEX